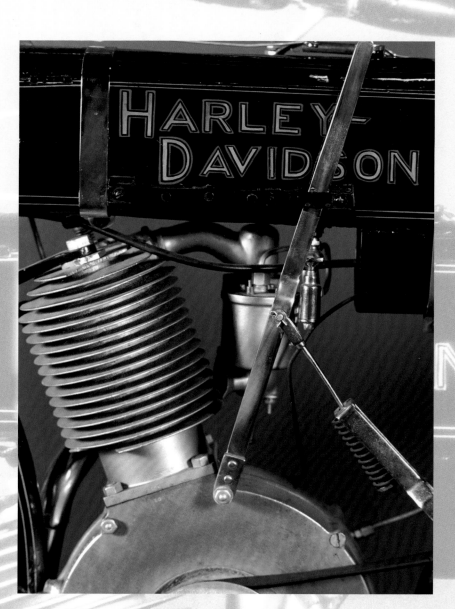

the great book of
Harley Davidson

vmb
PUBLISHERS

CONTENTS

Text and Photography
Albert Saladini and Pascal Szymezak

Graphic Design
Patrizia Balocco Lovisetti
Clara Zanotti

An imprint of White Star, Italy

© 2003, 2005 White Star S.p.a.
Via Candido Sassone, 22/24
13100 Vercelli, Italy
www.whitestar.it

ISBN 88-540-0393-X
REPRINTS:
1 2 3 4 5 6   09 08 07 06 05

© 2002 White Star S.p.a.
Harley Davidson
A way of life
A hundred year old myth
New up-dated edition

ISBN 88-8095-838-0

© 1999 White Star S.p.a.
Harley Davidson - Evolution of the myth

ISBN 88-8095-408-3

Printed in Korea

PART ONE

PART TWO

1 In 1903, Harley-Davidson's first three machines were equipped with the same one-cylinder engine.

2-3 Cyril Huze used a Harley-Davidson Electra Glide called "Miami Nice."

4 e 4-5 During their meetings, professional customizers professionisti present their masterpieces

6-7 The engine of an old Sportster.

8-9 Electra Glide model, fitted with Evolution engines, built in Canada.

5

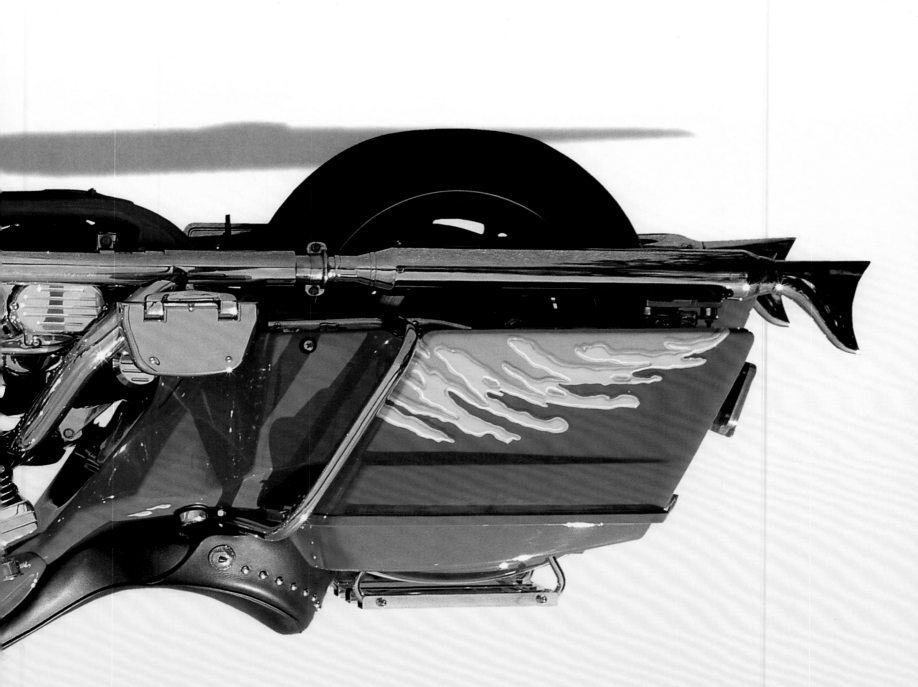

A HUNDRED YEAR OLD MYTH

HARLEY DAVIDSON

a way of life

PART ONE

INTRODUCTION

She is a true "grande dame" who, now that she is 100 years, has never developed a wrinkle and has demonstrated again and again that classics never go out of style. The color of her dress doesn't matter; what is important is the way her rhinestones are displayed. She has had the greatest lovers, all passionate, who have covered hundreds of thousands of miles for her and with her. She has always been looked at, examined, undressed with the eyes, and envied. She has won great prizes and wars; she has gone places others could not. Today, she is still captivating; she is celebrated and exhibited, dressed to please different tastes. Her return has upset the market, which is flooded by strong Japanese competition.

She fears no one. She is nearly 100 years old and, every morning when I wake her up and uncover her, I cannot help admiring her perfect line, which made my father dream and made me write this book.

Thank you, Mr. Harley. Thank you, the Davidsons.

Albert Saladini

Over the nine decades of its rich and eventful history, the Harley-Davidson Motor Company has won the affection and loyalty of a vast range of customers. Its motorcycles have been used for day-to-day transport, for touring, for racing, and simply for fun; they have been ridden by soldiers in two world wars, by the hippies and other members of the culture in the 1960s, by cops, and by crooks; and they have served as status symbols for stars and starlets. But whatever the nationality, profession, or social status of a Harley owner, he or she shares one thing with all the others—a devotion to the products of the Harley-Davidson Motor Company. For whatever your dream may be, a Harley will make it come true, and it will bring you into contact with others who share the same dream. It is this unique magic which wins the affection of Harley riders and makes their hearts beat faster as soon as they feel the first throb of a Harley-Davidson engine.

My own Harley conjures up feelings to which only she has the key—sensations that re-awaken memories of wide-open spaces, of past journeys, of pure happiness. This book is intended as a tribute to this automotive goddess, whose history is as old as the century but whose charms remain as potent as ever; I offer it up, with gratitude, to a machine which has shared my most cherished moments of freedom and joy.

Pascal Szymezak

12-13 "Wise"—relatively traditional—modifications on the look are quite frequent, both in Canada and the United States. In Europe, Australia, and Japan, radical changes are often seen on models fitted with Evolution engines, as for example on this Canadian motorcycle, whose frame, bodywork, and mechanical elements have been carefully finished.

HARLEY-DAVIDSON: PAST AND FUTURE

Not so long ago, there were those motorcyclists who believed that Harley-Davidsons were obsolete machines, relics from another era. They never took the time to examine or appreciate Harley-Davidsons, and few journalists made an effort to provide them with any information on the subject.

But in the last few years, there's been a growing enthusiasm about Harleys, along with an increase in the number of Harley owners. Companies that not so long ago disparaged the Milwaukee brand now manufacture motorcycles that imitate the Harley-Davidson look or that are, at the very least, strongly influenced by Harley-Davidson, with an engine architecture similar to that of the V-Twin. Riders are abandoning their ordinary sport bikes and heavyweight motorcycles for big Harley-Davidsons. Is the change some kind of turning point in the history of motorcycle manufacturing, or just a fashion decision? Either way, it underscores the sound thinking of the team

at Harley-Davidson, who have relied on Harley-Davidson's heritage and its brand image to win over customers tired of the parade of novelties proposed by other manufacturers over the years. Today Harley-Davidson finds itself a leader in the world of custom and deluxe touring bikes, closely watched by its competitors, who strive to incorporate Harley concepts into their own machines.

A quick look at the history of Harley-Davidson shows that the company has always been ahead of the curve in utilizing state-of-the-art techniques. Back when production of Harleys began, the bikes were already fitted with twist grips — unlike European and Asian motorcycles, which only began offering riders twist grips in the middle of this century. In the 1920s, the first machine to be equipped with a side stand and an electric lighting system (other brands still used acetylene headlights) was a Harley. And it was a Harley-Davidson that inaugurated the use of valve tappets with hydraulic return — even before the system was adopted for any mass-produced American car.

Another Harley-Davidson innovation, in 1981, was the adoption of a Kevlar fiber toothed belt secondary transmission on stepped pulleys. At the beginning of the century, the company had replaced the belt secondary transmission on its motorcycles with a chain transmission, while other manufacturers stuck with belts, which, at that time, skidded, broke, and required constant adjustment. Fittingly, Harley-Davidson was the first motorcycle company to go back to this early type of secondary transmission, which thanks to new, improved materials now has the advantage of requiring little maintenance. The tension needs to be readjusted only when the rear tire is changed, and the system can hold up for tens of thousands of miles — a big improvement over a chain secondary transmission, which not only makes the rear part of the bike dirty, but requires continuous maintenance and frequent replacement.

Apart from the fact that the Harley-Davidson engine offers an incomparable sensation of controlled power, formidable thrust even at low speed, considerable torque, and the feeling of a real living engine, the main thing going for Harley-Davidsons is their look. The Harley look changes somewhat from model to model but can be recognized by a long, raised handlebar, two half-tanks with the dashboard and speedometer located on top, a twin seat, plastic saddlebags, and a calm heavyweight motorcycle line — in short, all of those things that the people who now copy Harley-Davidson once mocked about this legendary brand. Harley Davidson, the oldest continuously operating motorcycle manufacturer in the world, in operation since 1903, has managed not only to preserve its most ingenious technical innovations over the years — the use of hydraulic tappets, for example, or toothed belt transmission — but to combine these innovations with new improvements, like the adoption, in 1984, of an engine made entirely of aluminum. Over time, Harley-Davidson has upgraded its techniques to keep up with scientific progress but has nevertheless maintained the Harley spirit and the Harley look.

Just talking about Harley-Davidsons isn't enough. You have to ride one of these motorcycles to fully understand what it offers to riders, what it lets them discover and share — to understand what it is to commune with a machine that will remain unique through the years and will give you renewed pleasure from the moment its wheels first turn each day.

Here is a motorcycle that doesn't look or act its age. Its very longevity is its charm.

14–15 The impressive evolution of Harley-Davidson machines shows through clearly in the comparison between a 1913 single-cylinder and a modern FXR Super Glide II. Designed for the open road, these cruising motorcycles are the dream vehicles of today's knights of the road.

FROM LOUIS GUILLAUME PERREAUX TO HARLEY-DAVIDSON

On Sunday, April 5, 1818, a vehicle called a draisienne, fitted with a back steam boiler and named "Velocipédraisiavaporiana," allegedly made its debut in the Luxembourg Gardens in Paris. The draisienne, a vehicle dating back to the end of the eighteenth century, was made entirely of wood (frame, wheels, and spokes) and looked like a bicycle without pedals, propelled by pushing with one's feet. Later, Pierre Michaux and his children had the idea of fitting some pedals to the draisienne's front wheel.

On December 24, 1869, L. G. Perreaux gave the Michaux family a small steam engine, which could be fitted to their "velocipedes" and, in 1870, the first "steam velocipede" was tested between Paris and Saint Germain en Laye over a distance of 16 kilometers.

In 1879, an Italian called Murnigotti patented a two-wheeler powered by a 0.5 horsepower four-stroke engine — but the machine was never built.

On November 10, 1885, Gotlieb Daimler and his assistant, Wilhem Maybach, first tried a motorcycle with a wooden frame and wheels, driven by a 0.5 horsepower four-stroke internal combustion engine and capable of attaining a speed of 12 kilometers per hour. From 1894 on, the first relatively consistent production of motorcycles began, thanks in particular to Hildebrandt and Wolfmüller, who manufactured a 1488 cc two-cylinder model, two thousand units of which were made. The brands multiplied in the United States and after a few years, there were about a hundred and fifty American manufacturers, the best known of which were Thor, which also built engines for Indian, Merkel, Peerless, and Yale. The immensity of the territory, combined with rapid industrial development, favored competition. In addition, copying between manufacturers led to the invention of increasingly sophisticated and technically reliable designs.

With the passage of time, however, the market stabilized, and the number of companies decreased as a result of competition, economic risks, wars, and mergers. In the end, the last fifteen great American manufacturers disappeared one after another, as a result of joint ventures, foreign takeovers, or bankruptcy due to faulty production. The consequence of this phenomenon was that only two manufacturers survived till the end of the Second World War: Harley-Davidson and Indian, which was founded in 1901, two years before Harley-Davidson. But gradually Indian was obliged to enter into partnerships and to distribute first the British brand Vincent, then others such as A.J.S., Matchless, Norton, and Royal Enfield, before it finally suspended production in the U.S. in 1953. In 1959, the Indian Company was taken over by Associated Motorcycles, the British maker of Matchless, A.J.S., and Norton. The Indian name was used through 1962. After that, several unprofitable attempts to relaunch this prestigious brand were made, most recently in 1994, when a company based in Albuquerque, New Mexico, manufactured an Indian prototype. But at the present time, Harley-Davidson alone is still functioning as an active and particularly dynamic American brand in the United States.

THE UNITED STATES AT THE BEGINNING OF THE CENTURY

The United States has been in full economic swing since the beginning of the century.

Two important factors favored industrial development: the massive influx of immigrants and the country's natural resources. Specialized and particularly well-mechanized businesses accounted for more than half of the farms; and immigrants rapidly formed an effective labor force. At that time, only one third of the population lived off agriculture, while the other two thirds were shared among industry, trade, the professions, and transport. Purchasing power as well as consumption increased so much that sale on credit developed and advertising became a very widespread promotion technique.

At the beginning of the century, the United States had almost seventy-six million inhabitants, of which twenty million lived west of the Mississippi. The 220,000-mile railroad network was longer than that of all the European countries put together.

In 1903, the U.S. automobile industry had 180 manufacturers (though this number fell to 44 within 23 years). The inevitable concentration benefitted Chrysler, General Motors and Ford, who manufactured more than 80% of all automobiles. Nearly twenty million passenger cars travelled the American roads. Air transport, too, uttered its infant's cry in 1903, with the Wright brothers' first flying tests. All these means of transportation obviously played a critical role in the economic development of the country at the beginning of the century.

The motorcycle industry experienced a concentration similar to that which occurred in the automobile industry, both in the United States and in Europe.

The major difference between these two industries lay in the level of profit, which was far lower for the manufacturers of two-wheelers.

But the founding fathers of the American motorcycle industry did not consider money a priority: they were idealists, passionate people who dreamed and, after visualizing their designs on a drawing board or in a sketch, built what they believed to be the ideal machine on which to cross this enormous country.

The beginning of the century seemed to justify them; in 1910, the number of motorcycles registered in the United States soared to 86,400.

16 center At the beginning of the twentieth century, trolley rails and horse-drawn carriages made it difficult to travel through a city like Milwaukee by motorcycle.

16 bottom When the first motorcycles appeared, they ran side by side with the most common transportation of the time: the horse.

17 top In the early twentieth century, the streets of Milwaukee, like those of any other city of the time, were used more by pedestrians than by engine-driven vehicles.

17 bottom The first two-wheel engine-driven vehicles to appear on the market were bicycle frames adapted to incorporate engines.

16 top Louis Guillaume Perreaux-Michaux's light motorcycle was the first to be patented in the world, in 1868. It weighed 61 kg and had a small steam engine, which allowed it to achieve the speed of 15 kilometers per hour. This unique motorcycle now belongs to the Ile de France museum in Sceaux.
Photo: Robert Grandseigne.

FRIENDSHIP GENERATES A LEGEND

In 1880, in Milwaukee, William S. Harley was born into a family of British immigrants from Manchester. At the age of fifteen, he started working for a bicycle manufacturer. He had a talent for mechanics and drawing, and a few years later, at the age of twenty-one, he became an apprentice draughtsman in a metal treatment factory. It did not take long for him to show his talent for invention: being fond of fishing and wildlife photography, he conceived a system which allowed him to take shots of birds in their natural environment. In the factory where he worked, he became good friends with an old schoolmate named Arthur Davidson, who was employed as pattern-maker. Arthur's family had emigrated to the U.S. from Aberdeen, Scotland, in 1872.

Arthur and William shared the same passions: nature and everything concerning mechanics. From the automobile to the bicycle, they read all the specialized journals, which also devoted numerous articles to the new means of transport: the motorcycle. From the beginning of the century, William S. Harley and Arthur Davidson had a strong desire to

19 This 1910 archive photo displays the four founders, left to right: William A. Davidson, Walter C. Davidson, Arthur Davidson, and William S. Harley.

join the large family of motorcycle pioneers. For the time being, they did not try to come up with a name for their future creations, but rather they tried to put their ideas into practice, though they were greeted with skepticism from their peers, who believed that such a project could never succeed.

Arthur's brother Walter, while keeping his job with the railroad, also worked very actively on the launch of the company. Even though he proved to be very good at business, it is as a racing rider that he later became famous and contributed to the prestige of the brand. A third Davidson brother, William A., who joined the team as manufacturing technical manager, also played a key role.

At the beginning of their adventure these friends built three prototype engines, one of which had enough power to drive a small boat. Unfortunately, neither drawings nor elements of these three first engines have survived.

It was in about September of 1900 that the two friends undertook a study of mechanics, with a special focus on motorcycle engines. The result proved

profitable; by the beginning of January, 1901, four engines were ready to be fitted on the frames of entirely classical bicycles. Their carburation was far from satisfactory, because a system for regulating the fuel supply was still to be found. Since starting is always difficult, their business remained modest both in terms of equipment and financial support, but they were determined to improve. In order to obtain the money needed for research, Arthur Davidson found an additional job and, in doing so, met another engineer, Ole Evinrude, who specialized in boat engines and would help in the development of certain parts. On another front, a German immigrant called Emile Kruger, who worked at the same factory as Arthur Davidson and William S. Harley and who had been employed by Aster Concern of Paris, had the technical drawings of the De Dion petrol engines, which were built in France. His technical knowledge, William S. Harley's experience in bicycle manufacturing and Arthur Davidson's plans to build a small air-cooled petrol engine all combined to speed up their project by rapidly solving a number of problems.

THE DREAM COMES TRUE
1903: THE BEGINNING OF A GREAT STORY

20 The first workshop for producing Harley-Davidson motorcycles was a simple 10-by-15-foot wooden building. In 1904 its size doubled, to provide enough space to build the eight machines that the company would make that year.

21 The first Harley-Davidsons were painted black and decorated with gold stripes and red and gold lettering, as seen on this 1906 model. That same year, the catalog boasted a second color: the famous Harley-Davidson gray, which would be linked to the history of the line.

Arthur's brother Walter, who was twenty-six in 1902, worked for the railroad, having started out as apprentice engine driver in Milwaukee, and then worked in Kansas and Texas before returning to Illinois. One day in Parsons, Kansas, while he was repairing a locomotive, his work was interrupted by the arrival of some mail, including a letter from Arthur inviting him to come and drive the latest prototype he'd built together with William S. Harley. Since Walter already had to go to Milwaukee for a wedding, he decided to try the first Harley-Davidson on that occasion. But the motorcycle was still in pieces when he arrived. Arthur's invitation had in fact been a lure; Arthur and William were relying on the services of a specialist like Walter to put the final touches on bike. Seduced, Walter had no difficulty accepting the invitation to collaborate on the project, but only in his free time.

The designing and manufacturing continued rapidly, despite the need to machine each part by hand, because the prototype had to be ready for tests planned for the spring of 1903. When the family house became too small for such an enterprise, a mutual friend lent them his garage and his tools (including a lathe and a press), and they were able to complete their first motorcycle, which could at last be tested. Among the various anecdotes, there is a legend saying that the carburetor of that first motorcycle was made from a tin of tomatoes, which is not contradicted by any documents, historical or current. In any case, it held the road fine, thanks to its 400 cc, 3 horsepower engine. The transmission was through a leather belt, which was compact, easy to fit, and gave a pleasingly smooth drive. Its speed, which was calculated at around 25 mph, proved quite reasonable, but the engine power was still insufficient to overcome mild inclines in one go. That "two-wheeler" also revealed to them that an engine adapted to a bicycle frame did not make a real motorcycle, because the transmission, brakes and steering were designed to cope with the strength of the cyclist's leg, not with the power of an engine.

William S. Harley sat down again at his drawing board to study what would be required for a supporting structure to replace the excessively weak frame of a bicycle. It was also necessary to change the wheel size and to increase the bore and the engine stroke, as well as the magneto flywheel diameter, which was raised from thirteen to thirty centimeters.

22-23 *Walter C. Davidson, the first president of the Harley-Davidson Motor Company, after winning the Federation of American Motorcyclists Endurance Run in 1908.*

Every part had to be studied separately and built to withstand serious stresses, to eliminate the risk of breakage or deformation.

It was at that time that Walter Davidson, Sr. took up the dream of his brothers and William S. Harley and joined their venture. He was responsible for making the tools needed for the construction of the engine. Moreover, to give even more family character to the project, it was the Davidson brothers' aunt Janet who decorated the bike in the Harley-Davidson colors. The badge logo she created would be used until 1925. The color inside the letters would sometimes change, but the initial red would never be completely abandoned, and can still be found on some current models. When that first bike was due to be launched, its creators wondered about the final name to give to their brand: Davidson-Harley or Harley-Davidson? That the latter formula was chosen was due initially to its sound but also to the fact that William S. Harley designed that first model.

For Harley enthusiasts, the year 1903 is crucial in the story of this prestigious brand. It appeared in all the ads and was mentioned in all the articles describing this legend. In 1903, William S. Harley and the Davidson brothers introduced their first motorcycle, whose manufacture remained, by force of circumstances, confidential. Three motorcycles had been made and sold by the summer and the autumn of 1904. Remarkably, these three one-cylinder and belt-driven motorcycles were sold even before they were made. The first of them had a career which is a famous part of the brand history: its purchaser, a Mr. Meyer, rode it for 6,000 miles before handing it to its second owner, one Lyon Georges, who rode it for over twice at distance, covering 15,000 miles. The next owner, Mr. Webster, covered the even greater distance of 18,000 miles, and that was not the end, because Louis Fluke then reached a total of 12,000 miles. Finally, the last rider of that early Harley, Stephen

Sparrow, surpassed all his predecessors, by adding 32,000 miles to those already covered.

That model was equipped with a 2 horsepower, 24.7 cubic-inch engine, with a 3 x 6 inch ignition coil and a carburetor. It could run at speeds from five to forty-five mph.

The transmission was still based on a 1¼ inch flat leather belt, the tank had a capacity of one and a half gallons, the wheels had a diameter of 28 inches, and braking was by back-pedalling; this model, in black, sold for $200. It was a success for Harley and the Davidsons, one which they did not hesitate to use as an example for advertising the qualities of their machine, the first of which, they pointed out, had covered more than 100,000 miles with its original bearings.

23 top This 1910 photo, now in the Harley-Davidson Motor Company's archives, shows the four founders, whose varying talents complemented each other.

23 bottom In 1904, only eight motorcycles were sold. In 1906, fifty machines came out of the Harley-Davidson Motor Company workshop.

As for the second model, in gray, the manufacturers focused particularly on the driver's comfort and decided to eliminate the open exhaust. This bike offered such a high-quality ride that it was rapidly baptized "The Silent Gray Fellow."

After these successes, the partners were convinced that they should not rest on their laurels and that they must further develop their business. Despite material difficulties due to the lack of money, they decided to double their workshop area; they had outgrown the famous small wooden shed, which was never intended for their purpose. Thanks to these arrangements, Harley-Davidson ended up manufacturing eight "Silent Gray Fellows" in 1904. Then, when Walter Davidson, Sr. finally left his job with the railroad to join his brothers' business, it became clear that the team needed to improve its technical knowledge in order to create a more solid base for the company. This induced William S. Harley to take a course in the field of combustion engines at the University of Wisconsin, in Madison. Everything seemed poised to ensure that the small motorcycle manufacturer

THE HARLEY-DAVIDSON MOTOR COMPANY IS FOUNDED

would not remain small for long.

The choice that William S. Harley and the Davidson brothers faced at this point proved very simple: either their small factory could remain as it was, in which case it was bound to disappear one day, or they could take the risk of expanding.

We know which direction they decided to follow: on September 17, 1907, four years after the launch of its first motorcycle, the Harley-Davidson Motor Company was officially registered at the U.S. Trade and Company Register

24 top Dating back to the first decade of the twentieth century, this picture shows the manufacturing team. The Harley-Davidsons they were building came equipped with a one-cylinder engine, one of which appears on the left.

24 bottom In 1907, the company enlarged its factory to meet the growing demands of motorcyclists who wished to drive Harley-Davidson models.

25 Incorporating improvements such as the addition of chrome-plated elements, this one-cylinder X8A accounted for most of the Harley-Davidson motorcycle sales in 1912. It had a 30 cubic-inch (491 cc) one-cylinder engine with a belt-tensioning lever fixed on the right of the fuel tank. The free-wheel lever, new to this model, was the ancestor of the modern clutch, its mechanism housed in the rear wheel hub. A magneto lighting system was attached to the right-hand side of the motorcycle.

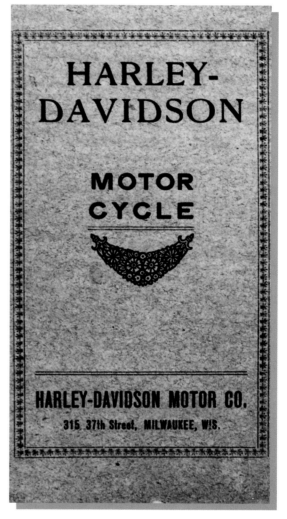

HARLEY-DAVIDSON

MOTOR CYCLE

HARLEY-DAVIDSON MOTOR CO.
315 37th Street, MILWAUKEE, WIS.

Office. It was no longer a matter of overseeing a small family workshop but of managing a real factory.

In fact, while in 1904 Harley-Davidson manufactured only eight motorcycles, in 1906, fifty machines left their workshop. With such growth, it was no longer possible to remain in the small wooden shed, even though its original size had been doubled. Soon men and machines were working in a large building in Milwaukee's industrial area, along Chestnut Street (later changed to Juneau Avenue) and 27th Street. The move was largely made possible by the support of James McLay, an uncle of the Davidson brothers and a beekeeper, who agreed to finance the new building, and that of their sister, Elisabeth, who invested a substantial sum and became the owner of several parts of the business.

The new structure demanded a meticulous distribution of roles, although each person could intervene in all sectors. The management team, as it was given to the Trade Register Office at the time, was as follows:

President: Walter C. Davidson, Sr.
Vice President and Works
Manager: William A. Davidson
Secretary and General Sales
Manager: Arthur Davidson

Chief Engineer and Treasurer: William S. Harley

Walter and William A. Davidson were appointed to the first two posts mainly because they were the only two who had to provide for a family. In fact, as a result of the excellent relationships he was able to build with the employees, to whom his door was always open, William A. Davidson was soon considered the heart of the company. One fact illustrates the point: whenever the workers needed part of their salary in advance, he granted it to them and noted the amount in the small notebook he always had with him. But it was a pure formality; he very rarely asked for reimbursement.

His brother Walter was not happy with

his post of president, and started attending a specialized training course on hot metal working.

Arthur took charge of commercial development and started to assign salesmen to several large cities: New York, Philadelphia, Chicago, Atlanta, San Francisco, and Los Angeles.

William S. Harley finished his university studies in 1908, with a degree in engineering. He then attended some courses on oxy-acetylene welding.

These small details show just how

26 As the factory grew, machines could be assembled more efficiently, and production increased considerably. As it standardized jobs, Harley-Davidson would consolidate its reputation, diversify its production, and improve its models over the first two decades of the twentieth century.

26-27 In 1914, Harley-Davidson offered a 35 cubic-inch (573 cc) one-cylinder motorcycle with a chain secondary transmission, fitted with a new starting system. Now the motorcycle no longer started by pedaling or by running at its side.

determined each man was to do his best in his field, to ensure that Harley-Davidson motorcycles would not become simply ordinary motorcycles and that the brand would continue to develop.

While studying at the university, William S. Harley continued with his research to improve the one-cylinder engine that had enabled him to launch the brand and had been praised by their customers. This motorcycle, which had an initial 165 cc displacement, was improved from year to year until it was fitted with a 4 horsepower, 550 cc engine, capable of running at a speed of 36 mph.

By 1918, this model had been technically upgraded: the power of models 6A, 6B, 6C, Series 6, was increased to 30.17 cubic inches, with an increased wheel diameter, as well as a cylinder which grew from $3^5/16$ to 4 inches and was available with one or three gears. In 1918, its manufacture was stopped, apart from a few motorcycles made on special requests, perhaps for customers looking for spare parts. After fifteen years on the scene, with 2500 units manufactured, this model, which began in a small wooden-walled workshop and had its success in a real factory on Juneau Avenue, deserved to retire.

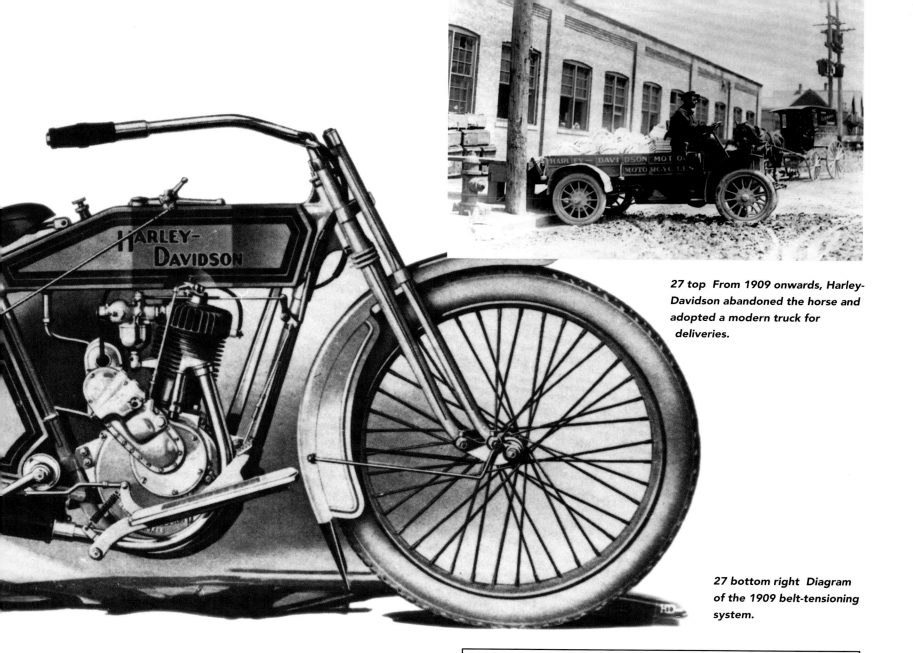

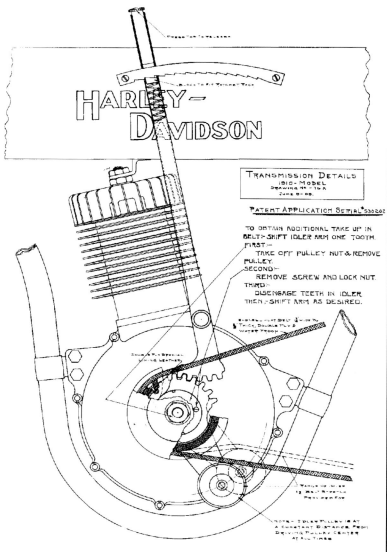

28

THE V-TWIN ERA

The first Harley-Davidson V-Twin appeared in 1909. One important detail must be mentioned here: this engine was not invented by the American company, and Harley-Davidson was not alone in adopting it. But the company kept and improved it, and it contributed to the brand's image over time. Thanks to its shape — an upside-down triangle — this engine fitted the bicycle frame, as was the case of the Harley-Davidson Motor Company "5D" model, in 1909.

Engineers easily established that an engine built with only one cylinder was naturally limited, mainly in its displacement and therefore in power, in such a way that it could withstand neither stresses nor an excessive efficiency.

The single cylinder, in existence since 1903, could be inclined both forwards and backwards. This positioning left room for a second cylinder, which in turn increased the possibilities of the engine, by keeping a single reinforced crankcase and fitting a modified timing distribution system control shared by both the cylinders.

Harley-Davidson adopted a forked connecting rod for this first model, which was fitted with the famous "V-Twin," thus doubling the engine displacement and obtaining greater efficiency. The two cylinders were set at 45 degrees, with an inlet valve on the head and an exhaust valve at the side.

This two-cylinder engine had a displacement of 850 cc (50 cubic inches), whereas the one-cylinder model did not exceed 500 cc. This new model had all cable controls: the accelerator and the spark advance were located at the level of the grips.

The 1909 "5D" model had a magneto and a 28-inch wheel, which could be requested as an option.

The "5D" model reached 62 mph with neither clutch nor gear box. In comparison with the one-cylinder model, the two-cylinder model kept pedals and a bicycle chain on the right, as well as a leather driving belt on the left, but its horsepower was increased by three.

Yet there were several technical handicaps: there was no tensioning pulley, the leather belt was inclined to slip, and the rider had to turn off the engine every time he wished to stop his motorcycle.

28 The first prototype of the Harley-Davidson V-Twin was unveiled during a motorcycle show in 1907, but the model was not actually produced until 1909. Design flaws slowed production, but from 1911 on, the V-Twin reappeared in the catalog and rapidly met with success.

29 top Head of the engineering department, William Harley proudly presents the first page of the Dodge City Daily Globe, announcing Harley-Davidson's victory in a 200-mile race.

29 center Since its first configuration in 1909, the Harley-Davidson V-Twin adopted a new exhaust outlet called the "pocket valve," which replaced the atmospheric valve taken from the old De Dion engines. V-Twin production stopped in 1910, but later a few modifications made these valves reliable and efficient. Shown here is a personalized machine from the mid-1920s.

29 bottom As early as 1914, the Harley-Davidson Motor Company promoted its motorcycles through advertising, boasting the merits of its models and attracting more customers by establishing specialized dealers who were able to maintain its machines.

This did not prevent the "5D" model from launching Harley-Davidson on the path the company has followed for almost 100 years.

In 1909, when the newly graduated engineer, William S. Harley, finally returned to the factory, he was convinced that production could only benefit from his scientific and technical knowledge. It was actually in 1908, on his drawing board, that he had conceived, in theory, the first two-cylinder engine. At first glance, it seemed that one had only to add a cylinder to the existing engine, but experiments showed that the new engine had to be particularly solid to withstand vibrations and other damage caused by the poor state of the roads, especially over the long distances which motorcycles might cover. As mentioned earlier, this engine, which went into production in 1909, had two cylinders positioned at 45 degrees and valves placed at the sides; it also generated greater torque than the one-cylinder model, especially at low speed. As with the one-cylinder model, the engine was extremely robust thanks to heads which were an integral part of the cylinders, and an inlet valve with an external rocker arm, which was articulated on the cylinder head. This allowed the rotation speed and engine compression to be increased. Even in its first tests, the new engine generated very large vibrations; this phenomenon would become part of the Harley-Davidson legend.

In 1910, the Harley-Davidson production catalog included, in Series 6, three 30.17 cubic-inch one-cylinder engines, the 6D V-Twin with 49.48 cubic inches, 6.5 horsepower, and 28-inch wheels. In 1911, Series 7 consisted of the same models (references: 7A, 7B, 7C for the one-cylinder and 7D for the V-Twin).

In contrast, Series 8 of the following year offered four one-cylinder and three two-cylinder models, the 8D, the X8D, a 49.48 inch displacement, and the X8E with 60.61 cubic inches and with 7 to 8 horsepower. This last model, which was supposed to be a sports model and which could only be driven by expert drivers, was the only one to have a clutch and a free rear wheel. On this V-Twin, entirely researched and designed by William S. Harley, a chain, which was tensioned thanks to a lever located on the left side of the tank, replaced the original leather belt.

The year 1912 marked the release of the geared V-Twin engine, where a chain-tightening lever was modified for this use and could also operate as a gear lever.

That year, another great novelty was introduced to customers: the seat was no longer a simple bike saddle with its two vertical spiral springs, but a real seat with a shock absorber fitted inside a tube which was an integral part of the frame.

30 top left The "Motorcycle Truck," later called "triporteur," reached the market in 1915. It met with huge success and was used by a wide variety of customers.

30 top right Keen on its brand image, Harley-Davidson developed a magazine for dealers and committed itself to advertising through quality catalogs.

30-31 and 31 top The "Motorcycle Truck" carried a large wooden trunk with a top cover, fixed on a directional chassis. It was driven with a handlebar, like a motorcycle. These machines were praised as a practical way to make deliveries. Less expensive than cars or trucks, they ended up providing excellent company publicity. Harley-Davidson manufactured them on order, with paintwork which included the logos of the companies purchasing them.

30 bottom The imagination of Harley-Davidson enthusiasts proved ebullient, which even surprised company officials. Take for example this 1917 ancestor of the skidoo.

32-33 *This is how motorcycles sent by the Harley-Davidson Motor Company were packed in 1916.*

In 1913, Harley-Davidson created its own racing service. Technical responsibility was entrusted to William Ottaway, who previously worked in the motorcycle department of Aurora Automatic Machine Company, in Illinois. Ottaway was also a racer, and when he went to work for Harley-Davidson, he had a reputation as a winner and an innovator in the motorcycle field. It was hoped that Ottaway's qualifications and his racing experience, together with William S. Harley's knowledge, would benefit the Milwaukee factory. He worked on technical improvements, specifically, the implementation of new systems which would allow the engines to perform better and to further withstand stress. In particular, his research resulted in an increase in the engine speed. He also conceived a new gear-changing mechanism, which then enabled Harley-Davidson motorcycles to move heavier loads, such as passengers in a sidecar. These early modifications appeared on the 1914 Harley-Davidson models, such as the "10B," which was equipped with a single cylinder and a single gear, and the "10C," which is the only one-cylinder engine that has two gears. In the same year, a V-Twin engine, referred to as "J," with 61 cubic-inch displacement, had two gears and a chain transmission. Ottaway permanently improved the qualities of this engine, increasing its power by 30%. In 1915, he implemented a foot-start system by means of a kick lever, eliminating the need to pedal.

During this period, the motorcycle became increasingly popular, thanks especially to the sidecar, which became widely used. Sidecars were produced by the Rogers Company, an American manufacturer which sold 2,500 of them to Harley-Davidson in 1914 and which doubled its production over the following year. Americans were discovering a new, reasonably priced means of transportation for more than one person. In 1915, these motorcycles were fitted with components still used today, such as a choke for cold starts, two-gear transmission, and back brakes.

In that period, single-cylinder engines enjoyed their last hours of glory. Over the years, the technology had improved to 30.17 cubic-inch displacements and 4.34 horsepower, but it was time for this model to be consigned to memory and to make room for new models which would forge the future of the Milwaukee motorcycle. During this time, the Harley-Davidson Motor Company continued its efforts to improve the revolutionary 1909 V-Twin engine. Bill Ottaway had given it a displacement of 61 cubic inches, or 1000 cc, which was very impressive for that time. The technological developments achieved in racing would continue to benefit production models. In 1917, Harley-Davidson put Model "17" on the market. A real bench mark for Bill Ottaway, this bike had an engine with four valves per cylinder and unique 54-inch wheels. Unfortunately, it was far from perfect: it was not fast and the rider had to lean either forwards or

backwards, according to his physical build, in order to balance it. However, by increasing the caster angle, Bill Ottaway found a solution to this problem.

Two years later, a 37 cubic-inch engine, the "Sport Model," was launched on the American market. Fitted with a four-stroke engine, it had a displacement of exactly 584.02 cc (6 horsepower) and could rotate at up to 4500 rpm, thanks to ball bearings on all the big ends. The engine flywheel was closed inside a sealed case. This three-gear Flat-Twin motorcycle, which had a chain transmission that was set by removing the back wheel, was manufactured between 1919 and 1922. In August of 1919, during a 1,012-mile run from New York to Chicago, it distinguished itself, ridden by Julian C. "Hap" Scherer, who covered the distance in thirty-one hours, twenty-four minutes.

Harley-Davidson continued at the same pace and won further endurance

33 top In 1918, Harley-Davidson became the most important motorcycle manufacturer in the world. Its success was due particularly to the V-Twin, which proved to be suited to being ridden alone or with a sidecar, which was then quite popular.

At that time, most of the motorcycles manufactured in Milwaukee were exported: war and the economic situation on the continent had forced European countries to reduce or even stop their national production. This was the case of England's Triumph, a company which had been founded in 1903, too, by two Germans, Siegfried Bettmann and Maurice Schulte. Since 1912, though, their 548 cc single-cylinder engines were manufactured by a branch based in Detroit.

races, with respectable records for each of them. Credit for the most spectacular of the trials must be given to Edwing Hogg, who crossed Death Valley. For his race across this 150-mile desert, Edwing Hogg chose a Sport-Twin, which was thoroughly overhauled by the Harley-Davidson service department before his departure. He crossed Death Valley a number of times, during which his only complaint was the large number of punctures. Once more, the Sport-Twin and Harley-Davidson had lived up to their reputations.

In 1920, motorcycle manufacture increased by almost 4,000 and reached the sum of 27,040 machines. Harley-Davidson motorcycles had been fitted with a magneto dynamo that allowed the battery to recharge when running, which was impressive, but the most impressive improvement of this era was the fact that the motorcycle could start even if the battery was dead.

33 bottom William A. Davidson and William S. Harley, on their way back from a fishing party (a sport they both particularly enjoyed), realized their combination of a Harley-Davidson and a sidecar was an ideal vehicle for leisure rides and short journeys.

THE COMPANY'S TECHNICAL AND COMMERCIAL POLICY

The success of the V-Twin and the growth of production spurred the managers to increase the number of sales people. In 1910, this led to the creation of a proper network throughout the United States.

Arthur Davidson was personally in charge of selecting the future dealers according to very strict criteria and making in-depth investigations to determine their professional qualifications, reputation, and inclination to build up good customer relationships.

Since most of them were bicycle dealers scarcely competent in mechanics, Harley-Davidson provided them with training in the new field so that they could better inform their customers and ensure good after-sales service. Some of the early salespeople, such as C. H. Lang, belong to the Harley-Davidson legend. Lang was one of the brand's first dealers.

34 top A good-looking girl, a Harley-Davidson, and a romantic drive-what else could one desire to be happy? This Harley-Davidson cliché still exists today.

34 bottom Harley-Davidson received a medal for creating vehicles that promoted communication between rural areas.

35 top Harley-Davidson dealers became more and more important. The character of their operations contributed to the company's image, especially in terms of service long after the motorcycles had been delivered.

35 bottom Harley-Davidson has been publishing a magazine, The Enthusiast, to promote the company since 1916.

From 1912, he alone was selling 800 motorcycles per year. (Total production in 1912 was 3,852 motorcycles.) In order to attract customers, he introduced a very appealing credit system. Thanks to his aptitude for trade, his activity did not slow down, and he became, in the space of four years, the most important Harley-Davidson dealer in the whole country.

But Arthur Davidson was not content with a network of dealers only inside the United States, so he built other networks in Australia, New Zealand and Europe (in England, Italy, France, Germany, Spain, Sweden, Denmark. . .). By 1921, Harley-Davidsons could be purchased in sixty-seven countries around the world. Some European manufacturers, seeing the public's interest in the motorcycles from Milwaukee, did not hesitate to copy the brand.

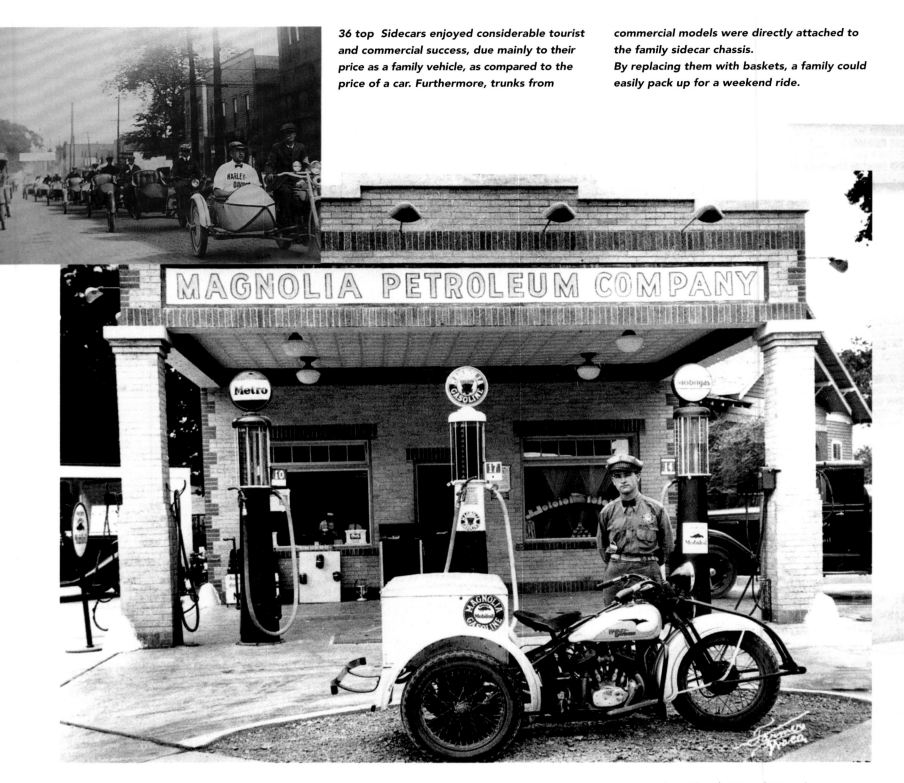

After the Great War, the French Harley-Davidson importer launched a small 123 cc single-cylinder motorcycle which looked like the "Silent Gray Fellow." Produced from 1923 to 1928, it was sold in France under the name of "Harlette-Geco."

To improve its commercial performance and set itself apart from its competitors, the Harley-Davidson Motor Company began publishing several magazines.

In 1912, the brand created *The Dealer*, a report to bind the company and its dealers, which was published until 1916. That same year, the company launched *The Enthusiast*, available in English and Spanish, which kept dealers and customers informed of all the novelties coming from the factory.

This paper also dedicated a few pages to miscellaneous reports which were in some way connected to motorcycles; it is still published today.

Harley-Davidson, like other manufacturers, also advertised in the first U.S. magazines aimed at fans of this increasingly popular sport: *Bicycling World*, *Motorcycle Illustrated* (published in Illinois), *Motorcyclist* (Los Angeles), and *The Western Bicyclist*.

All of them reported on the sporting events taking place around the country and presented the new models and accessories. It is worth pointing out that the motorcycle was an increasingly popular means of transportation in the United States until 1908, when Henry Ford launched his famous Model T. Since car production was still very limited, automobiles were a lot less affordable than motorcycles: a

motorcycle sold at $250 to $290, whereas it took $900 to buy a Ford T. The drawback of the motorcycle was, obviously, the smaller number of seats, but it was possible to fit a sidecar for less than $100, which explains the success enjoyed by these vehicles.

In 1920, after seventeen years of existence, thanks to their technical and commercial performance, Harley-Davidson outstripped Indian, which had been America's premier manufacturer until then. An investment of $3.5 million allowed the company to further expand the factory on Juneau Avenue (to 542,258 square feet) and to equip it with modern machinery. Thanks to the improvements, the factory, with 2,400 employees, was able to produce more than 30,000 motorcycles per year.

36 bottom During the 1930s, Harley-Davidson-based commercial vehicles diversified, in particular thanks to the Servi-Car.

37 top The Servi-Car became enormously successful with the American law enforcement authorities. The police used them for their urban corps: in the Servi-car, two policemen could ride together, one marking wheels to check parking duration of cars along the street.

37 bottom The Harley-Davidson sidecars won many races, not only in the United States but also in various other countries. Their legendary reliability encouraged many teams to undertake dangerous and spectacular journeys. Ordinary people, too, used them daily to get through any weather and across any type of ground.

38 *The Dudley Perkins dealership opened its doors in San Francisco in 1914. Today, it represents the oldest Harley-Davidson concession in the world. Still managed by the Perkins family, it has become legendary. It has changed as the brand has changed, responding to the market and to riders' demands, supplying motorcycles and all the accessories, clothes, and gadgets one can imagine, all marked with the Harley-Davidson logo.*

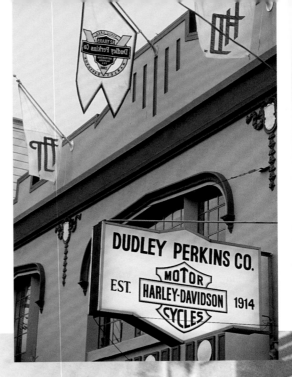

39 New Harley-Davidson dealerships, as well as those who have been operating for years, have to stay sensitive to the changing brand image. As a result, although the exterior of each shop is personalized, inside the customer finds himself in familiar territory. The layout of each dealership is familiar, but business style can be dictated by the personality of the dealer.

40 top To support sales, the Harley-Davidson Motor Company has published several magazines. In 1912, it launched *The Dealer*, a bulletin intended for concessionaires, sold until 1916. In 1916, it introduced *The Enthusiast*, which continues to keep dealers and customers informed. The company has consistently used advertising to communicate with future customers, placing ads not only in newspapers but also in new specialty magazines.

Harley Davidson

„The Silent Gray Fellow".

„**IMP**".

„The Only Real Cyclecar".

Compleet met kap, lantaarns en gereedschap, **f1285.-**

Vraagt catalogi A en C en proefritten aan de
Importeurs voor Holland, Koloniën en België:

Delftsche Motoren-Handel, Kolk 3, DELFT.

40-41 Harley-Davidson executives, as well as their heirs, had to be motorcycle enthusiasts. While they were all still young, Gordon, Walter, and Allan Davidson made a stop at the Dudley Perkins dealership in San Francisco in 1929.

Harley-Davidsons, like all the other motorcycles of that time, developed little by little. From simple utility machines used for transport, they gradually became leisure vehicles appealing to younger people. Racing played an important role in this process.

41 left Harley-Davidson promotions boast about the qualities of each machine and give information about the development of the company.

41 right Motorcycles and planes often appeal to the same enthusiasts. Here, Harley-Davidson focused on this theme, comparing the sensations of the pilot with the driver. Many plane pilots of the time actually traveled by motorcycle when they were on land.

The 1915
Harley-Davidson
Three Speed Twin Will
Climb a 60% Grade.

THIS powerful machine has taken a Harley-Davidson and sidecar up a 45 per cent grade without a murmur, a grade nearly twice that of the steepest hill to be found in most localities.

The 1915 Harley-Davidson twin motor is guaranteed to develop eleven actual horse power (37½% more than the 1914 Harley-Davidson twin). This exceptional power in conjunction with the new Harley-Davidson three speed gives the rider more power than he really needs. If the going is rough, sandy, snowy or muddy, he can shift into intermediate gear and run mile after mile without overheating the motor.

These three-speed gears are cut so perfectly that they do not make a

sound. The rider will find the Harley-Davidson transmission as silent in low or intermediate gear as in high gear. It is possible to shift from intermediate to high gear or to slam into low gear, any time, anywhere, without fear of clashing or stripping of gears. This is positively prevented by an ingenious device.

There are many other features which add to the comfort, durability and economy of the 1915 Harley-Davidson, fully described in our catalog which will be sent upon request.

More Dealers for 1915

Additions to the Harley-Davidson factories enable us to add more dealers for 1915. If, as a dealer, you are situated in a locality where we are not represented and feel qualified to represent the Harley-Davidson in keeping with the Harley-Davidson name and reputation, get in touch with us at once.

Harley-Davidson Motor Company
Producers of High Grade Motorcycles for Nearly Fourteen Years
407-B Street   **MILWAUKEE, WIS., U. S. A.**

TWIN THRILLS

BREEZE away, carefree, over the roads and highways on a speedy Harley-Davidson. Soar over the hills—zoom down into the valleys!

Only flying can compare with the sheer thrill of motorcycling.

A Harley-Davidson costs little to buy and almost nothing to run. It makes motorcycling one of the most inexpensive of sports.

What glorious good times you and your motorcycle will have together! Twilight jaunts with "the bunch" — week-end trips of hundreds of miles — wonderful vacation tours!

Your nearby Harley-Davidson Dealer wants to show you the great 1931 models, and tell you about his Pay-As-You-Ride Plan. See him today.

Ride a
HARLEY-DAVIDSON

Mail Coupon for Free Literature!

HARLEY-DAVIDSON MOTOR CO.
Dept. MM, Milwaukee, Wis.

Interested in your motorcycles. Send literature.

Name.....................................

Address.................................

My age is ☐ 16-19 years, ☐ 20-30 years,
☐ 31 years and up, ☐ under 16 years.
Check your age group.

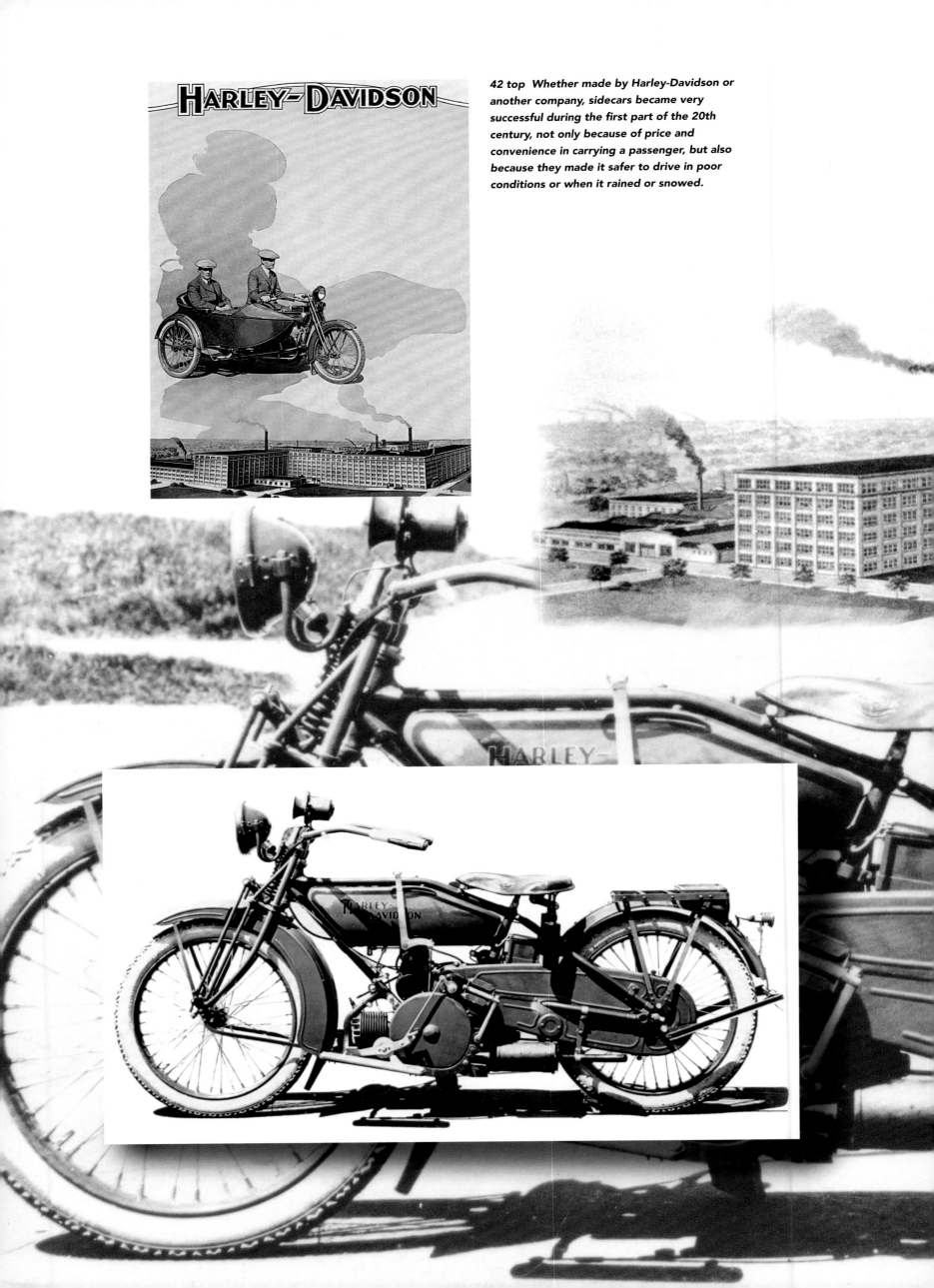

HARLEY-DAVIDSON

42 top Whether made by Harley-Davidson or another company, sidecars became very successful during the first part of the 20th century, not only because of price and convenience in carrying a passenger, but also because they made it safer to drive in poor conditions or when it rained or snowed.

42 bottom The Flat-Twin Sport model, introduced in mid-1919 as Twin Sport, had a 35.6 cubic-inch capacity. From 1920 on, Harleys were fitted with an electric system and, in 1921 (the model shown here), with a new fuel tank whose design resembled that of the Big Twins. This model, which became the Electric Sport Model, was only manufactured until 1922, since it did not give Harley-Davidson a competitive edge against the sportiest Indian machines.

42-43 In 1920, the Harley-Davidson Company was the biggest motorcycle producer in the world, measured both in size and in the number of motorcycles produced per year. In 1926, the Harley-Davidson factory on Juneau Avenue had been a monument of Milwaukee for a decade.

43 bottom Exploded view of a Harley-Davidson 74 cubic-inch V-Twin (1200 cc), produced in 1924. The first 74 c.i. V-Twin engine was unveiled in 1921 and appeared on the market in 1922. At the same time, a 61 cubic-inch (1000 cc) model was in the catalog as well.

44 top and 44 center right Fitted with baskets adapted to specific jobs, Harley-Davidsons with sidecar frames proved great commercial successes, performing jobs that ranged from simple deliveries to servicing broken-down vehicles.

44 center left In their marketing message, Harley-Davidson emphasized that their motorcycles were the perfect answer to customer needs of the time. It was possible to ride solo, or a leisure or commercial sidecar could easily be attached, simply by replacing the boot on the frame.

44 bottom left This fork head, appearing in the Harley-Davidson catalog during the first half of the 1920s, became popular as a screen against bad weather. While it could affect road handling when riding solo, it proved excellent when the motorcycle was coupled to a sidecar.

Media Drug Stores! In Philadelphia and Sub-
rbs, Media Drug Service is as quick and easy
a telephone call. Here's how.

Katydid! In Kansas City, Mo., the Katydid
Candies are rushed to watering mouths this
sure and certain Harley-Davidson way.

Burleson Tire Co., San Antonio, Texas, know the sweet fruits of rendering quick and reliable
vice to "stuck" motorists. A flat tire is a flat tire 'til it's fixed. These boys fix 'em — and,
rybody's happy.

Note the simplicity
and sturdy con-
struction of this
new windshield.

LAUGH
AT THE COLD
THIS WINTER!

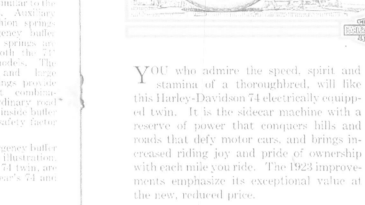

The Single Unit Electric System as used by Harley-Davidson has been in successful operation for consecutive years. Today, nine out of ten Harley-Davidson motorcycles, sold in the United States, are electrically equipped. The superiority of the Harley-Davidson type Single Unit System is further attested by the fact that it is the ignition used for U. S. Army aeroplanes and is standard equipment on such cars as Packard, Cadillac, Marmon, Stutz and Pierce-Arrow.

Riding Comfort is built-in the Harley-Davidson Motorcycle

The front fork springs with auxiliary buffer springs, the air-cushion saddle and the patented Ful-Floteing seat post of the 1923 Harley-Davidson assure genuine riding comfort.

In addition to the fore-going, there is a new fork on the 61" machines, similar to the 74" models. Auxiliary center cushion springs and emergency buffer and recoil springs are used on both the 74" and 61" models. The fork-side and large center springs provide a resilient combination for ordinary road conditions. In rough going the heavy inside buffer springs come into play and as a final safety factor positive stops are provided.

The auxiliary center cushion and emergency buffer and recoil springs, (shown in front fork illustration, under horn) so successful on last year's 74 twin, are now regular equipment on both this year's 74 and 61 twins.

The Ful-Floteing seat post is an exclusive and patented Harley-Davidson feature of eleven years success. The springs in this Ful-Floteing seat post can be easily adjusted to the weight of the individual rider.

The large, roomy, form-fitting, well padded air-cushion saddle adds to the riding comfort and pleasure of the Harley-Davidson.

YOU who admire the speed, spirit and stamina of a thoroughbred, will like this Harley-Davidson 74 electrically equipped twin. It is the sidecar machine with a reserve of power that conquers hills and roads that defy motor cars, and brings increased riding joy and pride of ownership with each mile you ride. The 1923 improvements emphasize its exceptional value at the new, reduced price.

Double Your Motorcycling Pleasures with a Harley-Davidson Sidecar

Harley-Davidson Motorcycles and Sidecars — the Choice of Skilled, Experienced Mechanics

HARLEY-DAVIDSON

45 In 1922, the first Harley-Davidson 74 cubic-inch (1200 cc) V-Twin was launched. This motorcycle's mission was to boost sales by offering greater power than the 61 cubic-inch model. While the 61 was better for riding solo, advertising promised that the 74 could generate 18 horsepower, making it the ideal engine for driving sidecars and carrying a passenger.
A strong market demand prompted manufacturers to develop sidecar machines and improve them over the years.
Sidecars had to compete with cars produced in assembly lines.
In 1923, Henry Ford launched a basic version Model T at about $300, with a devastating impact on the motorcycle industry. In 1922, a Harley-Davidson JDS Sidecar Twin sold for $390.
In 1923, the Harley-Davidson JD Solo was offered in the catalog at $330.

46 top Whether solo or with a sidecar, the Harley-Davidson was supposed to convey the spirit of discovery. The company wanted to convince the public that it was the ideal machine for traveling reliably, whether to the far corners of the earth or around the block, which is where most owners would drive it.

46 center and bottom A communication medium was needed—to convey the Harley-Davidson image, to portray the traveling spirit linked to these motorcycles, to inform potential owners of sports model performances, and to spread the news about innovations and improvements. Of course, the company already communicated with the public through specialized journals and high-circulation newspapers, but it needed its own publication. The Enthusiast appeared for the first time in 1916.

46-47 The Enthusiast addressed both dealers and users. It began by broadcasting Harley-Davidson's military contribution during World War I. Still published quarterly today, it is distributed by dealers.

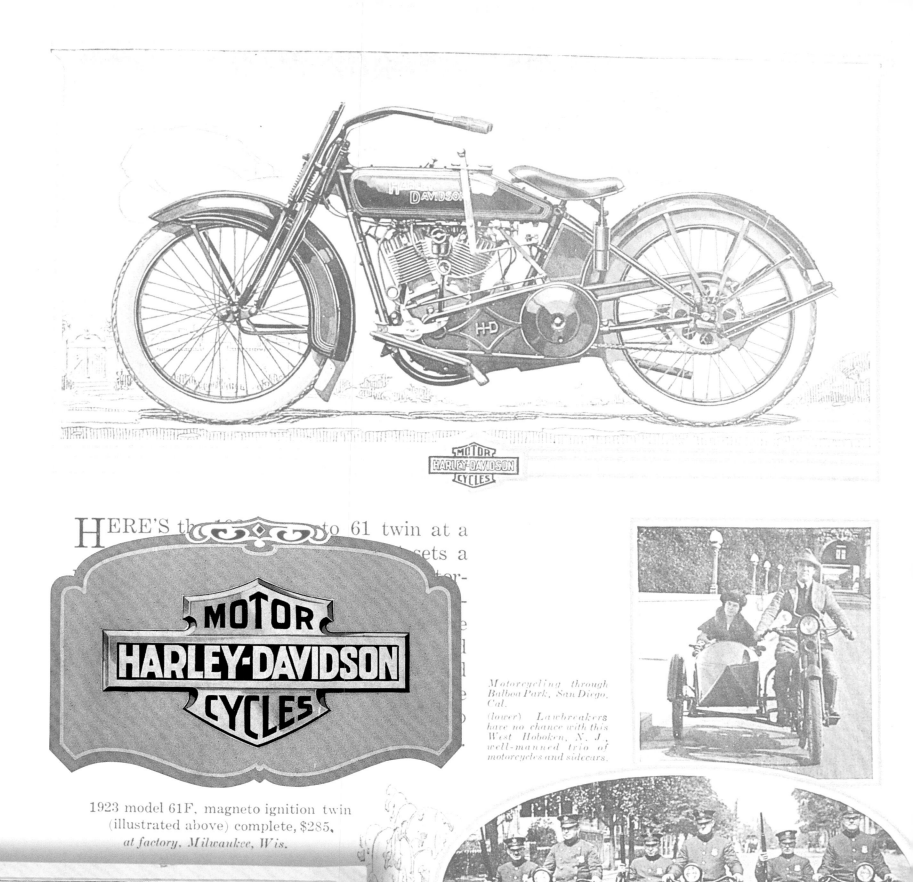

HERE'S the ... to 61 twin at a ... sets a ...

1923 model 61F, magneto ignition twin
(illustrated above) complete, $285,
at factory, Milwaukee, Wis.

Motorcycling through Balboa Park, San Diego, Cal.
(lower) Lawbreakers have no chance with this West Hoboken, N. J., well-manned trio of motorcycles and sidecars.

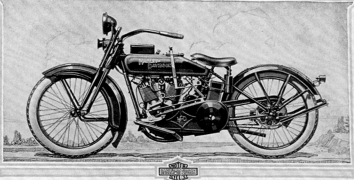

THIS 1923 Harley-Davidson 61 electrically equipped twin is a greater value at a greatly reduced price. The 61 electric model is now equipped with the double-action, shock-absorbing front fork springs, silchrome exhaust valves and all the other big 1923 new improvements. In addition to its ability to pull a sidecar, this 61 model is winning more friends, each day, as a solo mount, through its ease of handling.

1923 model 61J, electrically equipped twin
(illustrated above) complete, $305,
at factory Milwaukee, Wis.

Go to that fishing paradise with a sidecar outfit
(lower) Victor and victim homeward bound.

than 900 Police Departments

47 Before the Servi-Car, police officers used
the Harley-Davidson sidecar, since it allowed
the rider to be ready to take action, to open
fire if necessary, or simply to mark the tires
of parked cars.

48 top Finding a one-cylinder Harley-Davidson in this condition is quite rare. The collector has chosen to preserve this one in its original state rather than renovating and updating it.

48 bottom left The first sidecars were used like cars, and they adopted a similar look. Early marketing messages tried to ensure the comfort of a sidecar, since they targeted people who wanted a car but could not afford one.

48 bottom right Certain collectors—along with those who simply own and love their old Harley-Davidsons—still ride their classic bikes for pleasure. They also take part in rallies and shows. Sometimes, as here, they make real journeys.

49 It is worth noting the valve systems and the position of the plugs, features which were applied to the other American motorcycles of that time. The famous scoops in the tank permitting the passage of the inlet valve were later used by certain modern designers for aesthetic reasons when they transformed their Harley-Davidsons.

Harley-Davidson
MILWAUKEE U.S. of A

1918
Ladies
Standard

HARLEY-DAVIDSON
BICYCLES

The war created a demand for bicycles, too, and spurred the Harley-Davidson Company to produce them starting in 1917. Since this kind of two-wheeler was no longer imported from Europe, which was at war and whose industry suffered as a result, a complete line of Harley-Davidson bicycles was put on the market from 1917 to 1921 including, apart from the usual models for men and for racing, models for women, young girls, and children. There was also a special version for boys of ten to sixteen years of age, as well as a bicycle with a reinforced frame to which it was possible to add an engine — in other words, a return to the origin of the motorcycle. These bicycles, manufactured entirely by hand, were offered at prices ranging from $30 to $40; however, after the war, the Harley-Davidson Company

50-51 In 1919, in order to attract young customers, Harley-Davidson started manufacturing bicycles. The company made the most of its brand image, banking on the reliability, quality, and patriotic image of their motorcycles to sell bicycles. Similar to their "big sisters," the motorcycles, Harley-Davidson bicycles were painted army drab. Their quality was excellent, but production stopped in only a matter of years because the retail price was too high.

focused exclusively once again on its main activity: the motorbike. Once the war was over, the demand for Harley-Davidson bicycles decreased, and the company decided to abandon this area, concentrating their investment instead in the development of their racing models and those for the average consumer.

HARLEY-DAVIDSON PUTS ON ITS FIRST FIGHTING UNIFORM

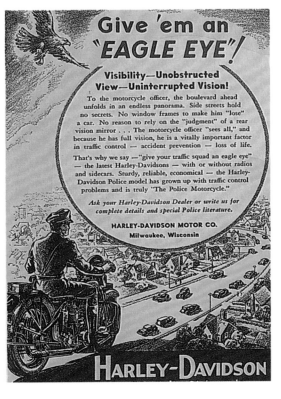

Having begun to build up his sales network, Arthur Davidson turned his attention to the various public service departments whose employees might be likely to use his two-wheelers for their work. In 1909, during an annual postal conference, he presented a motorcycle designed to speed up the distribution of mail. A contract was agreed to and signed, as was one with the telephone company, which ordered 700 motorcycles, not to mention the police, who would use this new means of transportation to maintain law and order.

In 1916, Harley-Davidson launched its first army motorcycles in a conflict on non-European soil, during a punitive expedition led by General John J. "Black Jack" Pershing against the Mexican rebels led by Pancho Villa. Since Mexico's President Francesco I. Madera lacked the military force to face the rebels, he authorized the Americans to enter Mexico to put an end to Pancho Villa's uprising. General Pershing's troops failed, but this was not a defeat for the Harley-Davidsons, which had been tested for the first time on a real battlefield and had performed successfully.

In 1914, war broke out in Europe. Initially, the United States kept its distance from the conflict. But it was difficult for President Woodrow Wilson to remain neutral for long. The Germans torpedoed American ships during submarine fights, ignoring any right to neutral navigation. The United States declared war on Germany on April 6, 1917, and sent in two million soldiers under General Pershing. The United States also granted $10 billion of credit to the Allies.

During these difficult years, Harley-Davidson equipped a number of its

machines with military equipment. In particular, William S. Harley was put in charge of studying the military's needs and adopting the necessary armaments for the missions the two-wheelers were to undertake on the European field. Twenty thousand motorcycles were used in this conflict. Although not all of them came from Harley-Davidson, the participation of the brand was far from negligible. During this period, the Harley-Davidson Motor Company established the Harley-Davidson Service School (which closed in 1941) to train mechanics to repair, in situ, the breakdowns that were the result of hard and demanding use. Beginning in 1917, the school soon stopped accepting Harley-Davidson dealers in order to reserve places for war recruits. Almost 300 soldiers attended the school before the armistice on November 11, 1918.

These military motorcycles, which

became renowned in Europe in only a few years, allowed Harley-Davidson to gain an excellent reputation. Seven thousand of them were sent to France, and certain collectors still have them today. The models reserved for France had a simple ignition magneto and acetylene lighting supplied by a compressed gas bottle placed in the center of the handlebar.

Before the war, Harley-Davidson had used German electrical systems made by Bosch, still a well-known brand today. But once the conflict started, it was no longer possible to equip motorcycles with this system; an American manufacturer was put in charge of devising an equally good system. In this way, engineers were forced to manufacture technologically excellent parts, which would benefit the whole automotive industry.

52-53 Public authorities, like private companies, rapidly replaced horses with motor vehicles, among which sidecar motorcycles gained a good market share. The U.S. Post Office even published a stamp bearing the image of a Harley-Davidson. Police, who used Harley-Davidsons to preserve the order, posed for pictures like this one.

In 1917, one of Harley-Davidson's military contributions was to train soldiers to be mechanics, specializing in on-the-spot motorcycle repairs.

The first Yank and I to enter Germany.

A CORPORAL AND HIS MECHANICAL MOUNT

On November 8, 1918, a few days before the armistice, while the German soldiers were marching towards their borders, an American messenger, Corporal Roy Holtz, driving a motorcycle with a sidecar, led his captain on a mission to the north of Belgium. The bad weather and the fighting forced Holtz to travel by night, and, having lost his sense of direction, he headed east. Attracted by the lights of an isolated farm, he stopped to ask for directions, only to discover that the farm was in fact a German headquarters. The two Americans were taken prisoner. Luckily, their imprisonment lasted just two days, for the armistice was declared on November 11. Once free, the captain and Corporal Holtz split up. The corporal headed west on his bike and met the German troops who were retreating. Thus, Roy Holtz was the first American soldier to penetrate into Germany. . . seventy-two hours before his American friends.

On November 12, 1918, somebody living on the banks of the Rhine took a photograph of a man on a motorcycle, but establishing the motorcyclist's identity was very difficult. It was a full twenty-five years before Roy Holtz (who in civilian life was an electrician near Milwaukee) was identified as the man in the picture. In 1943, the photograph appeared in The Enthusiast, and in 1944, Holtz went to the Harley-Davidson offices to get a copy of the picture, which had been published in many American newspapers and had become a famous image, symbolic of the end of the war.

In 1917 and 1918, Harley-Davidson produced 45,230 models. The factory manufactured five different commercial models, two single-cylinder and three V-Twin, of which one type had one gear and the other two types, F18 and J18, had three gears and a displacement of 60.34 cubic inches. Unfortunately, the war brought hard times to the American motorcycle industry and some small manufacturers, unable to obtain certain parts from Europe, were forced to shut down.

54-55 On the 12th of November, 1918, after an amazing but true experience which he shared with his captain a few days before, Corporal Roy Holtz was the first American to penetrate Germany after the end of World War I.

54 bottom Whether ridden solo or with a sidecar, Harley-Davidsons offered soldiers significant advantages over horses.

55 William S. Harley, together with soldiers, tested the performance of motorcycles built for World War I.

THE DÉTENTE AFTER THE CONFLICT

From 1904, Harley-Davidson motorcycles took part in many races, but unlike other brands such as Indian, Pope, and Thor, the factory contributed neither to the preparation of race models, nor to their financing. Yet Harley-Davidson benefited from the commercial implications of the numerous victories won by their bikes. In 1913, for the company's tenth anniversary, William S. Harley finally decided to set up a racing service.

President Walter himself rode a Harley-Davidson to victory in an endurance race lasting two days. It was the first official American race organized by the Federation of American Motorcyclists (F.A.M.), which would later become the American Motorcycle Association (A.M.A.). In 1908 there was a two-day endurance race that began in the Catskill Mountains and ended in Brooklyn. There were eighty-four participants and twenty-two brands represented, but half the drivers and their motorcycles were eliminated during the first day of the race.

56 top *Harley-Davidsons rapidly managed to dominate dirt-track races, but the company didn't establish a racing department until 1914. Until then, these races were won by avid riders who had modified their machines by themselves.*

56 bottom *Ralph Hepburn, astride an 8-valve Harley-Davidson after a series of victories. Hepburn won the 100-mile race in 1:07:05.4, the 200-mile race in 2:07:54, and the 300-mile race in 3:30:03, all at Dodge City, Kansas, on July 4th, 1921.*

Walter Davidson managed to stay the course without difficulty and won the race with an entirely mass-production single-cylinder motorcycle.

After this first endurance event, Walter Davidson took part in another race, the Economy Run, which began on Long Island, New York. He won again. His victories boosted sales, and the publicity surrounding him resulted in an increase in the number of dealers. On Independence Day, July 1914, Harley-Davidson's motorcycles won 23 races. Leslie "Red" Parkhurst won the One Hour National Championship in Birmingham, Alabama. In 1915, a rider named Floyd Clymer won the World Dirt Track Title on a two-cylinder model fitted with eight valves and two exhaust outlets per cylinder prepared especially for the race.

While the war was raging in Europe, Harley-Davidson and Bill Ottaway continued to win victories on the race track. They also organized a race in Venice, California, at which the main motorcycle brands would compete. The best drivers were there, and Bill Ottaway, a master of organization, chose drivers capable of taking the top positions.

56-57 *Board track races became very popular in the 1920s. Many board track riders became famous, and many spectacular accidents took place on these oval wooden tracks. Builder Jack Prince specialized in the construction of these wooden tracks from 1908 to 1925.*

57 top *Eddie Brink in 1927, astride the "Peashooter," a 21 cubic-inch (350 cc) one-cylinder Harley-Davidson. In the same year, Brink died on a board track, by falling in front of Joe Petrali.*

57

THE 1921 RACER

Perhaps anticipating the rising costs of racing, as early as 1921, the Harley-Davidson Motor Company did not really intend to invest in expensive research in order to manufacture a new, stronger, and more efficient engine designed to win races. At the time, most of the circuits were entirely covered in wood with banked curves, called "board track," or they were simply compacted earth with flat curves, called "dirt track." However, the company did decide to develop a mass-produced "V-Twin" engine with a few modifications to guarantee its durability while making it more efficient. The main modification concerned the cylinder heads. Each cylinder had two intake valves and two cutouts, controlled by means of tappets and rocker arms, driven by a single camshaft housed in the timing case.

This engine was built thanks to the experience and knowledge of a specialist, Harry Ricardo. In the meantime, an English rider, Freddie Dixon, fitted two carburetors on his racing bike with more than satisfactory results.

The "Racer" of the early days had only one carburetor though there were three versions of this eight-valve engine. They cannot be confused with each other, for each was different and corresponded to the needs of the rider.

This engine fits inside a frame, nicknamed "Keystone"; a lower element formed by two plates sandwiched the engine block. Don't look for brakes: at that time, brakes were not allowed on racing bikes, because their use was considered dangerous for the other competitors!

The "Racer" was fitted with a primary and secondary chain transmission with an intermediate pinion which adapted the chain tension by means of a cam. This superb bike was reserved for professional drivers, and its prohibitive price ($1,500) was three times greater than that of any other racing bike. That alone was enough to disuade non-professionals.

Since no more than a dozen of this model were built, some of which were sent overseas to distinguish the brand from the competition on European circuits, this has become a very rare collector's piece. Willie G. Davidson owns a superb copy built by Steve Wright. The one shown in these pictures, however, belongs to an Italian collector who is well aware of the value of his treasure, even though the frame is not original.

60-61 The Racer, a Harley-Davidson adapted from the touring model, was fitted with a 61 cubic-inch (1000 cc) 8-valve engine. From early on it stood out, winning races when ridden by Otto Walker. It was the first machine to go faster than 100 miles per hour during a one-mile board track race at Fresno, California, on February 22nd, 1921. On that day, riding this motorcycle, Otto Walker won every competition in which he entered.

SMOKEY JOE

In 1904, one year after the first Harley Davidson was built in Wisconsin, Joe Petrali was born in San Francisco. Born on February 22, Petrali had an early, boundless admiration for motorcycles. His passion was encouraged by a neighbor called Dewey Houghton, who was a mechanic. Houghton's motorcycle, was a Flanders, an American brand manufactured for the few years between 1911 and 1914. Fitted with a 499 cc single-cylinder engine, its general appearance was similar to that of the "Silent Gray Fellow," which had come out a few years earlier. Dewey Houghton looked after his motorcycle very carefully, and sometimes he would demonstrate the meticulous technique required for tuning the Flanders engine.

Joe Petrali's father gave his son his first motorcycle, an Indian, when Joe was thirteen. This motorcycle had been ridden hard for a number of years on compacted earth tracks. Nonetheless, Joe had already developed a taste for speed and victory, and was determined to get his bike ready for racing. Working with an Indian dealer from California, he prepared well.

In 1918, Joe Petrali won the 500 cc category of the Economy Run, a race where one needed to cover the longest distance using the minimum amount of fuel. On that day, Joe managed to run for 175 miles on less than a gallon, thus claiming the national record and inscribing his name in the history of American racing.

This victory on his very worn-out motorcycle was followed by other successes, and Petrali soon attracted the interest of motorcycle racing patrons, who realized that, despite his tender age, he had the makings of a great rider. When, in August of 1922, "Shrimp" Burns, the official Indian rider, was killed during a race in Toledo, Ohio, Joe Petrali took over. During one long race, a bad fuel mixture caused serious carburation problems in the eight-valve engine. Inspite of this, the young champion finished the race second. This was an enormous achievement, especially when one considers that he was competing against drivers much older and more experienced than he. When he was 16, Petrali had left California to move to Kansas City. He worked there as a

mechanic for a motorcycle dealer, Albert G. Crocker, who also manufactured his own brand from 1936 to 1941. Crocker took advantage of some of the research and development done by the major brands, using a number of Harley-Davidson and Indian parts in his V-Twin engines. Crocker hired Petrali based on the young man's

reputation, and he was not disappointed. For a board track race in Altoona, Pennsylvania, Indian had guaranteed Petrali that his personal engine would be overhauled, prepared, and refitted on to its original frame in time for the start. But on the day of the race, due to a shipping error, his engine had not arrived.

Making the best of a bad situation, Joe borrowed the Harley-Davidson of a rider who had been injured during the tests. They agreed to share the prize money in the event that Petrali won the race. During the race, Petrali was so focused on winning that he didn't notice when another rider had to stop to change his front tire and lost two laps. Seeing the same rider in front of him later in the race, Petrali struggled to pass and went two extra laps, not realizing that he'd already won.

His fame was increasing and in 1921 Harley-Davidson hired him away from Indian and made him their official rider. In his new role, he continued to claim victories in races as varied as the flat track,

the board track, and the hill-climb. When Harley-Davidson interrupted its sporting activity from 1926 to 1931, Joe Petrali turned to the Excelsior Supply Company, which manufactured motorcycles in Chicago from 1907 to 1931. With the collaboration of Ignatz Schwinn, Joe Petrali built a series of Excelsior V-Twins called "Super X." During this period, but before his Excelsior was ready, Petrali entered a race in Springfield, Illinois, riding a 350cc single-cylinder Indian. During the race, his

friend and rival on the circuits, Eddie Brink, lost control of his bike coming out of a curve, skidded, and slammed into Petrali's Indian. Eddie Brink was killed on the spot; Petrali suffered a massive head injury and a seriously torn lip. Thanks to the intervention of a young doctor and Petrali's own strong constitution, he was soon back on his feet and ready to start racing again.

Four years later, when Petrali was twenty-seven, the managers of the racing group at Harley-Davidson resumed their activities and rehired him for an important series of races. Once again, Joe Petrali became a full-time Harley-Davidson employee, and his experience as both a mechanic and a rider was important to the company.

62 Joe Petrali first raced on an Indian. Later, he gained a name for riding Harley-Davidsons and then stole victories for Excelsior, from 1926 to 1931, until that company shut down. In 1931, Harley-Davidson returned to racing and engaged Joe Petrali again. His invincible style stood out on the dirt track0, on the board track, and in hill-climbing.

62-63 Joe Petrali gained immortal glory by riding this Harley-Davidson OHV 61, powered by a Knucklehead 1000, at Daytona Beach, Florida. In 1937, he set the 136.183 mph record on the sands of Daytona Beach—a record which was never equalled before such attempts came to an end.

In 1935, when Petrali was thirty-one, he won thirteen races valid for the national championship. In only one day of racing, he filled his record book — after winning the 1-mile race, he snatched the 5-, 10-, 15-, and 25-mile races on the same circuit in New York. It was on this day that he was given the nickname "Smoky Joe," referring to the cloud of dust he left in his wake.

At that time, the Harley-Davidson Motor Company was just finishing work on a new V-Twin generation, the Series E. Knucklehead Twin, a 61 cubic-inch (1000 cc) OHV with rocker arms, whose conception was partly due to Smoky Joe. But it had not yet been properly fine-tuned when President William A. Davidson decided to launch it in an attempt to balance the Harley-Davidson accounts.

To advertise this product, Harley-Davidson launched a massive campaign which would make the Knucklehead and Joe Petrali famous throughout the world. Harley-Davidson built an unusual-looking racing motorcycle with a full front wheel, a narrow fork, a tank furnished with a thick pillow on the top, and a small fairing, or more precisely, a fork head, which was fabricated, under William S. Harley's direction, in a tank built especially for the purpose. The engine itself was a Knucklehead with short and direct exhaust pipes. The ignition was by magneto, which had a double carburetor and a highly efficient camshaft. Then came an enormous media blitz, with pictures of the rider and his motorcycle before they left to set a new speed record at Daytona Beach.

On March 13, 1937, surrounded by fans, journalists, and organizers, Joe Petrali was timed at 124 mph. He could have done better, but certain aspects of the bike

worried him, such as the fairing, which made the front lighter at high speed, and the odometer, which impaired visibility.

Within the hour, these elements were eliminated or improved and Petrali set off. He broke the world speed record again, this time with a speed of 136.183 mph, a record which has never been beaten or even equalled on a beach.

Other brands in the world tried to beat the record, but without success.

There is still so much talk about it today that the speed is strictly limited on Daytona Beach, making it impossible to attempt another record on this sandy track.

A year after this performance, Petrali once again avoided serious injury in an otherwise devastating accident, and he finally decided to put an end to his career as a rider, at the age of thirty-four.

He went back to manufacturing race cars for a few years, then he began working for the millionaire Howard Hughes on the construction of his legendary plane "The Spruce Goose." Smoky Joe passed away of natural causes at the age of sixty-eight.

64 Joe Petrali proved to be an extraordinarily talented rider, with a good sense for mechanics that helped him capitalize on innovative systems which his competitors did not dare try. His distinctive riding technique, effective in any type of race, won him a considerable number of victories.

64-65 When Joe Petrali broke a record at Daytona Beach, his motorcycle, fitted with a Knucklehead engine, appeared like this— without its fairing. The fairing, shown during press conferences and used during his first attempt, proved dangerous, since it unbalanced the motorcycle.

RED PARKHURST

An integral part of the Harley-Davidson legend and American motorcycling history, he cannot be separated from the history of world records.

The first motorcycle races took place on oval tracks covered in pine, similar to the flooring used in houses.

Drivers reached high speeds and sometimes lost control, killing themselves in accidents that also caused injuries to the rows of spectators. Many amateur drivers competed on this deadly surface. One among them, a Harley rider, regularly stood out. Leslie Parkhurst, a native of Colorado, was born to win, and because of his ginger-colored hair, was given the nickname "Red."

The racing group at Harley-Davidson understood that hiring this young rider as an official member of the team could only bring further success, helping to consolidate Harley's already well-established reputation. Red Parkhurst agreed to race for Harley-Davidson on normal tracks, and he added significantly to the numerous victories of the Harley-Davidson Motor Company — until he suffered a serious concussion. Luckily, there were no long-term effects, and the great racer recovered.

When the beginning of the Great War put a sudden stop to the races, at least for brands such as Harley-Davidson, Indian, Excelsior, and a few others, the drivers had to wait for better days and to be patient, often taking jobs that had nothing to do

with their passion. Leslie Parkhurst worked for a coal mining company located in the same city as Harley-Davidson until 1919. After the war, he did not want to resume racing but changed his mind after a discussion with Bill Ottaway. He had his new start at a race held in Portland, Oregon, with new and much more powerful bikes. Red Parkhurst remained a leading figure in the company and a top racer. He added the 5-, 10-, and 25-mile races to his records in successive stages.

One of this great rider's qualities was his faithfulness to the brand. Even though he received many offers, some of which were very appealing, he remained with Harley-Davidson, and his loyalty won him the respect of many factory managers and race officials.

Leslie "Red" Parkhurst left racing very late, and was hired by Firestone — a solution that allowed him to stay in touch with motor sports, especially the two-wheeled variety.

66 Red Parkhurst, whose official career began when he attracted the attention of the brand-new Harley-Davidson racing department in 1914, rapidly started scoring victories for the company. He raced again for Harley-Davidson after World War I and retired as the world's first motorcycle celebrity.

66-67 In 1926, Harley-Davidson introduced a new machine, equipped with a 21.10 cubic-inch (345.73 cc) one-cylinder engine. Referred to as "BA," this motorcycle became known as the "21 single," named for its 21 ci OHV engine. The racing model derived from this machine was the famous "Peashooter," so called because of the sound it produced. Variations on this motorcycle continued to be produced, including adaptations with side and overhead valves.

HARLEY-DAVIDSON SUFFERS THE GREAT DEPRESSION

HISTORY AND IMPLICATIONS OF THE CRISIS

The crash of the New York Stock Market in late 1929, which devastated the U.S. economy, obviously had an enormous impact on the world of American motorcycle production. Despite bankers' efforts to curb this crash, its aftereffects were felt until 1933. It caused many bankruptcies and triggered an incredible social crisis, with the number of unemployed in the U.S. rising to 15 million in 1933. Shortly before the crash, at the beginning of 1929, newly elected President Herbert Hoover had made a speech in which he said, "The American society is about to beat poverty forever." He was referring to the economic indicators at that moment: an industrial

The NEW HARLEY

NEW LOW PRICE $320 at factory

THE REMARKABLE NEW 74 TWIN FOR 1932

growth of 64% between 1919 and 1929, and an economic boom in the building and the automobile sectors. In the United States at that time, there was one car for every five people. Advertising encouraged people to spend more and to purchase luxury items. What is more, between 1923 and 1929, although companies profits grew more than 60%, the average worker's salary increased by only 11%, thus widening dramatically the gap between production and potential consumption.

Hoover had thought the United States possessed enough economic power to overcome its difficulties, but it took Franklin Delano Roosevelt's election in 1932, and his decision to repeal Prohibition and announce the measures known as "the New Deal," for the situation to improve.

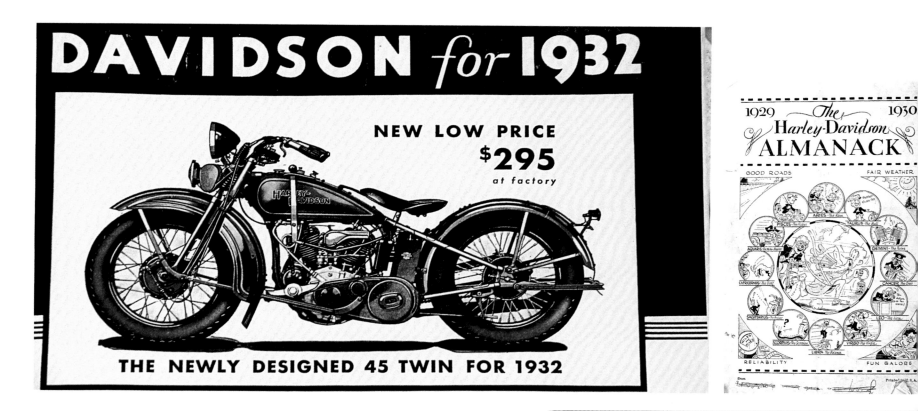

DAVIDSON *for* 1932

NEW LOW PRICE
$295
at factory

THE NEWLY DESIGNED 45 TWIN FOR 1932

1929 *The* 1930
Harley-Davidson
ALMANACK

GOOD ROADS   FAIR WEATHER

RELIABILITY   FUN GALORE

68 *The 74 cubic-inch (1200 cc) VL Sport Solo model with side valves, which was introduced in 1930, had 15 to 20% more power than earlier models. From 1933 on, it sported more attractive paintwork than plain olive green.*

69 *In July 1928, Harley-Davidson introduced its Model D, equipped with a 45 cubic-inch V-Twin engine. Presented as a 1929 model, it enjoyed a long, brilliant career, despite the fact that it was launched just as the Great Depression began.*

He put the budget in order, launched works funded by the Federal government, reduced agricultural production, thus raising prices, and relaunched industry. Thanks to the measures adopted between 1933 and 1934, in 1937 American industrial production managed to regain the level it had been at in 1929. But in 1940 there were still eight million unemployed. Only America's entry into World War II, in late 1941, would eventually bring full recovery to the U.S. economy.

Despite these economic hardships, in 1929, the Harley-Davidson company produced its new 45 cubic-inch, side-valve engine, which they called the "Flathead." It was both powerful and versatile, and the company hoped that it would become its new workhorse. The Flathead was an immediate success and remained so for many years: not only did it manage to go through the Great Depression and World War II, it equipped the Servi-Cars until 1974. In 1930, the company introduced the VL74, whose creation set a new standard for touring motorcycles. It still had side valves but the engine was enlarged to 1200 cc. The company also produced a 30 cubic-inch (500 cc) single-cylinder engine manufactured until 1935.

In 1932, a three-wheel utility vehicle, which would become very popular with the police and other civic departments, appeared in the catalog, listed at $450. It was, of course, the famous Series G Servi-Car, which, with its V-Twin 45 cubic-inch (750 cc) engine, would be manufactured for more than forty years.

70 top and center left William H. Davidson, who was to be president of the Harley-Davidson Motor Company from 1942 to 1971, winning the Jack Pine Enduro in 1930.

70 center right To boost sales, Harley-Davidson offered a new range of colors and ornamentation from 1923 onwards.

70 bottom left The Servi-Car, equipped with the 750 cc (45 cubic-inch) side-valve engine, was first listed in the Harley-Davidson catalog in 1932. It soon became popular for law enforcement and other professional purposes.

70 bottom right The Harley-Davidson line was already amazingly varied and the company was good at advertising this fact. It offered vehicles for any use, bragging that even women could easily ride a Harley-Davidson.

Nevertheless, despite these successes, Harley-Davidson continued to experience the same economic crisis as the rest of the country. In the same year the Servi-Car was introduced, Harley-Davidson registered a very sharp drop in production, manufacturing only 7,217 motorcycles. The drop continued in 1933, with 3,703 bikes coming out of the Milwaukee factory. Luckily, the level of production recovered in 1934, and rose to 11,212 motorcycles.

In that period, motorcycle manufacturers experienced overwhelming difficulties and nearly all disappeared from the market, because leisure activities had taken a back seat to professional migrations and the public was no longer as interested in the motorcycle. The car also absorbed a considerable share of motorcycle sales.

It was a period of scrimping and saving. Sales dropped dramatically, and some employees worked only two or three days a week. This reduction in working time helped to avoid massive layoffs.

Given the economic climate, Harley-Davidson had to use a great deal of ingenuity and imagination to sell its new models, not to mention the rest of its line. The manufacturing methods also improved considerably and nothing was left to chance. Each promising idea was thoroughly analyzed before being implemented. Despite this cautious approach, a number of technical improvements were made: aluminum pistons, interchangeable wheels, a better electrical layout, thanks to a new ignition coil and, finally, warning lights, to help riders check the bike's operation.

71 *This new type of tank decor appeared in 1934, but it was only available for two years, since Harley-Davidson was becoming aware that variations in color and logo could boost sales.*

In 1933, Harley-Davidson decided to brighten up its motorcycles. It gave them a cost-effective but attractive new look simply by varying the colors and decorations. The khaki color of the mudguards, the tanks, the odometers and the frames was replaced by variegated colors, which were further brightened up by new logos.

But the motorcycle manufacturers' situation became increasingly worrisome; in 1933, overall motorcycle production, all brands included, dropped to 6,000 units. Harley-Davidson did its best to avoid bankruptcy.

The American automobile industry and its suppliers registered an 80% drop in production, and they too found themselves in a very delicate situation. In 1933, one estimate reported 100,000 registered bankruptcies. With exports reduced to nothing and unprecedented price cuts, the United States was experiencing the worst economic catastrophe in its history.

Gradually, the Harley-Davidson Motor Company emerged from the chaos. In 1936, the company offered a few new models. That year also introduced of the famous

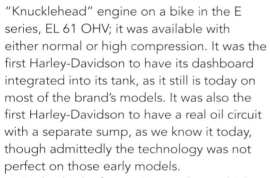

"Knucklehead" engine on a bike in the E series, EL 61 OHV; it was available with either normal or high compression. It was the first Harley-Davidson to have its dashboard integrated into its tank, as it still is today on most of the brand's models. It was also the first Harley-Davidson to have a real oil circuit with a separate sump, as we know it today, though admittedly the technology was not perfect on those early models.

It also had a four-ratio gear box, which was a technical improvement that left its competition at Indian in the dust. This machine offered more power by doing away with the side-valve system, and it met with the success it deserved.

The FL Special Sport Solo, a 1200 cc model which had a 74 cubic-inch, high-compression Knucklehead OHV V-Twin engine, was put on the market in 1941, originally to meet the requirements of various police forces. This model's successful career, together with that of the 1000 cc model, the EL 61, continued until the appearance of the Panhead engine in 1948. But, before that event, the Harley-Davidson Company would play an active part in the Second World War.

72 The Knucklehead was presented during the summer in 1936. It had an overhead valve, 1000 cc engine that provided more power than the Flathead it replaced. In 1937, Harley-Davidson adopted the technique of fixing the dashboard on the top of the tank—a practice still followed today.

73 A vintage picture, taken to promote the Knucklehead. Here (from left to right) Arthur Davidson, Walter Davidson, William S. Harley, and William A. Davidson are meant to be inspecting the very first Knucklehead 61 coming off the 1936 assembly line.

74 top The Harley-Davidson name gradually became synonymous with motorcycling in the U.S. By the early 1940s, there were only two big manufacturers competing with each other: Harley-Davidson and Indian.

74 center and bottom Those Harley-Davidsons that were outfitted with the Flathead, the famous side-valve engine, helped to build the myth of Harley-Davidson as a legendary motorcycle. After World War II, army motorcycles, sold by Americans in Europe or left as contributions to reconstruction, rapidly developed a strong Harley-Davidson following among overseas motorcycle fans.

75 In the United States, Harley-Davidsons fitted with side-valve engines were real collectors' pieces. Army motorcycles proved to be rarer in the U.S. than in Europe after World War II. Nevertheless, Harley-Davidson always took its place at important shows, represented by the big 74 cubic-inch (1200 cc) and 80 cubic-inch (1340 cc) side-valve engine models.

76 left Because of Harley-Davidson's military commitment during World War II, all civilian motorcycles produced between 1941 and 1946 were identical. Technological and aesthetic detailing came second to the company's commitment to the war effort.

76-77 top Once indispensable among police and other professionals, Servi-Cars today are still sought after, both as collectors' pieces and also as working vehicles. Often they are renewed and decorated according to their owners' tastes.

77 bottom left From 1936 on, Harley-Davidson offered a series of motorcycle accessories that could be attached right on the assembly line. A purchaser could pick up a machine at the dealer's, already personalized to his taste.

77 bottom right This exploded view of the Knucklehead engine shows its operations, above all its cylinder head lubrication. Early Knuckleheads had a few lubrication problems, which were rapidly solved on the models in the following years.

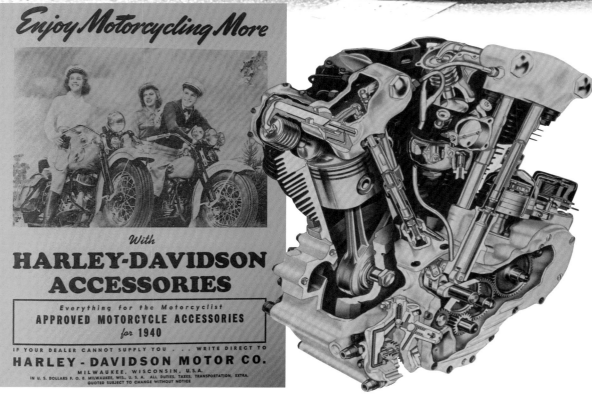

A Great War Followed

In September 1939, twenty-one years after the end of World War I, Europe experienced the beginning of its second conflict. President Roosevelt asked the American people and the Congress to be ready to intervene, if necessary. On November 4, 1941, America entered the fray. The United States lifted the arms embargo and began producing an exceptional amount of military equipment bound for the Allies. Annual costs for war equipment climbed from $17 to $50 billion, and the United States became a veritable arsenal for the Allies. In the space of four years, the U.S. produced 95,000 airplanes, 3 million tons of warships, 80,000 artillery guns, and nearly 90,000 Harley-Davidsons.

The WLA 45 models, a military version of the WL 45, were the most widely manufactured Harley-Davidson motorcycles used in the conflict. Another type of motorcycle, the XA, with a Flat-Twin engine modeled on that of the German BMW, appeared as a military vehicle. It was able to compete with the European machines, but its career did not extend beyond the war.

Times of upheaval are often times of innovation as well; during this period, Harley-Davidson did not only manufacture motorcycles. Willys, the famous manufacturer of another American legend, the Jeep, planned to build 5,000 small, cross-country cars — a sort of mini-Jeep — that would be powered by 750 cc XA engines.

These Jeeps were to be air-lifted to Europe, but the war came to an end before completion of this important order, and the production of X engines did not exceed 1,000 units.

At the conclusion of the Second World War, Harley-Davidson revealed a military secret regarding another military vehicle: the company had supplied certain Canadian mini-tanks with two 61 cubic-inch Knucklehead V-Twin engines.

78 A World War II armed division. These soldiers are equipped with 750 cc WLAs decorated with division colors and provided with the standard equipment, including holsters attached to the motorcycle forks.

78-79 and 79 bottom Harley-Davidsons could be found in all facets of armed conflict. Many pictures showed how riders could use their motorcycles as shields, although a tank full of fuel and oil did not provide the ideal protection.

80 Motorcycles were used for escorting convoys, as rapid liaison, and by the military police, but they were rarely found at the front or on reconnaissance. Jeeps stole the limelight in this phase of conflict.

However, this project remained experimental and the machines never saw full military service.

In recognition of the Harley-Davidson Motor Company's contribution to the U.S. war effort, it was awarded the U.S. Army-Navy Production Award, known as the "E" award for excellence.

With the war over and military requisitioning at an end, civilians bought up the stock of available WLAs: nearly 15,000 Harley-Davidson WLA 45s were sold at a unit price approaching the original price of $500. During the '50s, some of WLAs were still sold for as little as $80. Thanks to the strength and reliability demonstrated by these war-time motorcycles, the Harley-Davidson reputation was reinforced in Europe, and as a result, the company renewed efforts to establish its brand.

Despite its war-time success, it would be eighteen years before Harley-Davidson won another Army contract. The order was for a model called the XLA, which was a Sportster fitted with rigid fiberglass bags and a windshield. Although this was the last true Harley-Davidson to be used by the Army, on October 10, 1987, Harley-Davidson bought the manufacturing rights for single-cylinder 350, 500, and 560 cc motorcycles from the Armstrong Company. These were real cross-country models, which were used by security patrols and escorts, communication and reconnaissance services. The vehicles, fitted with Rotax engines, were never sold to the public.

80-81 *Sidecar prototypes were built for the Army but this type of vehicle was rarely used in the Second World War, as Jeeps proved more efficient and agile on all types of terrain.*

81 bottom *The President of Harley-Davidson Motor Company, William H. Davidson, proudly accepts, on behalf of all the company employees, the Army and Navy "E" Trophy, as a reward for the war effort.*

"WLA" AND "XA :
TWO REFERENCE POINTS

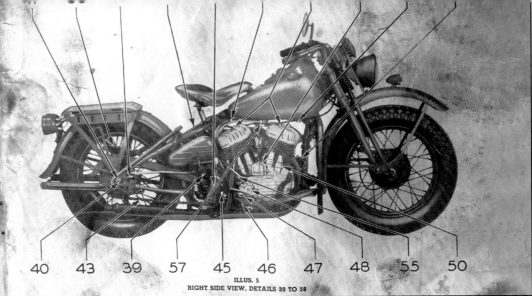

40   43   39   57   45   46   47   48   55   50

ILLUS. 5
RIGHT SIDE VIEW, DETAILS 39 TO 58

9   21   20   22   31   32   33   35   24   25

26   28   27   29   34   30   36   37   23   38

ILLUS. 4
LEFT SIDE VIEW, DETAILS 19 TO 38

82 In addition to the WLA model, Harley-Davidson supplied the Army with a descriptive motorcycle manual and a troubleshooting guide in case of breakdown.

11
6
14
2
13
4
9
3
8

15
17
10
1
16
5
12
18
7

ILLUS. 3
TOP VIEW, DETAILS 1 TO 18

8

Top Vie...
(CONTRO...

1. THROTTLE C...
open throttle; tur...
throttle control gr...
engine will co...
in fully closed...
should be ma...
2. SPARK...
vance, turn...
operation...
ing and m...
ing un...
eng...

71. W... star...
clutch with an ed...
w... junction ad...
j...
movement and y...
effort on the part...
ment should be m...
4. GEAR SHIFT...
dicated on tank s...
neutral and clutch...
Fully release clutch...
5. REAR BRAKE FOO...
adjusted so brake does...
pushed down about an in...
effect at least an inch be...
rear wheel to make sure br...
dragging. When brake adjust...
they should be made by the...
Detail 53).
6. FRONT WHEEL BRAKE HAND...
properly adjusted, lever will move free...
quarter of its full range of movement befo...
begins to take effect; if adjusted with less free...
ment brake is likely to drag. Keep brake control wire
well oiled for easy action.
Always use rear brake in conjunction with front
brake when bringing motorcycle to a stop. It is better

Steering damper should be adjusted so it does not
take noticeable effect until handle is nearly straight
... Each must turn freely when lever is in released

SPECIAL TOOLS
FOR SERVICING WLA (SOLO) MODEL
HARLEY-DAVIDSON MILITARY MOTORCYCLE

THIS LIST COVERS REQUIRED HARLEY-DAVIDSON SPECIAL TOOLS. IT DOE
NOT INCLUDE STANDARD SHOP TOOLS NEEDED SUCH AS STANDARD OPE
END AND SOCKET WRENCHES AND OTHER MISCELLANEOUS TOOLS.

TOOL ILLUSTRATION	NAME OF TOOL	FEDERAL STOCK NO.	HARLEY-DAVIDSON N
	SPARK PLUG WRENCH	41-W-3334	11929-40
	TUNGSTEN POINT FILE	41-D-1410	11840-X
	THICKNESS GAUGE	41-G-407	11974-X
	VALVE COVER WRENCH		11806-31
	SET OF VALVE TAPPET ADJUSTING WRENCHES	41-W-3573	11904-X
	HEAD BOLT WRENCH	41-W-185	12047-30-5

82-83 and 83 Used on all types of terrain, the WLAs proved to be remarkably versatile. About 88,000 such motorcycles were produced for the Army.

As evidenced by the "E" award the company was given at the end of the war, like many American companies, Harley-Davidson played an important role in the conflict. For a second time, William S. Harley had the responsibility of adapting Harley-Davidsons to the harsh conditions of war. From 1939 on, Harley-Davidson trained its mechanics to be ready for all eventualities. Their duty was to guard against potential failures and to maintain the WLAs on the battlefield.

Every four weeks, almost fifty trained mechanics completed the training course at the school located at the company premises on Juneau Avenue. The U.S. Department of Defense signed a contract with the Harley-Davidson Motor Company and with the Indian Company for the manufacture, almost exclusively for the war, of about 88,000 WLA 45s, a military version of the Harley-Davidson WL 45. By modernizing its production techniques, Harley-Davidson was able to supply this large number of motorcycles. The Harley-Davidson Motor Company decided to expand its production area and capacity by renting supplementary space in the area near its factory. Moreover, it organized its workers into shifts so that they worked round the clock. By these means, the company's assembly lines were able to produce enough WLA 45s and WLA 74s, not to mention all the spare parts. In fact, the WLA 45's role in the liberation of Europe won it the nickname "Liberator."

All the tests on these military models were carried out at Fort Knox under the supervision of military personnel and, until his death from a heart attack on September 18, 1943, William S. Harley). The wheels were interchangeable and had an 18-inch diameter. The tires were 4 or 5 inches wide, and the rider was protected from the spray by very large mudguards, fitted at the highest possible level to prevent the mud from blocking the wheels. The large and well-protected air filter enabled the bikes to cross shallow fords. A steel plate was fitted under the lower part of the frame to protect the engine, and the chain was also protected by a large, strong guard. An internal lubrication system allowed cooling during long periods of use at low speed. A rugged metal luggage rack was provided to house a two-way

radio weighing 40 pounds. On the right front, a gun holder was fixed for a Thompson machine gun or a light automatic carbine. On the left part of the fork, a metal box acted as counterbalance and contained magazines and ammunitions.

Certain WLAs were also equipped with a hand-cranked siren, operated by a shaft that rubbed against the rear tire. This surplus weight prevented these WLAs from going faster than 50 mph, and its acceleration was equally reduced. The motorcycle behaved well on the battlefields, though, not least because it was easy to maintain. Harley-Davidson also manufactured 20,000 WLAs for the Canadian army under the designation WLC and also ELC. In the Canadian versions, a few elements changed position as

compared to the American and European models: the gear lever and foot clutch were moved to the right, while the brakes were moved to the left, on the handlebar.

The U.S. Army was so impressed by the performance of the German BMWs and the Zundapps that, in the spring of 1942, they asked Indian and Harley-Davidson to come up with a similar motorcycle with equivalent performance capability. The XA, which could out-perform the WLA, was suggested as its replacement.

84 Since the WLA was the Harley-Davidson model most often ordered by the Army, it was produced in large quantities. By the end of World War II, it was possible to find many WLA spare parts in Europe.

HARLEY-DAVIDSON WLA.45 SOLO MOTORCYCLE

85 While the European motorcycle industry was devastated by the conflicts of World War II, WLAs with spare parts for 30,000 had been shipped to the European territory. So several countries, including France, chose the Harley-Davidson WLA as their army motorcycle.

86-87 Today, many WL and WLA models appear in exhibitions, shows, and meetings in the United States. Some have been modified, while others have been restored exactly to their original state, as if they were coming out from the assembly lines of the Milwaukee factory. Sometimes their owners dress in the military style of the time, parading their motorcycles in a spirit dating back to the early 1940s.

The XA increased the stock of military equipment, and its engine was inspired significantly, not to say entirely, by the BMW flat two-cylinder of that time. Most details were copied by simply transforming the European measurements into inches. As previously mentioned, in the end, only 1,000 models of this motorcycle were built. Fitted with a fork bordered by hydraulic shock absorbers, their cost to the U.S. Army was less than $1,000 per unit. After the war, civilian customers were eager to own this motorcycle, which appeared revolutionary, but only 200 XAs were turned into civilian models and preserved by collectors. Thus, the XA did not manage to depose the 45 degree V-Twin, which had prevailed since 1909 and which was already available in different versions.

88 top During World War II, Harley-Davidson's training school for mechanics enrolled only soldiers, teaching them to solve motorcycle problems in the field.

88-89 and 89 American soldiers were impressed by the efficiency of German motorcycles, especially their reduced maintenance requirements despite intensive use on difficult terrain, such as sand. As a result, they asked for similar motorcycles. Thus the XA, a copy of the BMW, appeared. About a thousand motorcycles of this type were built.

RETURN TO CIVILIZATION

END OF A CONFLICT AND ECONOMIC COMPETITION

Before Harley-Davidson could resume large production volumes, they had to rebuild what the war had damaged. The Harley-Davidson Company encouraged its agents to reestablish the dealer network again, but the dealers needed to be persuaded that the company was still efficient and serious about business, that the war was really finished, and that the models currently being manufactured would still attract the public. The commercial and entertainment press and *The Enthusiast*, the already celebrated company magazine, spread the Harley-Davidson message far and wide. Beyond reassuring dealers, this message was also aimed at once again attracting civilian customers, who had been relatively neglected during the war. Meanwhile, a new fashion, one on two small wheels, invaded the United States and became

especially popular among students seeking a cheap means of transportation. A company from Lincoln, Nebraska, called Cushman, which belonged to the Johnson-Evinrude group, began marketing the scooter in 1944. After the war, the 4.8 horsepower Cushman sold for about $150, and to help them to rebalance their accounts, many Harley-Davidson dealers started selling this successful product.

Harley-Davidson was less than enthusiastic about this situation. In the spring of 1947, the managers in Milwaukee threatened to allow only official dealers and not franchise holders to sell their motorcycles. Thus they forced dealers to choose to represent either Harley-Davidson or Cushman. This conflict was heightened at the end of 1947, when Harley-Davidson began offering a model that broke somewhat with the Harley-

Davidson mold. It was a small motorcycle fitted with a 124 cc two-stroke single-cylinder engine. Its appearance was faithful to the Harley-Davidson spirit and, like the Hydra-Glide, its tank was graced by an entirely chrome-plated, water-drop-shaped logo with Harley-Davidson carved in black.

This motorcycle marked the start of a production of small-displacement motorcycles, which charmed a new group of motorcyclists, who found these light bikes to their taste: women.

By diversifying their production and improving their Milwaukee factory, which had again become too small to work efficiently, Harley-Davidson gradually resumed a normal production pace. In 1945, the Harley-Davidson Motor Company bought some buildings located a few minutes from Milwaukee for $1.5 million.

90 top In 1948, in order to gain greater market share, Harley-Davidson built a small, 125 cc three-stroke one-cylinder motorcycle, the S Lightweight, inspired by the German DKW.

90 bottom The last Knucklehead, with a newly designed tank logo and a new dashboard, was built in 1947.

91 top The Servi-Car, still produced during the war, went through an evolution of improvements, such as this 1948 model. Practical accessories were added to answer the needs of those who used it for business.

91 center Before World War II, during the war years, and immediately after the end of hostilities, Harley-Davidson continued producing side-valve engines. Their civilian versions were available with various capacities: 45 cubic inch (750 cc), 74 cubic inch (1200 cc), and 80 cubic inch (1340 cc). All three models are still very popular today, and are often exhibited at shows. Their excellent reliability allows them to be customized and used by their owners fifty years after their original manufacture.

91 bottom Since war production was a priority for Harley-Davidson, the 1941—1946 civilian line did not develop and for five years had practically the same look. This type of tank, with this logo, appeared on all those civilian motorcycles, whether they were equipped with a Flathead or a Knucklehead engine.

From 1949 onwards, Harley-Davidson's new flagship engine, the Panhead, was fixed on a frame fitted with a telescoping fork, replacing the old Springer.

FEATURING THE 1949 MODEL

The **Enthusiast**

A MAGAZINE FOR MOTORCYCLISTS OCTOBER 1948

MOTORCYCLING—
World's Greatest Sport !

Ride a
HARLEY-DAVIDSON
HYDRA-GLIDE

THE lure of motorcycling is like nothing else in this world. Once it's in your blood . . . brother, you'll never be the same again! From then on, nothing can ever equal the fascination of cruising down a scenic country road with a Harley-Davidson purring quietly under you . . . the he-man thrill of soaring up a steep hill like a climbing jet . . . the breathless feeling of levelling off for the straight-aways . . . the sense of power and freedom you get whenever you settle back in the saddle and "give 'er the gun!" In no other sport are friends so loyal, gals so glamorous. Nowhere is fun so easy to find as at exciting race meets, hillclimbs, gypsy tours and other club events. A Harley-Davidson is your ticket to endless good times, to happy, healthful outdoor enjoyment. You can own one on easy terms. So why not get started now? See your dealer today.

Ladies Riding Breeches & Jodphurs

The 260,000-square-foot premises were located on Capitol Drive in Wauwatosa; today, they house production of the Harley-Davidson V-Twin engine line. In 1949, they enabled the company to embark on the manufacturing of new models, including the Hydra-Glide. The Hydra-Glide had the first hydraulic fork and was driven by the new generation of Panhead V-Twin, fitted with aluminum heads and adjustable hydraulic tappets. This post-war model is considered the ancestor of the Electra Glide and, today,

Harley-Davidson is keeping the Hydra-Glide spirit alive with the "Heritage Softail Classic" model. But more difficulties were ahead. Walter Davidson died in 1942, and another founding member of the brand, William S. Harley, passed away the following year. In February 1942, the company presidency was assumed by William Herbert Davidson, William A. Davidson's son, who had started working for the company in 1928 as a worker. Because of his background, he was familiar with all the stages of production and

marketing. Moreover, he was an excellent rider who successfully took part in many races for the brand; in 1930, driving a 750 cc Model DLD, he won the "Jack Pine Endurance Race." Despite William Herbert Davidson's involvment, some members of the Davidson family were not attracted by a career in motorcycles, and gradually the people responsible for the good operation of the company changed. Additionally, in 1946, despite the difficulties involved for new importers, foreign motorcycles arrived on the American market.

92-93 and 93 In 1948, the Harley-Davidson Motor Company replaced the Knucklehead engine with the Panhead, fitted with aluminum cylinder heads and hydraulic tappets. Two versions of this engine were immediately available: the 61 cubic-inch (1000 cc) and the 74 cubic-inch (1200 cc) models.

THE BRITISH
INVASION

94-95 The Hydra-Glide had accessories and equipment to counter the English motorcycle invasion, but it proved to be heavy and inefficient compared to its rivals. In 1955, a new model which had higher compression and a more efficient camshaft was introduced: the FLH Super Sport.

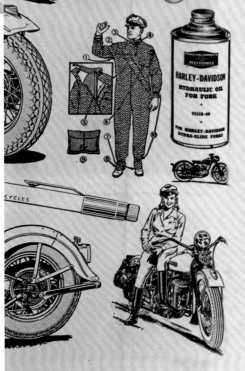

Norton, Royal Enfield, BSA, and Ariel are all British brands which have faded into history, although collectors and enthusiasts continue to find pleasure in riding them. These British motorcycles, which started arriving in the United States after the end of the war, were the first serious competitors from abroad. Despite lines that were less majestic than Harley-Davidson's, they appealed to American motorcycle riders for their sporty appearance and for certain technical improvements, such as the foot gear shift and the hand clutch — techniques which were later adopted by the American brand. They were of interest to the motorcycle dealers, too, because favorable tax laws encouraged their importation.

In 1946, some Ariels, a British brand which first went into production in 1902, a year before Harley-Davidson, started to show up on American highways. This brand had begun by manufacturing tricycles powered by De Dion Bouton's engines. During the Second World War, Ariel also made motorcycles for the army, using 347 cc engines with rocker arms. Afterwards, Ariel and BSA merged. BSA, which had begun manufacturing motorcycles in 1906, continued to produce parts for both brands until 1970, and produced BSA motorcycles until 1973. Triumph, which started off in the same year as Harley-Davidson, was the premier British manufacturer for a long time. Nearly 10,000 of these British motorcycles were sold on the American market in 1947.

The A.M.A. responded to this British threat by enacting regulations favoring motorcycles made in the United States. Harley-Davidson also responded by releasing, in 1949, the Hydra-Glide. This model boasted many innovations and was destined to have a brilliant career. Production resumed its ascent again with 16,222 bikes in 1946, 20,115 in 1947, and 29,612 in 1948. After 1948, it settled on an average of 15,000 to 20,000 motorcycles per year. Profits were also consolidated by the sale of clothing and of accessories that allowed riders to personalize their bikes. In order to develop this commercial sector, Harley-Davidson organized races where the best-equipped and most original motorcycles received awards. Over the years, the motorcycles presented at these events came to look like real works of art, reflecting their owners' unique personalities and abilities.

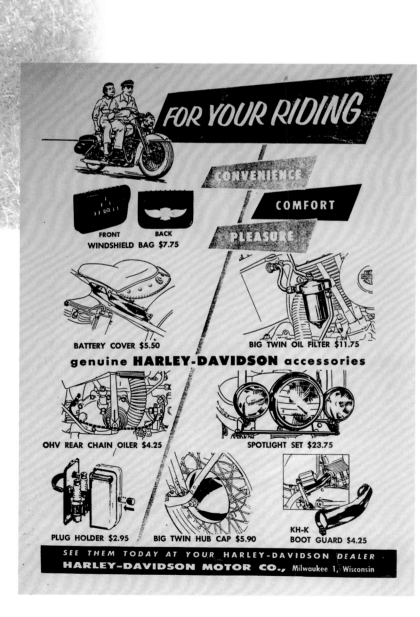

HARLEY-DAVIDSON'S RESPONSE

In 1948, a year after the Harley-Davidson Company bought the Wauwatosa factory, it presented its new 125 cc light single-cylinder engine, the "S" Model, which was produced until 1952. It could reach 49 mph and was an economical model for those who just wanted to cover short distances, and do so at very low cost. Also in 1948, the Panhead was launched to replace the Knucklehead. That same year, at a large meeting of American and foreign dealers, the company's production manager, Gordon Davidson, announced that he hoped to increase Harley-Davidson production. Production in 1948 did grow to—29,612 motorcycles—but the following year it dropped back to 23,861. The downward trend continued into the new decade, dipping to 17,168 in 1950, then reaching a low point in 1955, when the company produced just 10,686 motorcycles. Despite these problems, the Harley-Davidson Motor Company launched a number of 21 and 30.5 cubic-inch light motorcycles to try to stop foreign brand penetration; but fighting on both fronts, it also reaffirmed its commitment to the large V-Twin models,

which were, in many ways, the ideal machines for this big country.

Even so, by 1950, 40% of the motorcycles registered in the United States were foreign brands. William H. Davidson tried everything he could to convince his dealers to double their efforts to promote the American bikes. In particular he tried to reinforce that Harleys alone were suitable to the weather and geography of the country. The company also made a big effort to prove that the new S model, derived from the German model "DKW," was a strong machine in keeping with the Harley-Davidson tradition. Harley-Davidson managed to deliver about 4,708 of this small-displacement motorcycle in the first year of its production.

After the war, European countries needed to relaunch their economies. Building on the success of their smaller bikes, British manufacturers then began building bigger bikes to compete directly against the large V-Twin, in terms of both performance and reliability. As a result, in 1949, Triumph launched its "Thunderbird," with a displacement of 650 cc, and Norton brought out a 500 cc. But these

motorcycles failed to live up to expectations and never really threatened the great American tourer.

Confronted with the development of foreign brands, the Harley-Davidson Motor Company realized that it would once again have to fight to save itself.

Unfortunately, misfortunes continued. There were high-profile defeats during races like the Daytona Beach 200-mile race, where Norton entered four riders against the other British and American brands. Harley-Davidson entered its "WR45." Norton took the victory and Harley-Davidson was forced to face the

96 The Panhead engine was produced in the 61 cubic-inch (1000 cc) and the 74 cubic-inch (1200 cc) versions. In 1952, the smaller version was discontinued in favor of the larger, which was more efficient and met with more commercial success.

96-97 The Harley-Davidson Hydra-Glides, equipped with Panhead engines, were regularly improved by technical developments and modified to meet customer tastes. In 1952, the FL Sport Solo included a modern gear-change system with a foot selector lever and a handlebar clutch. For traditionalists, Harley-Davidson also manufactured a model with the earlier gear-change system.

fact that its motorcycles were no longer really competitive. On December 30, 1950, tragedy struck: Arthur Davidson and his wife were killed in a car accident. In that year, production decreased by 6,693 motorcycles. It is possible that this further drop was partly due to the implementation of the Marshall Plan, which was intended to jump-start European economies by granting them important financial help.

During this period, competition worried Harley-Davidson dealers, who asked the company for models equal in weight and power to those upsetting the balance of their trade, especially since they were forced to sell and repair only the brand from Milwaukee. Harley-Davidson's inflexibility ended up sitting badly with its distributors.

The dealers figured that they had to live; they believed that if Harley-Davidson refused to adapt to the new market, its obstinacy would bring it to a dead end. Despite the ban, certain dealers began to sell other brands, such as Triumph, for which there was then a large demand. It is worth pointing out that in 1954 Marlon Brando would ride a Triumph in *The Wild One*, a film based on the infamous incident in which bikers ran amok in a small California town.

In 1952, in response to foreign attacks and to customer pressure, Harley-Davidson launched the 45 cubic-inch Series K, which replaced the W series.

It had a sprung frame, rear shock absorbers, and a hydraulic front fork. Over the next year, it became available in several versions, such as the "KK" and the "KR," with a magneto and upswept exhausts for heavy motorcycle races; it was targeted to young sports customers. The model was adopted in 1956 by none other than Elvis Presley, who chose a "KH" (which was not yet the Sportster).

The May 1956 cover of the Harley-Davidson magazine *The Enthusiast* featured the King on his first red and white Harley-Davidson.

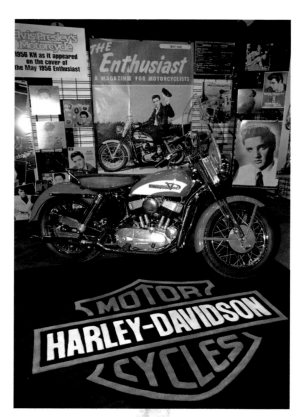

98 top This Model K Sport Model, with its 45 cubic-inch engine, appeared in the 1952 Harley-Davidson catalog. 1952 and 1953 proved to be momentous years for Harley-Davidson, not least Marlon Brando rode a Triumph in The Wild One.

98 bottom Series K replaced the W series from 1952 onwards. Until 1954 it had a 45 cubic-inch (750 cc) capacity, then the KH was fitted with a 55 cubic-inch (990 cc) engine Flathead, which it had until 1956.

98-99 In May 1956, on the cover of The Enthusiast, a new rock 'n' roll star named Elvis Presley appeared astride a Harley-Davidson KH.

100-101 Bikes with Panhead engines are often some of the best customized machines at shows. The engines are often restored to their original state or decorated with chrome, though always in a manner which respects the spirit of the time.

CREATORS ARE NOT IMMORTAL: THE SUCCESSION

By 1942, the Davidsons and William Harley had constructed a solid enterprise, and since the production of their first engine at the beginning of the century, the sacred brand form the Milwaukee had been a constant presence on roads around the world. During the preceeding forty years, many members of the families had worked for the company, to ensure strength and longevity. But now, foreign competition was not the only problem the company faced.

On February 7, 1942, Walter C. Davidson, Sr., president of the Harley-Davidson Motor Company, died at the age of 66; his death raised questions within the family group concerning the succession. It was not easy to determine the most

suitable person to represent such a well-established company. Walter Davidson left his three children, Gordon, Walter Jr., and Robert; his brother, Arthur Davidson; and his two sisters, along with his wife, Emma. Since 1907, over the thirty-five years of his presidency, he had come to personify the Harley-Davidson brand so much that it was difficult to entrust this responsibility to anyone else. Arthur Davidson, the founder, was 63 when the search for a president was taking place; however, his health was not good, and as mentioned previously, he and his wife would soon die in a tragic automobile accident. Although this did not affect the process of choosing an immediate successor to Walter Davidson, it did mean their were fewer family members

upon whom the company could rely when the difficulties increased.

The successor had to be diplomatic and flexible and, at the same time, retain the firmness of the first president of the company. Walter Sr. believed that a product conceived honestly and assembled accurately could be sold without qualms to the public. Although two of his sons were involved in the company — Gordon as Sales Manager, and Walter Jr., as Manufacturing Manager — neither of them wished to take on the responsibility of the presidency, and the third and youngest son, Robert, had chosen a career in a completely different sector.

Later, Gordon would leave his job with the company and his brother, Walter,

102 The second and third generations of Davidsons astride their motorcycles: William H. Davidson and his sons, John (at his right) and William G. (at his left), later known as Willie G. Davidson.

103 left Willie G. Davidson, just after winning an endurance race in 1952.

103 right The Davidsons gathered to celebrate the 90th anniversary of the Harley-Davidson Motor Company in Milwaukee in 1993. Mr. and Mrs. Willie G. Davidson (second and third from left) stand with their three children (from left), Karen, Billie G., and Michael. Karen and Billie G. work for the company.

would die of lung cancer, in 1967. In the meantime, William S. Harley decided to leave his position as chief engineer and wished to entrust this responsibility to one of his sons, William J. Harley. William J. Harley was happy to accept. He travelled to Italy often during the association with Aermacchi. In 1957, he was appointed vice president of the company, but he died of diabetes in 1971.

His brother, John E. Harley, who was educated at a military college, had the necessary motorcycle experience to train the soldiers of the motorized division at Fort Knox and in Georgia, but he died of cancer in 1976.

The Davidsons were more numerous as Harley-Davidson Motor Company share-holders than the Harleys, with a ratio of 70 to 3 so it is not surprising another Davidson was chosen to take over the role. In the end, William A. Davidson's son, William Herbert Davidson, was deemed to be the most appropriate choice, and he inherited the post of president of the Harley-Davidson Motor Company on February 23, 1942. Holding several diplomas and, in particular, a degree in business, he did not experience great difficulties managing the company. In addition, his uncle, Arthur Davidson, became president of the A.M.A. on January 20, 1944.

Today, despite all the changes over the years, the Davidson name remains within the company, now in the third and fourth generations; and at the end of the century, the person Harley enthusiasts are always eager to meet is William G. Davidson, the most visible symbol of the exciting, epic deeds of the two families.

Known as Willie, Davidson once dealt with the styling, the upholstery, the colors, and everything relating to the motorcycle of the year. He is currently responsible for important public relations and promotional activities for the brand, which he carries out in person at the great Harley-Davidson demonstrations and gatherings. His daughter, Karen, and his son, Bill, also work for the Harley-Davidson Company in Milwaukee, while another son lives in New York and works as a painter.

The V-Twins Follow But Do Not Resemble Each Other

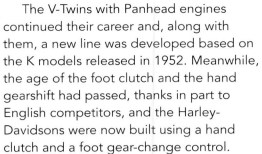

104 top and center *The Sportster stands out in a 1957 issue of The Enthusiast. It had become Harley-Davidson's strong suit, predicted to counter foreign competition and meet the expectations of customers seeking a lighter, more agile, and more efficient motorcycle than the Big Twin.*

104 bottom left *Exploded view of a modern Evolution-type Sportster engine.*

104 bottom right *The Sportster promotion campaign targeted those who wanted a motorcycle redolent of youth, performance, and leisure—a really modern machine.*

The V-Twins with Panhead engines continued their career and, along with them, a new line was developed based on the K models released in 1952. Meanwhile, the age of the foot clutch and the hand gearshift had passed, thanks in part to English competitors, and the Harley-Davidsons were now built using a hand clutch and a foot gear-change control.

The "KH" could achieve 56 horsepower, and its engine and four-speed gearbox, which was a bit weak, were encased in a solid block. The gear shift was located under the right foot and the clutch consisted of a lever fitted near the left handlebar grip. Despite the qualities of this motorcycle, the American customers, and the young in particular, could not resist the temptation of owning a British bike. In 1953, the direct American competitor, Indian, shut down: constant change in its management had led the company to bankruptcy. Harley-Davidson was now alone to face the strong foreign competition.

Model K left many customers disappointed, but the company was not daunted by one failure. The groundwork to create a light motorcycle had been laid; but time was short and a lot of work was necessary to make it more reliable. In 1954, Harley-Davidson released the Series KH Sports Twin, whose displacement of 55 cubic inches is equal to today's "883 cc." In the following year, the KHK Super Sport Solo was introduced. The external appearance of the "KHK" was similar to that of the "K," apart from the caster angle, which had been reduced to provide better stability at high speeds but it came fitted with a special kit which increased its performance.

The bike could reach 100 mph with 38 horsepower.

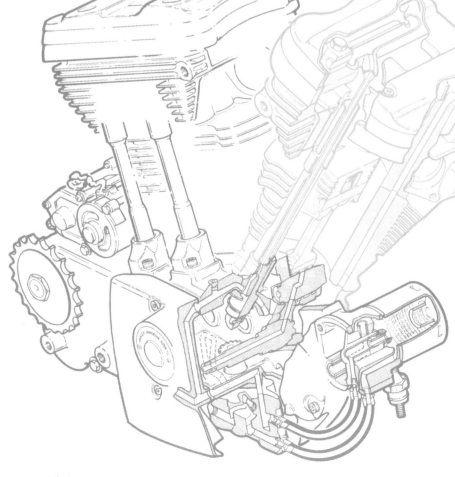

105 top The 1952 Model K, a modern version of the old W, was fitted with a foot gear selector and a handlebar clutch. Its gearbox was integrated into the crankcase.

105 center The XL Sportster, introduced in 1957, anticipated future generations of this consistently successful model.

105 bottom The small S Lightweight, introduced in 1948, was sold for 13 years, during which it was only slightly modified.

Production lasted for just two years. In 1956, a combined total of 1,253 "KH"s and "KHK"s were made and, in the same year, besides the two above mentioned models, the company introduced the specialty models the "KR," the "KRTT," and the "KHRTT," all of which had a displacement of 45 cubic inches and were sport bikes for cross-country races.

In 1958, these models stopped appearing in the catalog because, although the company still produced a few of the Ks, the new XL far outstripped them in terms of sales. Interestingly, this new motorcycle resembled the KH in certain details, such as the engine base. In 1958, the "XLH Sportster" underwent some important modifications: compression went from 7.5:1 to 9:1 and the valves became larger. Some Harley-Davidson dealers on the West Coast realized that this new motorcycle had interesting sports possibilities; at their request, Harley-Davidson conceived a lighter competition model.

Over the years, the Sportster underwent several technical improvements and has remained one of the top models in the Harley-Davidson line. Certain parts were later made in aluminum; new paints allowed it to preserve its youth and to adapt to customer taste. The introduction of discs meant changing the braking system slightly, and the electrical system changed to 12 volts. In 1965, the "XL" became "XLA," but only for the 1,000 units built for the U.S. Army. Subsequently, the kick-starter was abandoned, an electric starter was provided, modifying the sump, and the magneto was replaced by a coil ignition. In 1970, one year after the partial buyout of Harley-Davidson by American Machine & Foundry, came the launch of a model exclusively for sport, the "XR 750," which generated a buzz on the circuits and which many enthusiasts still dream of acquiring.

By 1972, over 82,000 Sportsters had been made since the model's release in 1957. Well conceived and reliable, since its creation, this model has been adapted to suit many types of riders and their myriad requirements.

Today, it is still so fashionable that the new Harley-Davidson customers opting for a Sportster as their first bike very rarely know that its basic conception has existed for more than thirty years. It is also the least expensive model in the range.

The "XLCR," a model in the Sportster line that was launched in 1977 with the name of "Café Racer," ended up being hunted by collectors because only 1,201 were made. Today, in exhibitions dedicated to collector's vehicles, this bike may fetch a price similar to that of a new "FLHTC."

In 1982, these light motorcycles underwent a great change, especially concerning the frame, which became even lighter and, in particular, more rigid. It also became capable of supporting a new tank with a 2^{1}/2 gallon capacity. In 1986, the Evolution engine appeared on the XLH 883 Sportster and XLH 1100. But in 1988, XLH 1100 was replaced by the 1200 XLH to provide more torque and power, and so to further differentiate it from the 883. At present, the Sportster 883 and 1200 are continuing their careers, albeit in slightly different versions, thus enriching the Harley-Davidson line.

106-107 The Sportsters, which appeared in 1957 with a 54 cubic-inch (883 cc) overhead -valve version, were the successors of the Flathead-type model K, although they were fitted with a crankcase including bottom engine and gearbox. Sportsters have been the company's longest-lasting and most consistently successful models.

Through the years, their technology has improved and their range has increased. In 1986, a whole aluminum engine called the Evolution was unveiled, similar to the aluminum Big Twins sold from late 1983 on. Sportsters with Evolution engines were immediately available in 883 cc and 1100 cc versions.

1953 : INDIAN DISAPPEARS, HARLEY REMAINS

In 1958, the heavy Harley-Davidson V-Twins underwent some important changes. The Harley-Davidson Company was aware that it was important to keep in the catalog a style of bike that had helped build the brand's image over the years. Even today, some people still associate the Harley-Davidson brand with a white motorcycle, such as an "FLH," with wide handlebars and a rear wheel with either rigid fiberglass or leather bags at the sides, ridden by a stiff, proud policeman on a solo seat, dressed in spotless new clothes; in other words, an old Hollywood image. However, beginning in 1941, this "FL" model was actually subjected to many modifications, although its displacement remained 74 cubic inches (1200 cc).

First of all, as mentioned earlier, the Knucklehead engine gave way to the Panhead in 1948. In 1949, Hydra-Glide telescoping hydraulic forks became standard. The FL series was augmented by the addition of the FLH in 1955, and, in 1956, this series was composed of six motorcycles. Despite their similar appearance, a few small but key differences helped distinguish one from the other. Models "FL," "FLE," "FLEF," and "FLHF," whose total production amounted to 5,806 in 1956, accounted for almost 50% of that year's output from the factory in Milwaukee. In 1958, the Hydra-Glide was renamed the Duo-Glide (in turn anticipating the Electra Glide), and the new model was fitted with rear shock absorbers linking the frame to the swinging arm. This modification increased comfort and improved the heavy bike's ability to hold the road; but the rear shock absorbers had not definitively been adjusted. Their position was still inclined too far forward, reducing their efficiency considerably. However, because the seat was fitted on two springs and the large tire ensured a great deal of comfort already, the designers of this new "FL" did not make life too difficult for themselves by undertaking complicated studies concerning the fitting of the shock absorbers.

The Duo-Glide, equipped with this practical, if imperfect new feature and a hydraulic brake on the rear wheel, benefitted immediately, not least because the bikes, which were less stressed, had an increased road life.

In 1958, a small 125 cc model, the "Hummer," appeared in the catalog and stayed until 1960.

At that time, Harley-Davidson had been around for fifty-five years and had experienced a happy period before the Great War, a lively battle against its American competitors, the Great Depression, a second World War, and finally, the arrival of foreign competition — all events during which four men, joined by a very solid friendship and driven by the same passion, had been able to create, nurture, and build what had become the oldest motorcycle factory in the world.

108 The Panhead appeared in the Harley-Davidson catalog with this shape until 1965, proving its versatility. It was the first Harley-Davidson engine to be adapted to Chopper frames.

109 top and center *The Duo-Glide replaced the famous Hydra-Glide in 1958. The main modification, from which the new name originated, was a rear frame equipped with dampers, giving a double shock-absorbing effect, one in the front from the telescoping fork and one at the back.*

109 bottom *The Enthusiast continued to boast Harley-Davidsons' merits, advertise accessories, and present new models.*

110 top Police corps used Harley-Davidsons, equipped with all the accessories they needed: radios, windshields, warning lights, sirens, saddlebags, etc.

110 bottom In 1958, accessories appeared such as saddle rails, which anticipated real seat backs mounted on sissy-bars.

Then, as the years went by, the new generation followed and even-greater difficulties began to present themselves. Consumer needs evolved as motorcycle owners became more knowledgeable and demanded new and updated products. The Harley-Davidson Motor Company was lucky to maintain a core group of loyal supporters who kept selling and riding their motorcycles but even so, change was on the horizon. The company may have just celebrated its 50th anniversary, but twenty difficult years were ahead.

The November 1959 issue of Floyd Clymer's magazine *Cycle* announced the arrival of a new brand of motorcycle on the American market, but it didn't predict the impact that arrival would have on the motorcycle field of the future. It was no longer a question of the danger related to the competition coming from Europe, but to that from Japan and a brand called Honda, which was hardly known.

Penetration of the market was very modest in the beginning. Honda very wisely settled on American soil with a small 50 cc motorcycle. This small capacity motorcycle worried no one, and most people didn't even pay attention to it. At the time, Japanese material was not renowned for its reliability.

The Japanese strategy was actually quite well thought out: they invaded the American motorcycle market by offering products at extremely low prices. Although this did not bring a huge profit, it was a cost-effective means of establishing brand recognition. Then, once the brand was well established, they began exporting heavy motorcycles, which often even copied American design.

There are those who think that Harley-Davidson played an important role in the success of the Japanese motorcycle industry. In 1929, when the yen lost half its value, American imports, notably the Harley-Davidson, became much too expensive for Japanese pockets. In 1932, Harley-Davidson sold a manufacturing license to the Japanese company Sankyo (at the time a pharmaceutical company, but a brand which can still be found on electronic equipment today) to

manufacture a sort of Japanese Harley-Davidson, called "Rikuo" (King of the Road).

In the 1960s, when Japanese motorcycles began posing a serious threat to the last U.S. manufacturer, it was up to William Herbert Davidson and his associates to devise a strategy for preserving the future of the brand.

111 center and bottom Duo-Glides which have been renovated and fitted out with historically accurate accessories are often shown in competitions. Many owners do not hesitate to improve the Duo-Glides' looks even further by using newly chrome-plated parts.

LOSS OF PERSONALITY

HARLEY AND THE ITALIANS

In the summer of 1960, the Harley-Davidson Motor Company started to negotiate with Aermacchi, an Italian company based in Varese. This step was aimed at finding an arrangement which would allow Harley-Davidson to distribute lightweight bikes that would compete effectively against the Japanese models.

Before World War I, the Aermacchi company, which had been based in Milan since 1912, manufactured planes in small quantities.

At the beginning of 1930, as orders

came to build warplanes for Mussolini's airforce, the company grew. Then, during the Second World War, it was almost destroyed. After the war, it reestablished itself more modestly in Varese and began to manufacture light cars; but it continued to suffer financial problems. Aermacchi thought motorcycles might be a more profitable business, and began manufacturing lightweight models. In 1960, Harley-Davidson purchased half of Aermacchi's bike division, forming Aermacchi/Harley-Davidson.

In 1960, as a result of the agreement with Aermacchi, Harley-Davidson marketed a scooter, the "Topper," equipped with an automatic gearbox, a belt drive, and a 165 cc engine. It remained in the catalog through 1964, but was not a great commercial success.

During the first years of cooperation with Harley-Davidson, Aermacchi took part in important races with a 250 cc motorcycle designed specifically for the purpose. In this period, other Italian models were also put on the American market and, in 1962, Harley-Davidson launched the BT Pacer Lightweight, a 175 cc motorcycle. This model was reliable and had a quality in line with the reputation the factory in Milwaukee had been forging for sixty years, but the competitors were simply offering more appealing and aesthetically sophisticated products.

(Incidentally, all through these years, Harley-Davidson realized that fiberglass was gaining ground and that the use of this material had become nearly indispensable to chassis conception

and to certain motorcycle accessories. In 1962, the company acquired 60% stock in the Tomahawk Boat Company in Tomahawk, Wisconsin, and reorganized it to make it suitable for the production of motorcycle elements. Harley-Davidson also used the opportunity to manufacture small electrical golf carts in this factory, but not for very long.)

1965 marked the end of the Duo-Glide, which was ousted by the Electra Glide and went to the museum to join the Hydra-Glide, the model which it in turn had once replaced.

The Electra Glide, whose name came from the fact that it had an electric starter motor, nevertheless preserved the kick-starter system. Its battery was 12 volts, rather than 6, and front and rear disc brakes replaced front and rear drum brakes. Until 1966, the motorcycle was equipped with a Panhead engine, which was then replaced by the new Shorelhead engine, which generated a great deal more power.

In 1970, the Electra Glide was finally given its modern and definitive appearance when its engine sump acquired the shape with which we are acquainted today and when it abandoned its magneto in favor of an alternator. This bike was also later equipped whit a new carburetor — in short, it benefited from many improvements. As for the Sportster, on one of its versions, in 1967, it was fitted with an electric starter.

In the early 1960's, the third generation, which had already been involved for a few years, was asked to accept greater responsibility for various sectors of the company. A few years earlier, William H. Davidson, who had been president of the company since

1942, suggested that his son, William G. Davidson, take on responsibility for the design department. In 1963, William G. accepted this offer; it gave him the opportunity to use his skills to contribute to the factory that he still considered a part of the family. It is worth pointing out that Willie G. had graduated from an art and design school in Pasadena, California. Before working for Harley-Davidson, he had already demonstrated his talents at Ford, the same company that had seriously worried his grandfather and his uncles at the beginning of 1900.

Having grown up among bolts, wheels, and V-Twin engines, and having taken part in endurance motorcycle races, he was aware of the needs of the company's customers. He accepted his father's offer and started working immediately. Although it seemed a good sign, Walter Davidson's son Gordon died in 1967, perhaps precipitating some of the company's imminent difficulties.

113

HARLEY FACES GREAT DIFFICULTIES

In 1967, Harley-Davidson became the target of Bangor Punta, a firm working in the railroad sector and specializing in the buyouts of companies threatened by bankruptcy. To prevent the brand from disappearing, President William H. Davidson accepted a proposal from American Machine & Foundry (AMF) to acquire Harley-Davidson for the amount of $21 million. AMF would retain control for the next eleven years. Rodney C. Gott, who acted on behalf of AMF and felt a particular affection for Harley-Davidson, became a member of the executive management for the new company group, called AMF/Harley-Davidson. For Harley-Davidson, it was the end of sixty-two years of private, family management.

The financial injection was indispensable. Harley-Davidson was equipped with old machinery and was incapable of producing a large number of motorcycles quickly and cost-effectively. Therefore it was unable to compete against the Japanese. In order to fend off the pressure from Japanese motorcycles, which were continually being improved, it became necessary to modernize production systems. However, it was imperative that a rapid growth in production go hand-in-hand with quality and reliability, two attributes which had shaped the Harley-Davidson reputation for decades. Furthermore, the company needed to set up a research department which would be able to quickly satisfy customers who were increasingly eager for new technological and stylistic improvements.

Three letters now appeared beside the Harley-Davidson logo on the tanks: AMF, and Harley-Davidsons began to be mass-produced. It was the only way to supply sufficient quantities to retailers and sufficient variety to customers. Thanks to this relationship with AMF and the change it entailed, once again Harley-Davidson production began to grow; in 1969, it reached 15,575 bikes, then 16,669 in 1970, 22,650 in 1971, 34,750 in 1972, 37,525 in 1973, 40,430 in 1974, and finally 34,255 in 1975.

But many faithful customers, especially in Europe, did not understand the change. Why was their favorite brand making bikes that were so indistinguishable from their competitors? What had happened to the unique Harley spirit? Rodney C. Gott soon understood that the production increase had been accompanied by a significant drop in quality and that Harley-Davidson could not compete against the Japanese on their own ground — that of mass-

114 top The MSR-100 appeared in 1971, under the name Baja 100. This small two-stroke 6 cubic-inch (100 cc) Harley-Davidson was not able to win the competition against the Japanese.

114 center Harley-Davidson tried to penetrate the scooter market with the Topper. Introduced in 1960 and fitted with a two-stroke 165 cc engine, it was listed in the Harley-Davidson catalog until 1965.

114 bottom The Sprint, a small four-stroke 250 cc motorcycle, was sold until 1969, when the capacity of the road model was increased to 350 cc. Made in cooperation with the Aermacchi/Harley-Davidson factory, this model would disappear from the line in 1975.

production. He inferred, from this analysis, that the only solution for the American brand was to keep developing the trump cards which had built its success and its legend: solidity, reliability, and quality. During this period, the Japanese reinforced their penetration with models which were as big as the Harley-Davidson V-Twin. In 1975, Honda presented the "Gold Wing" in the United States, a massive motorcycle with a flat 1000 cc four-cylinder engine, whose bulbous shape was close to the legendary Harley-Davidson.

Rodney C. Gott believed that Harley-Davidson's problems were caused by the Harley-Davidson family management, but the events that followed and the succession of different presidents proved that the source of the company's trouble lay elsewhere.

William Herbert Davidson had held the office of president for twenty-nine years; in 1971, he left the post, although he continued to work within the company as chairman for two years. In 1973, when he retired, one of his sons, John A. Davidson, Willie G.'s brother, took up the presidency.

114-115 and 115 Harley-Davidsons fitted with Shovelhead engines gradually stood out as deluxe touring motorcycles. They appealed to those who were eager to ride through America's wide open spaces on a motorcycle that provided maximum comfort. These riders did not hesitate to decorate their motorcycles with chrome plating, accessories, and specially designed radios.

116 left In 1976 Harley-Davidson celebrated America's bicentennial by selling machines with "Liberty Edition" tank decor. Posters commemorated the event, presenting Harley-Davidsons as American machines linked to images of freedom and escapism.

In the same year, the line was widely modified, both in terms of decorations, with new colors and logos, and in terms of frames and tanks.

But the factories in Milwaukee and on Capitol Drive were incapable of concurrently implementing these modifications and of increasing production, which amounted to more than 70,000 motorcycles in 1973. AMF owned a large factory producing military material in York, Pennsylvania. The management decided to move the manufacture of frames and assembly of the Harley-Davidson line in this factory, leaving the manufacture of engines and gearboxes in the Capitol Drive plant and in Milwaukee. The first motorcycle to come off the York line was a Sportster, one of the best-selling models of the Harley-Davidson range.

Unfortunately, this separated manufacturing process led to myriad

problems. While production increased in York, the factory in Wisconsin could not keep the same pace. Because each factory was managed in isolation, according to its own imperatives, there were problems in communication and coordination, and, consequently, irregular production.

Although some customers remained loyal, AMF/Harley-Davidson lost a lot of money, because the finished motorcycles revealed an increasing number of defects. As a result, in an increasingly tense atmosphere, AMF started to change the members of its management team, which led, finally, to a three-month strike. It proved difficult for the new head, Ray Tritten, to find reasonable solutions.

When Ray Tritten took over, there was no distribution plan, and stocks were badly managed; not to mention the complex production system and the divisions between managers.

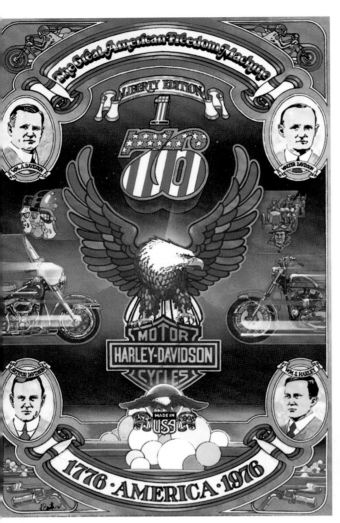

116 right The first Shovelhead engines appeared in 1966. They provided a ten percent power increase over the Panhead, while ensuring better lubrication and greater reliability.

117 Production of the SS 250 started in 1975. Equipped with two-stroke one-cylinder engines, these motorcycles were available in road and cross-country (SX) versions, with 175-and 250-cc V-Twin engines.

Tritten was able to solve certain problems. The only solution for Harley-Davidson was to improve the quality of its machines and make customers forget the simplicity of its mechanics as compared to the sophistication of Japanese bikes. (While it was true that Harley-Davidsons started easily, braked better and practically did not vibrate, the press dedicated only a very few articles to the American motorcycles, arguing that they lacked new features compared the continuous innovations of their foreign counterparts.)

Ray Tritten thought the best solution was to appoint a new head in Milwaukee, one capable of finding and introducing a new management policy likely to set this legendary company back on its track. After a search, L. Vaughn Beals, a disciplined and uncompromising man, was appointed president in 1977. He was completely new to the world of motorcycles, but was able

to understand the problems of a firm whose structure was so disorganized. The company needed a long-term policy rather than a day-to-day strategy; it needed to improve the existing motorcycles by making them more reliable; and to fight against the competitors with machines of equal performance. To this end new, technologically improved engines needed to be developed, without sacrificing the personality of the famous V-Twin.

Jeff Bleustein, who is the executive president today, was chief mechanical engineer at the time. He was put in charge of setting up a research department for Harley-Davidson. Jeff Bleustein thought it was essential to keep the characteristic sound of the V-Twin. A Harley-Davidson can be recognized from afar by this noise, which identifies the brand even before the water-drop shaped logo on the tank is within sight.

In the early 1980s, the management set up a project called "Nova," aimed at improving the V-Twin and then creating a new range of bikes and engines to compete against the Japanese. Today, these two objectives would appear almost impossible to accomplish, because a Harley-Davidson has really become inseparable from the V two-cylinder engine. However, at that time, Vaughn Beals and Jeff Bleustein easily obtained the budgets needed for the research from AMF and asked Porsche, in Germany, to study a new engine. Ten million dollars were spent on the "Nova" project. It ended with the abandonment of the Porsche prototype, which was built around a V 4 engine block.

In 1978, the research offices at Harley-Davidson were given an imperative: propose a design for a new engine, differentiating it from the Shovelhead. So, its rocker arm cover could not resemble that of the Shovelhead, and obviously, its production cost had to be reduced in comparison to its predecessor. It took 250,000 miles of testing this new V-Twin to reach the desired reliability before it could be fitted on the Harley-Davidsons, beginning in 1984. And the V2 Evolution was born. These six long years would demand a tremendous amount of tenacity from Harley-Davidson, as well as the strength to embark on a new adventure.

PERSONALITY AND INDEPENDENCE

THE ARRIVAL OF A MAGICIAN

Harley-Davidson has many faces, and while older people may think of police motorcycles when they hear the name, for younger generations it often conjures up the image of a chopper, the machine ridden by the bikers of the '60s and '70s. The film *Easy Rider,* starring Peter Fonda and Dennis Hopper, showed precisely this kind of motorcycle, in this case a completely transformed Electra Glide.

In 1971, Willie G. Davidson had been responsible for design within the company for eight years. After observing this new way of conceiving the motorcycle and especially the Harley-Davidson, he took his

red and blue geometrical and symmetrical patterns.

These modifications merely modernized the appearance of the Harley-Davidson, which remained practically the same in terms of its engine and frame. Its engine was a 1200 Shovelhead, so this bike could be considered the mixture of two motorcycles.

In 1972, the Sportster engine reached 1000 cc, thanks to a larger engine bore. In 1974, the Super Glide was given an electric starter as an option, and the range was completed by the "FXE," a designation indicating the motorcycle fitted with this

new accessory. Nevertheless, the standard FX model continued to be produced until 1978, a year in which 1,774 items were manufactured; up to 8,134 "FXE"s, were produced in the same year. All in all, the factory produced 79,700 Super Glides between 1971 and 1978.

The Super Glide lead the way for a whole series of models derived from that first creation of the design department head. So, in 1977, it was followed by the "Low Rider," then the "Fat Boy," and finally, in 1980, the "Wide Glide," which became one of the company's best-selling motorcycles.

pencil and sat at his drawing board. For the sake of reliability, he conceived a completely new but very economical model, which modified various elements of the models included in the range that year. The thin, light Sportster front and the heavy, stable Electra Glide back gave rise to a bike capable of satisfying different kinds of customers, but above all of injecting new life into the ranks of Harley-Davidsons.

The "Super Glide" did not particularly surprise the customers. The tank shape was still that of a water drop, the fork was still thin, the head-lamp simple, the handlebar like a cow horn, the twin-seat located on a streamlined and shaped mud-guard; its colors were borrowed from the American flag, consisting of a white background with

118 top In 1974, Willie G. Davidson (left) and William H. Davidson presented an entirely renewed Racer to Tony Hulman, who would show it in the museum in Indianapolis. Joe Petrali had been national champion six times on a motorcycle like this.

118 bottom In 1971, AMF/Harley-Davidson presented this Super Glide with its original design, particularly daring in those days. This motorcycle marked the beginning of what was then called "factory customization," with Harley-Davidson offering machines with special lines that distinguished them from mass-produced motorcycles.

Willie G. quickly understood what the Harley fans expected; they were not necessarily looking for fast motorcycles, but rather for machines with character and power, which would be able to maintain a certain style and personality over the years.

In 1984, after the Wide Glide, the Softail was put on the market. Since it incorporated the characteristics of the Super Glide, the Low Rider and the Electra Glide, it initially gave the impression that Harley-Davidson was releasing a 1958 model for nostalgia buffs, but this was not the case; and although the frame seemed rigid, it disguised two shock absorbers which ensured a comfortable ride, one of the reasons today there is a complete Softail line built around this frame.

During the '70s, while Willie G. Davidson put together and designed some adjustments for the new models, AMF/Harley-Davidson experienced an impressive increase in production. But the Japanese still produced and redesigned

more rapidly, thus obliging the dealers to drop the prices of the motorcycles left in stock. What is more, the American-Italian association found itself handicapped by the light motorcycles manufactured by Aermacchi, which were not able to stand up to the Japanese competition either.

In 1978, Rodney C. Gott retired from his post as AMF head and Tom York replaced him. Unfortunately, York did not understand the special relationship Harley-Davidson had with its customers.

As a result, York concluded both market share and profitability could be recovered if AMF built new models whose qualities and style corresponded to the Japanese fashion. Obviously, these proposals caused great concern amongst those who knew and loved the company.

Supporters of the company, who realized that the company's main strength lay in its personality, rallied togethet to put an end to the AMF and Harley-Davidson cooperation, so as to prevent the extinction of Harley-Davidson at the hands of Tom York. In 1980, Vaughn Beals tried to make the head of AMF understand that the sale of Harley-Davidson represented the best chance for its survival.

In 1983, the Nova project was finally abandoned. It was a huge financial loss, but where would it have led with such instructions? Surely to super-powerful, sophisticated but unoriginal motorcycles; to simply entering into direct competition with the Japanese manufacturers; to trying to be little more than the company that releases the fastest model and the fanciest fairing.

119 top The entirely black 1977 Café Racer was another customization of a Sportster. Unluckily for Harley-Davidson, this conception of the sports motorcycle was too advanced for those days.

119 bottom With this 1977 FXS, called the Low Rider, factory customization continued. The Low Rider met Harleyists' expectations more closely than the Café Racer of the same year. Thanks to its success, more models were derived from this motorcycle.

INDEPENDENCE AND RESCUE

Vaughn Beals, the son of an accountant from Boston and the person who would lead Harley-Davidson's return to independence, had studied aeronautical engineering at the Massachusetts Institute of Technology. He had worked for various companies before becoming a research and development engineer at and then head of an important aeronautical technology factory. Thanks to his diplomacy, once at Harley-Davidson, he managed to reinforce the team spirit and suggested that the other members of the executive management take on more responsibility. He motivated and helped the dealers by granting them some discounts. His objective was to consolidate

Beals left his post, but remained within the AMF group.

Then, on February 26, 1981, Beals gathered twelve other Harley-Davidson executives disappointed by the association with AMF to suggest that they should buy the company together. He knew that the asking would not be very high, because Harley-Davidson was considered beyond recovery. Vaughn Beals started discussions with Citicorp, the industrial credit company; these proved very difficult, as were the discussions with AMF.

By this time, Harley-Davidson had had six presidents in eight years. When Vaughn Beals launched the redemption operation, Willie G.'s brother, John A. Davidson, who became the head of the golf cart department, retired from the management team, thus leaving Willie G. as the last remaining member of the big family that had started the eighty-year-old enterprise.

Nonetheless, the difficult negotiations paid off, and on June 14, 1981, the contract of sale of Harley-Davidson was signed by the AMF president, Ray Tritten. At that time, the thirteen board members were as follows: John Hamilton, Jeffrey Bleustein, Kurt Woerpel, Chris Sartalis, Willie G. Davidson, James Paterson, Timothy Hoelter, David Lickerman, Peter Profumo, David Caruso, Ralph Swenson,

the customers who were still loyal to the brand and to lay the groundwork for a new start for the firm. He launched the 5-speed gearbox and various other improvements, but unfortunately, at the end of the '70s, financial problems meant many projects had to be abandoned. Eventually, Vaughn

Charles Thompson, and Vaughn Beals. Together they got on the road to make the long trip from York to Milwaukee. Harley-Davidson had returned, with difficulty, to a unique identity.

After this historical signature, some people criticized AMF very harshly for not

120 top With the signing of this document, the Harley-Davidson Motor Company recovered its independence, in June 1981.

120 bottom left The new owners and full-time employees of the Harley-Davidson Motor Company: (standing from left to right) John Hamilton, Dr. Jeffrey Bleustein, Kurt Woerpel, Chris Sartalis, William "Willie G." Davidson, and (sitting from left to right) James Paterson, Timothy Hoelter, David Lickerman, Peter Profumo, David Caruso, Ralph Swenson, Charles Thompson, and Vaughn Beals.

120 bottom right The first motorcycle produced by the independent Harley-Davidson Company was a Heritage Edition, decorated with a gold medallion on its oil tank cap.

121 left The Sportster XR-1000 evoked the racing XR-750 models produced for competition. This motorcycle, which became available as a limited series in 1983, contributed to the recovery of Harley-Davidson.

121 right The 1981 Heritage Edition, one of the first Harley-Davidsons other than the Electra Glide to come with a 1340-cc capacity. Although it was fitted with a modern Shovelhead engine, it developed a totally retro look, anticipating later Harley-Davidsons equipped with Evolution engines entirely made in aluminum.

taking better care of the classic company which had been in their stewardship. Others reacted more reasonably, taking into account the efforts AMF had made: if AMF had not invested money to develop the new Evolution V-Twin, or simply to build of the Super Glide and other newly conceived models, Harley-Davidson would have disappeared long ago.

At the moment the company recovered its autonomy, the motorcycle market in the United States was not at all favorable. Production fell again, to the consternation of its new executives. Additionally, certain Japanese motorcycles that had the same aesthetics, if not the same spirit of the heavy V-Twin arrived on American soil. They were sold for half the price charged by Harley-Davidson Motor Company.

At the end of 1981, Harley-Davidson found itself in the worst situation the company had ever known. Since certain parts became very difficult to find, most of the Harley-Davidson dealers opted for the sale of Japanese motorcycles and only a few remained loyal to the brand, perhaps as a result of some premonition. By waiting for better days, they showed their confidence in the thirteen executive managers.

In Japan, inventory was updated several times a year, allowing a thorough inspection of the parts in terms of quality and cost price. The ideal thing was to have the right parts at the right moment. It was also a matter of further involving the worker, of making him feel responsible, so that he watched over the execution of each assembly step and avoided becoming a robot. He had to check his production pace in order to remain in step with the rest of the manufacturing process. Each operation had its name.

1— The "EI" (Employee Involvement) was the complete participation of each employee in problem solution and quality control.

2— The "JIT" (Just In Time Inventory) was the reduction of expenses and quantities.

3— The "SOC" (Statistical Operator Control) was each employee checking his own work.

Harley-Davidson learned from the Japanese and implemented these three organizational and regulatory systems. Traditionalism and conservatism also had to be put aside in order to make way for a new method. The suppliers themselves had to accept these new working formulas and opt for a pace that was identical to Harley-Davidson's, so as to be able to deliver on time and with the required quality.

After this reorganization, only the necessary quotas were manufactured each day and immediately assembled on each

122-123 top *The classic image of the Harley-Davidson—fitted with the Panhead engine, linked to one- or two-up touring—was adapted to the fashion of the time in advertisements for new Harley-Davidsons in the 1980s and '90s. Advertisers used the same theme again for the Electra Glides.*

bike. The Harley-Davidson engineers responsible for the assembly, namely, those in the York, Pennsylvania factory, met regularly with the suppliers to discuss problems that had arisen during assembly or to define the qualities of an accessory worth following up. Thanks to the "Statistical Operator Control," the assemblers and the manufacturers could spot the specific problems at the beginning of production and stop the process before any motorcycles were rejected by the commercial service or by the customers. There were very few employees in the Harley-Davidson factories who had never ridden a Harley-Davidson. Many of them owned one, even several,

Commission took action for the first time to help the company. The I.T.C. submitted an official request to President Ronald Reagan aimed at increasing tariffs on imported Japanese heavy motorcycles (more than 700 cc) over a duration of five years (until 1988). The tariff amounted to 45% in 1983, 35% in 1984, then dropped to 10% in 1987, a year by which there were no more than 10,000 foreign heavy motorcycles on the American market. Since Harley-Davidson had regained its strength and the production pace of its best days, Vaughn Beals asked the government to lift the measure and to give free rein to the competition.

In 1983, at the beginning

of this relaunching, only part of the factory was being used for the manufacture of motorcycles; Harley-Davidson seized the opportunity and began producing metal racks for carrying Air Force bombs. The contract with the military was actually the company's most profitable and, during Ronald Reagan's presidency, provided more than $20 million per year. In effect, 40% of the company profits came from a sector which accounted for 20% of production. In 1984, the new V-Twin, "V2 Evolution," was introduced as part of the 1340 cc range. The Shovelhead, always a source of trouble, left room for a V-Twin capable of inspiring confidence in the Milwaukee motorcycle once again.

and when working on this legendary line, they did their best to manufacture a flawless product. They managed this by unifying "EI," "JIT," and "SOC," the working methods inspired by their competitors — the same competitors who had nearly managed to eradicate the Harley-Davidson brand from the world of motorcycle production.

But Harley-Davidson still had to become competitive in terms of price. This was not simple, because the Japanese were already in a strong position and had nothing to prove. Thus, it was difficult for the company from Milwaukee to appeal to foreigners and especially to reconquer its domestic market, which was the key to ensuring the company's recovery.

In September of 1982, responding to the request of the managers at Harley-Davidson, the International Trade

Some years earlier, Harley-Davidson had begun manufacturing special limited series of motorcycles to mark important American events, which was an efficient way to boost sales. The Milwaukee managers would even suggest to the retailers specific ways to promote the special editions. In 1986 came the Liberty Edition, celebrating the 100th anniversary of the Statue of Liberty, and on July 18, Vaughn Beals burst into the New York Stock Exchange driving a Limited Edition "Liberty" Super Glide to announce the Harley-Davidson share issue.

In 1986, Harley-Davidson bought the Holiday Rambler Corporation, one of the biggest manufacturers of leisure and commercial vehicles in America, which specialized in the manufacture of campers. The union lasted until the beginning of 1996, when Harley-Davidson sold back this department. The goal: to concentrate entirely on motorcycles, obtaining enough investment to increase production beyond 200,000 motorcycles per annum by the year 2003.

122 center *The Harley-Davidson Heritage Softail first appeared as a limited series in 1985, then it became part of the line in 1986. Its components were based on modern technology but its looks were openly inspired by the old Harley-Davidsons.*

122 bottom *The Low Rider was released in a limited series: it was fitted with a Shovelhead engine, painted black, equipped with belt primary and secondary transmissions, and called the Sturgis model, after the fortieth anniversary of the Sturgis meeting.*

123 bottom *Once the Electra Glide adopted the Evolution aluminum engine, it finally achieved the success it deserved as the ultimate grand touring machine, rapidly conquering America as "King of the Highway."*

FOUR FACTORIES, ONE MYTH

124 top and center The Harley-Davidson factory, manufacturing engines and gearboxes, is located in Wauwatosa, a suburb of Milwaukee, Wisconsin. Motorcycles are assembled at another factory, in York, Pennsylvania.

Harley-Davidson is now the leading heavyweight motorcycle manufacturer in the world, but recovery came after disaster. When analyzing the difficulties that it encountered in the late 1970s and early 1980s, the company tried to accurately assess the technical measures that helped it regain success. It was aware that problems did not arise from personnel so much as its construction techniques and manufacturing system.

In light of that understanding, as mentioned earlier, the company reorganized, following three strategies similar to those used by Japanese manufacturers: employee involvement, just-in-time manufacturing, and statistical operator control.

In 1978, even before the buyout, Harley-Davidson had become one of the first companies to start a quality circle program, encouraging employees to express their ideas, to solve problems, and to increase the quality and effectiveness of their own work. The company knew that only through its employees could it develop maximum efficiency. To begin with, each employee had to be recognized and respected. Then a team structure, organized around the company's goals, had to be established. Finally, a suitable incentive for achieving success had to be created.

That incentive involved the "just-in-time manufacturing" techniques, which Harley-Davidson labeled "MAN" (Materials As Needed). Before MAN, the company's techniques could lead to long delays, a big stock, and a rigid production system. MAN was a strategy by which the company could evolve.

124 bottom The oldest Harley-Davidson factory, and the one that best symbolizes the brand, is still located on Juneau Avenue in Milwaukee. It now houses the company's administrative and research offices, however, the research division projects the need to move to a new location by the end of the century, if they are to continue expanding the line.

First, Harley-Davidson developed a system to help it better predict customer demand. The company then reorganized its manufacturing system to group activities by category and reduce assembly times. The new system improved parts management and increased quality by allowing operators to follow a motorcycle through the whole manufacturing process, start to finish. It also permitted the rapid correction of errors and reduced the physical space needed for assembly.

The next step in reorganization was for operators to monitor parts constantly, identifying those needed and assuring more rapid restocking. With better control of parts acquisition, response rate increased and paperwork decreased.

These MAN policies could only be adopted with the full commitment and heightened awareness among all workers of everybody's responsibilities, at all levels of production. Through MAN, the company set up a real partnership with its suppliers: through the new "partners for profit" program they were given even more incentive to answer the needs of the company.

This program helped encourage suppliers to maximize quality and reduce manufacturing costs, just as Harley-Davidson itself was. During this process, Harley-Davidson reduced the number of its suppliers by half. Those who remained were promised a long and fruitful partnership.

Statistical operator control (SOC) also proved its effectiveness day after day, by constantly improving production and reducing manufacturing costs. Thanks to this method, the company could rapidly correct emerging mistakes and constantly improve quality. Statistics became tools that operators could use to solve their most urgent problems. Harley-Davidson imagined that the program would only last three years, but it has actually become permanent, making it more possible for the company to respond to emerging economic and technical imperatives.

125 Harley-Davidson's assembly lines were recently reorganized, incorporating state-of-the-art manufacturing technology, but production still depends upon the human factor.

The Factory in Wauwatosa

Any neophyte Harleyist imagines that all Harley-Davidsons are built and assembled in the famous factory in Milwaukee, on the corner of Juneau Avenue and 37th Street. That was where the Harley-Davidson story began, but it is not the only location where the great motorcycles are now built. Nowadays, the midtown-Milwaukee building houses Harley-Davidson administration, research, and design, although the company is awaiting the opening of a new research and development center. Most actual manufacturing takes place elsewhere.

Since 1969, Tomahawk, Wisconsin, 150 miles from Milwaukee, has been the manufacturing center for all the Harley-Davidson glass and fiberglass elements, including fairings, covers, saddlebags, and sidecars. Harley-Davidson bought the factory, once used to build boats, to benefit from experienced personnel and to avoid relying on an outside company for parts.

One challenge faced at the Tomahawk manufacturing plant was to match the colors of metal and fiberglass parts. Early on, such matches were impossible, which explains why, in the 1970s, the Electra

Glide's fork head and bags were black and white. Today, this problem no longer exists, and fiberglass bags and other elements are almost exactly the same shade as mudguards and tanks.

As for true manufacturing, only the painting of engine parts takes place on Juneau Avenue. But foundries and assembly teams for the 1340 cc, 1200 cc, and 883 cc engines are located just a few miles away, in the Milwaukee suburbs on Capitol Drive. Close to a thousand

employees work at this plant, manufacturing engine parts by hand. Strict planning avoids overproduction. Over the last few years, Harley-Davidson has also invested millions of dollars in automated manufacturing machinery, designed to produce reliable and high-quality parts. In the first area of the factory, engine parts are cast. Nearby, in the next area, men and women assemble those parts into engines.

Those engines will be fitted on motorcycle frames manufactured hundreds

126

of miles away, in another factory in York, Pennsylvania.

Engine assembly lines include quality control testing as well as manufacturing, guaranteeing the reliability of engines as well as transmissions.

On the V-Twin engine, for example, instrumented inspections are carried out intensively. The engines run for thirty minutes, then are dismantled and thoroughly checked. Certain tests are also conducted on V-Twins fixed to frames and made to react with transmissions, so as to simulate road behavior. Before being sent to the York factory, most of the engines get a coat of a special high-temperature-resistant paint. Chrome-plating and polishing take three-quarters of an hour; a finish layer of nickel and, sometimes, potassium bichromate is applied. Some parts—especially those with precise dimensions and high performance demands—are sent to York to be finished and tested.

126 and 127 The Wauwatosa factory, located on Capitol Drive, manufactures motorcycles' major elements, such as engines and gearboxes. Trucks deliver components daily, and the products they offload undergo daily quality control scrutiny. Similarly, at numerous stations throughout the manufacturing process, quality control experts examine parts, to preserve maximum reliability while increasing productivity.

In 1982, Harley-Davidson began welding frames, then assembling them in one operation, which ensured better-quality engine support and overall performance. Now these assembled elements are sent to 1425 Eden Road in York, where Harley-Davidsons come to life. The company first moved into this 400,000-square-foot facility in 1973, using it to assemble motorcycles and golf carts, manufactured during the time of the AMF association. Today the golf cart operation has been completely abandoned.

Harley-Davidson manufactures motorcycles according to market demand. In 1989, Harley-Davidson produced 55,000 motorcycles; of them, 8,100 went to Europe and 40,300 stayed in the American market. Production keeps growing. Volume of production in 1996 increased over that of 1995 by 12 percent, while 1995 volume had grown by 8.6 percent over 1994. In other words, production went from 490 machines per day in 1995 to 510 per day over the fourth quarter in 1996.

Most suppliers are based within one hundred miles of the Capitol Drive plant in Milwaukee. Since the early 1990s, 96 percent of the parts making up Harley-Davidson engines have been manufactured in the United States. The Milwaukee factory, like the one in York, operates on principles learned from Japanese car manufacturers.

The Milwaukee factory tries to produce the exact number of engines needed in York to fill orders from dealers and other sales forces. Each working unit has exactly the material required by the assembly chain to fill this demand, neither more nor less. Working plans are drawn up daily and, for example, once a shelf of one hundred engine parts is empty, that shelf returns to its starting point, indicating that there are now one hundred engines on the line. Another shelf takes its place and an order goes to the supplier—no paperwork or management discussion required.

The company has been operating like this for years. It is a strategy that relies on workers, established after the recovery of the early '80s, as management acknowledged its past mistakes. Now all workers have their own responsibilities and try to do as well as possible, since everybody is interested in results. Each line operator is responsible for the part he is assembling; he must not let a faulty part go to the following station. Everybody accepts and appreciates the responsibility granted by this "quality circle" approach. Thanks to this principle, operation costs have been reduced, space is being used more efficiently, and maintenance has been reduced to a minimum. Moreover, assembly lines have greater flexibility, permitting, for example, special or anniversary models to be assembled without changing the factory and line operation.

Aware that motivated operators build company strength, Harley-Davidson has encouraged teams on each assembly line. These teams can arrange the working space and the tools or equipment as they like, in order to obtain the best possible comfort and productivity. They plan their work by themselves, modernize and improve operations, and take charge of the tools and material they need. They work as individual units on the assembly line. Just as small businesses, they control the supply of materials and work with motivation to obtain coherent and continuous production. Thanks to this system, Harley-Davidson production and quality have

128 and 129 Harley-Davidson's engine manufacturing and assembly lines still depend on human operations, despite a big emphasis on automation. Company heads do not want to replace employees with machines, except in cases where machines can do dangerous jobs. Then, they believe, mechanization increases productivity without disrupting the team approach.

increased. At all levels of the organization, everybody tries to produce a product of the highest possible quality and during meetings, new ideas for improving or upgrading the product or the factory always come up. While many companies units are moving towards complete robotization, this is not the path chosen by Harley-Davidson. Although it uses some robotics, it considers the need of human supervision and control essential. Harley-Davidson is a living machine with its own philosophy. Robots are primarily used to carry out dangerous tasks, but the human factor remains vital in the conception of the company and its machines. Maybe this is the key to Harley-Davidson's unique spirit. These products do not resemble any other motorcycles, and every new Harley-Davidson rider benefits from the quality.

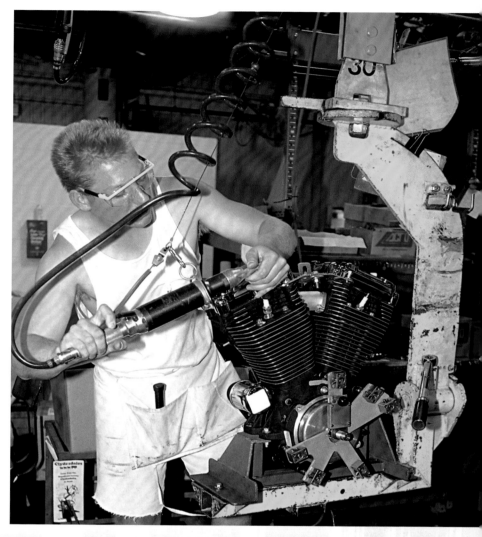

THE FACTORY IN YORK

The assembly factory moved to its new location in York, Pennsylvania, in 1974. The first thing a visitor sees is the warehouse where engines and transmissions arrive from Capitol Drive and wait their turn to be mounted on a frame, which determines the model. Boots, side bags, fork heads, and elements made out of fiberglass coming

powerful have a force of 60,000 tons. These huge presses transform thin iron plates into mudguards and oil or fuel tanks, while others cut away excess metal from around the parts.

Presses also fold the metal handlebars, leg guards, and bag guards to create the distinct models.

from Tomahawk also arrive at this warehouse.

Considering all the models under construction, several different stations are needed to assemble the hundreds of motorcycles completed here every day. As in Wauwatosa, parts arrive here as they are needed, so a large permanent stock has been eliminated. Certain elements made abroad as late as the end of the 1980s are now made in the United States, but a few elements, such as forks, carburetors, and electric circuits, still come from Japan.

The new system of just-in-time stock management has allowed a savings of nearly $40 million, not to mention the improvement of working conditions at York and the other factories. Each worker wears compulsory safety glasses as he works at one of the many machines. The biggest presses, hydraulically powered, are located at the beginning of the line; the most

130 top Since 1974, all Harley-Davidsons have been assembled in York, Pennsylvania. From 1998 on, however, Big Twins will come out of the York factory and Sportsters will be assembled in Kansas City.

Wheeled shelves fill up with these recognizable elements. Then they are either chrome-plated or polished before painting. Next they advance to the station where the frame—the only Harley-Davidson part that passes through the entire York assembly line—is assembled. All the oil and fuel tanks are welded, polished, and carefully examined before reaching the dust-free painting booths.

The Harley-Davidson factory has invested a fortune in its ultramodern painting unit. At first sight, it looks like a completely aseptic space laboratory. Whether visitor or employee, everybody must wear a white overall, shoe-covers, and

a cap to protect the hair, not to mention transparent safety goggles and face masks. To visit this famous Harley-Davidson painting lab, one must walk through a room with a sticky floor, which retains all the impurities attached to the soles of one's shoes. Then one must walk through a flow of hot air from several ventilation ducts, so that all possible dust is removed. Then one enters the futuristic laboratory, where everything is automated and human intervention is limited only to the supervision of machinery and to the management of computer programs that run the equipment. In short, mechanical operations accomplish the following procedures: the metal parts are first accurately cleaned, through degreasing, washing, rinsing, and finally drying. Robotic arms, which look like spiders, keep parts in the right positions. Each of them can adapt to the special shape of any Harley-Davidson part in need of paint—tanks, mudguards, covers, etc.

130 bottom and 131 On the assembly line, frames are first fixed on supports. Afterwards, they follow a track to various stations, receiving all the elements necessary to complete a Harley-Davidson by the end of the line. Machines then test the engine, gearbox, transmission, brakes, electrical system, etc., before the bike is packed for shipment.

After these preparatory stages, paintwork is also carried out by robots inside sealed booths. This factory is flexible enough to allow paint colors to be changed very rapidly. At the end, there is an inspection unit, where all the colors that have been applied are checked. Fresh, filtered, and moisturized air continuously flows through the painting unit for ventilation.

The maximum daily capacity of this unit is 400 motorcycles of one color or 270 if colors or models change mid-production. This factory also includes the laboratories that produce the paints, as well as quality-control labs that test the finished products. Each paint layer is baked in a furnace at a temperature of 300° for about twenty minutes before being covered with another

finishing coat. The body of certain models is decorated with colored borders.

In the penultimate operation, a sticker with the Harley-Davidson logo is applied on the fuel tank, and the whole motorcycle is painted with high-temperature varnish. In the final assembly line station, a large number of supports ready to be loaded with motorcycles moves slowly along a metal conveyor.

A Dyna Glide, a Softail, or an Electra Glide frame, accompanied by an identification number, is solidly fixed to each support at the beginning of the chain.

Due to move to the new Kansas City factory at the end of 1997, Sportsters have their own assembly line. Although Sportster manufacture is different from that of the Big Twin, the operations are similar.

Once the secondary transmission has been fixed, the V-Twin and its gearbox are fitted on the frame. By using jigs, the assemblers can tighten the bolts without risking damage to the engine. Several stations are needed to finally complete the assembly of the engine and the rear wheel.

A day of assembly at York is not dedicated to a single model. The Ultra Electra Glides follow the Softails, sometimes preceded by a few Dynas, all along the line. Some workers specialize in the assembly of forks and brakes.

Others fix the radio and tape players onto the fork heads and do the wiring for tail and headlights, oil pressure and fuel gauges, the horn, and the starter.

At the end of the line, each motorcycle is examined. Test rooms simulate five miles of road conditions. Everything is inspected: brakes, shock absorbers, gears, horn, lights, and indicators.

Motorcycles are placed on wheel supports, operated by the rear wheel. Then they are packed or remain in the hands of the engineers for a few hours, so that they

can repair or replace a faulty part detected in the test room.

After quality testing, the Harley-Davidson motorcycles, enveloped in large, thick, transparent plastic bags, are placed on wooden boards. They are fastened down with belts, protected with small wooden arches, and packed in a huge cardboard box. Thus they leave the factory, bound for their final destinations in the U.S. or abroad.

In the United States, dealers can call on specialists who are trained to maintain and

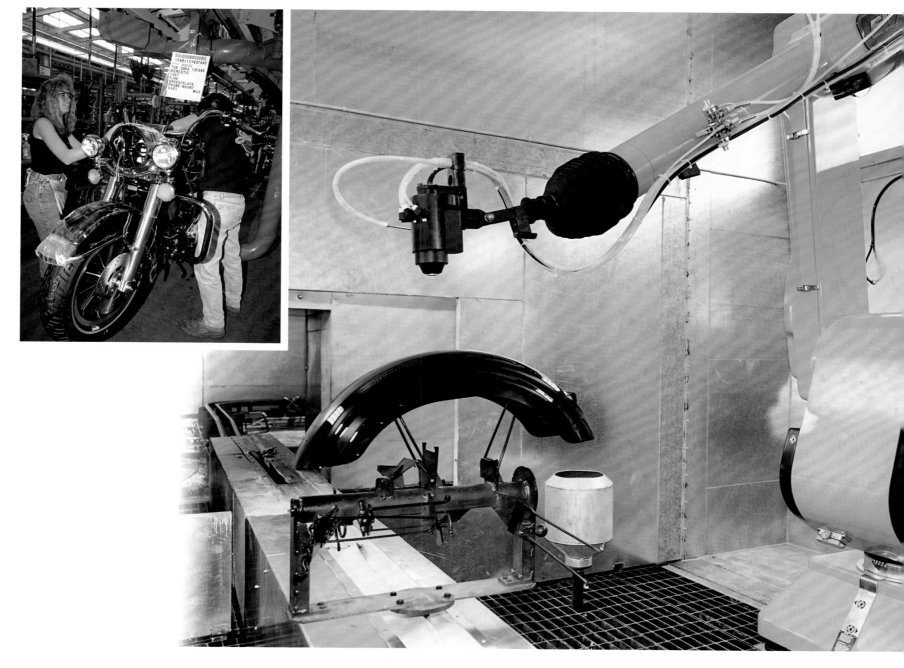

133 *The painting department of the Harley-Davidson factory in York is a top-quality unit, more like a laboratory than a common painting station and rarely accessible to visitors.*

repair the various V-Twin models of the Harley-Davidson range.

These mechanics follow three-month training courses in various schools; the main school, located in Phoenix and Orlando, is called the "Motorcycle Mechanics Institute." This school's training programs, sponsored by Harley-Davidson, are intensive courses, twelve weeks long, designed to provide a mechanic with the knowledge and experience needed to work on the engines, transmissions, clutches, shock absorbers, and electrical components of the Harley-Davidson. Courses are also taught in restoration, focusing on models dating from 1936 to 1969. Another school, the American Motorcycle Institute (AMI), founded in 1972 in Daytona Beach, Florida, trains mechanics to work on Harley-Davidsons, other brands of motorcycles, and boats as well.

In the middle of the 1990s, American dealers complained that they did not have enough Harley-Davidsons to sell.

New arrangements promise to enable the company to increase production, reaching a goal of 200,000 motorcycles per year in 2003, the date of the company's 100th anniversary. At present, many American customers have to wait several months for their Harley-Davidsons, depending on the models they have ordered—sometimes more than a year. Such a market situation goes far to explain the high prices currently paid for secondhand Harley-Davidsons, which are sometimes even more expensive than new motorcycles.

A Museum for a Great History

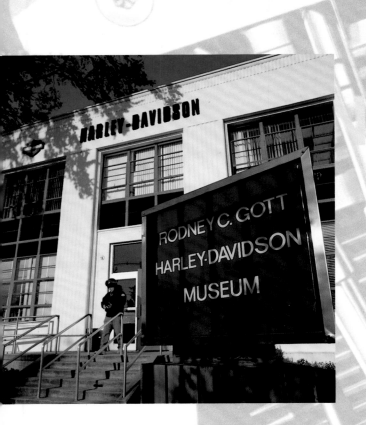

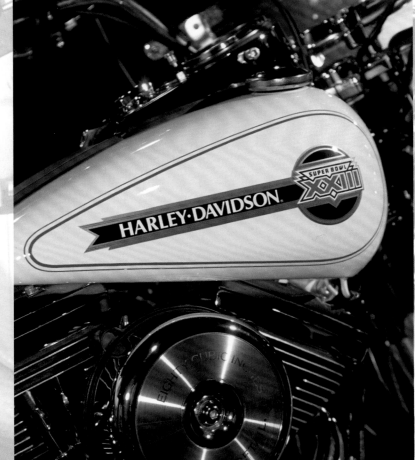

134 top The entrance to the Harley-Davidson Museum in York, same address as the motorcycle assembly plant.

134-135 The new 1997, FLSTS Heritage Springer stands out at the museum entrance, along with a sports model, the Buell, based on a Sportster engine.

135 bottom The Harley-Davidson York Museum overflows with posters, newspaper clippings, leaflets, and some photographs showing the major executives of the Harley-Davidson Motor Company with celebrities and some not, as is the case here. From left to right: Ralph Swenson, Charles Thompson, Vaughn Beals, and William "Willie G." Davidson.

Think Harley-Davidson, and you think the United States. These motorcycles are inextricably linked to the wide-open spaces—to deserts, to the Rockies, to Hollywood, to Texas, to the highway, and to dreams of escape, shared by generations of fans. Those who want to relive every twist and turn of the great Harley-Davidson adventure should visit the Rodney C. Gott Museum in York, Pennsylvania.

At the end of a large field, one can see some white-walled buildings, "York Division" in black letters on one of them. At the corner, a big gate opens to a simple entrance, then six steps climb to a double-windowed door.

There you are, approaching the legend. Next you find yourself in a small entrance hall.

Mystery and impatience grow. Go back to the past and admire the first lady from Milwaukee. She waits for visitors, behind the museum's big wooden sliding door. She is there, proud and brilliant, embodying the century of memories displayed in the museum before you.

136 top, 136-137, and 137 top The first Harley-Davidson frame, with a curved front tube, was drawn directly from bicycle frames of the time. The original paintwork of the first models was black, red, and gold, but from 1906, gray also became available.

136 bottom A solid gold rendition of the first Harley-Davidson model, released in 1903.

138-139 *The V-Twin started its career with Harley-Davidson in 1909. The first available engine of this type had a 49.48 cubic-inch displacement. In 1912 it became available with 61 cubic inches (1000 cc) and a roller chain drive. The wheel size, ranging from 26 to 28 inches, could be changed as a function of owner weight. In 1914, footboards were introduced, along with a clutch and brake pedals.*

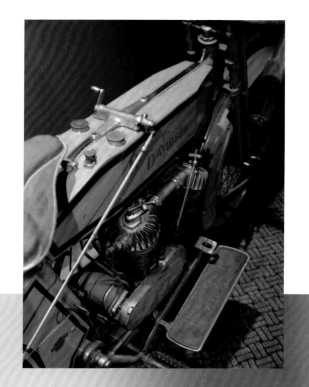

140-141 The two-cylinder 61 cubic-inch
11 J model gained new pieces of equipment,
such as a three-speed transmission with the
lever fitted on the tank. This motorcycle had a
sophisticated electrical lighting system with a
two-bulb headlight, a taillight, a horn, and
ignition. These new components were all
optional, and most users preferred to keep the
acetylene system, already fully tested. This
model sold for $310.

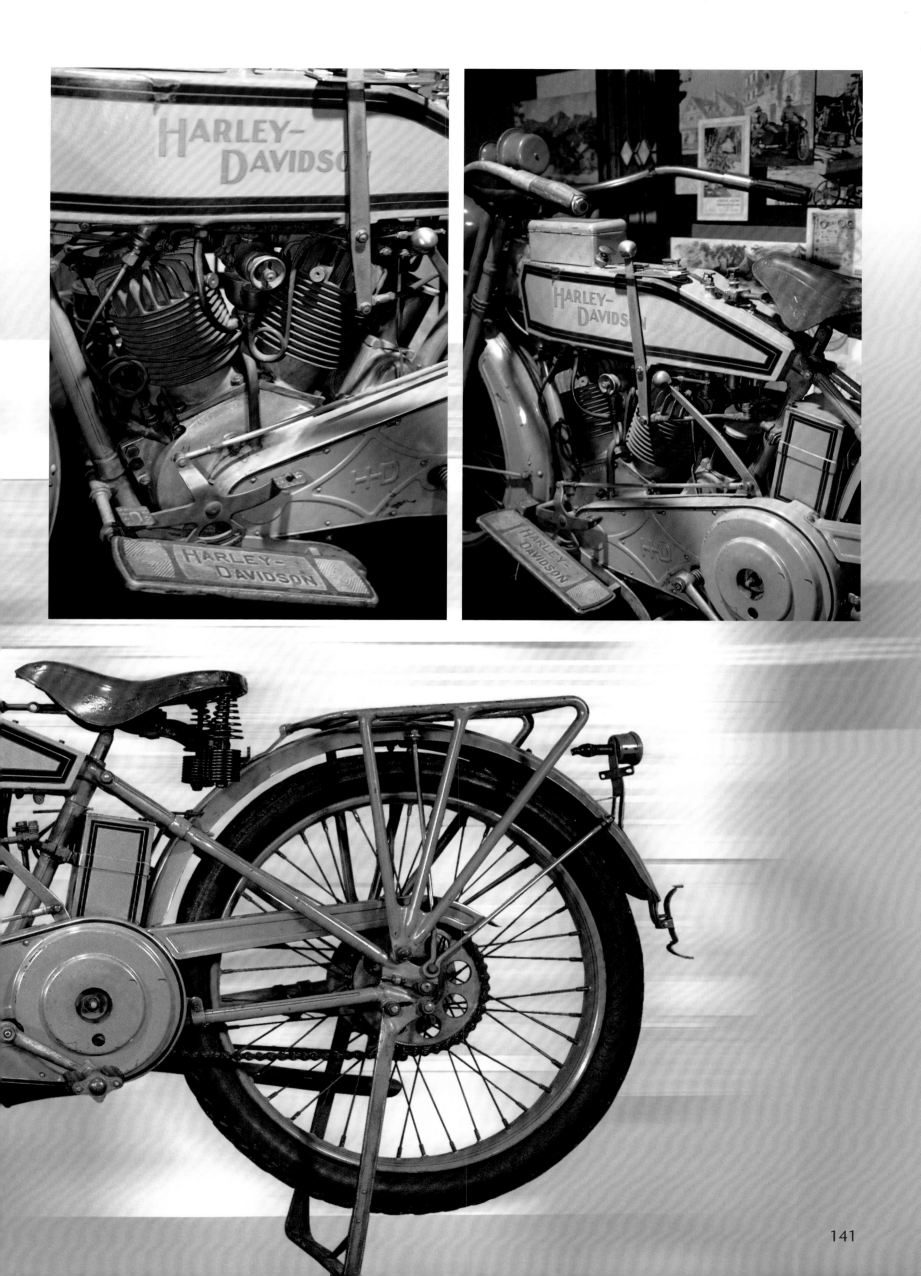

142 The 1918 two-cylinder J model was the world's first motorcycle to be used in military conflict. The gas bottle, located between the two handlebar grips, powered the headlight and horn. Equipped with a sidecar, this type of motorcycle was driven to Germany by Corporal Roy Holtz on November 12, 1918. It was propelled by a 7-horsepower 988.83 cc displacement V_Twin engine, with a three-speed gearbox and simple train gearing. Changing gears meant disengaging the clutch. The transmission was based on a roller chain. Primary and secondary drive chains, covered by sealed drawn steel guards, could be adjusted separately. With its automatic carburetor and throttle, the V-Twin started easily. Three carburetor fittings ensured a better mixture at every speed. Drum brakes worked like internally expanding brake shoes, worked by a pedal on the right footrest. The brake drum had an 18.85 cm diameter and was 2.3 cm wide. The fuel tank held over two gallons; the auxiliary tank held three-quarters of a gallon and the oil tank held four quarts. A curved steel frame, especially designed and reinforced to allow the attachment of a sidecar, supported the whole.

143 The Sport Twin model was a real novelty for the Harley-Davidson Company. The 35.6 cubic-inch model was introduced in mid-1919, and was provided with a 6-horsepower motor that could achieve 45 to 50 miles per hour. Over the first few years of production, it sold for $335, but four years later the price went down to $275. Thanks to a crankshaft counterweight, this two-horizontal-cylinder engine could operate at 4500 rpm. It was fitted with ball bearings for the main engine bearings and the connecting rod small end bearings. It had a magneto flywheel housed in a sealed case. The oil level in the gearbox was kept constant, thanks to an automatic lubrication system. The transmission design, which included lubrication by oil steam coming from the crankcase, was supposed to ensure longer chain life with less maintenance. A high-voltage magneto mounted on the top of the crankcase powered the ignition and was easily accessible. This model was only manufactured from 1919 to 1922, because Harley-Davidson found that it didn't win enough customers away from the Indian V-Twin Scout.

144-145 This machine, introduced in 1922 under the model names 22 F and 22 J, lasted for six years of production. The electrical systems of the two models differed: 22 F was fitted with a magneto and 22 J had dynamo. Available with engines of 61 and 74 cubic inches, the motorcycle sold for as much as $390. This machine was powerful enough to be combined with a sidecar. Its gas consumption rate was reasonable, as a gallon of gasoline would run sixty miles. This low gas consumption ensured it a good fuel distance thanks to its 3-$\frac{1}{2}$-gallon gas tank. It had a four-quart oil tank and good front and rear lighting systems, with a six-volt battery positioned towards the rear. An aluminum gearbox and pistons made for better heat dissipation and greater power. In 1928, a front brake introduced in addition to the existing rear brake, was located at the right foot. The decorations on this model echoed the graphics of the first Harley-Davidsons. During the 1920s, design improvements reduced engine vibrations by half, thus improving the V-Twin's duration. In 1924, aluminum alloy pistons were introduced, developed after lengthy testing, which meant even further improvements in performance. These lighter pistons, four rings, and drilled connecting rods lightened the

1923

moving parts and made the engine more powerful. Since these engine parts were easier to cool, too, high speeds could be maintained over longer distances without danger of overheating. Cooling did not demand too much oil, and the newly designed rings, pistons, and axles resisted wear longer than the old cast-iron parts, thus increasing reliability.

In 1924, both machines—those fitted with old pistons and those with new—were offered in the Harley-Davidson catalog. Models with aluminum pistons could achieve higher speeds than those with cast-iron pistons: ten miles per hour faster solo and twenty with a sidecar. As for lubrication, an Alemite system efficiently allowed the hand pump to send the lubricant at a 500-pound pressure to the desired point.

In 1924, the exhaust doubled its volume and the kickstart system was improved. Motorcycles with electric systems had a 6-volt generator, an accumulator, a headlight, a taillight, an electric horn, and a hand switch with an automatic alarm signal; fuses, housed in a box, protected these new systems. These motorcycles were painted olive-green and decorated with broad maroon stripes and gold pinstripes. An ammeter, speedometer, auxiliary brake, and luggage rack were available as optional parts. The handlebar was manufactured from a single piece of tube with a diameter of an inch, ending in rubber grips. The grips housed the controls, operated by double steel wires sheathed and hidden in the handlebar.

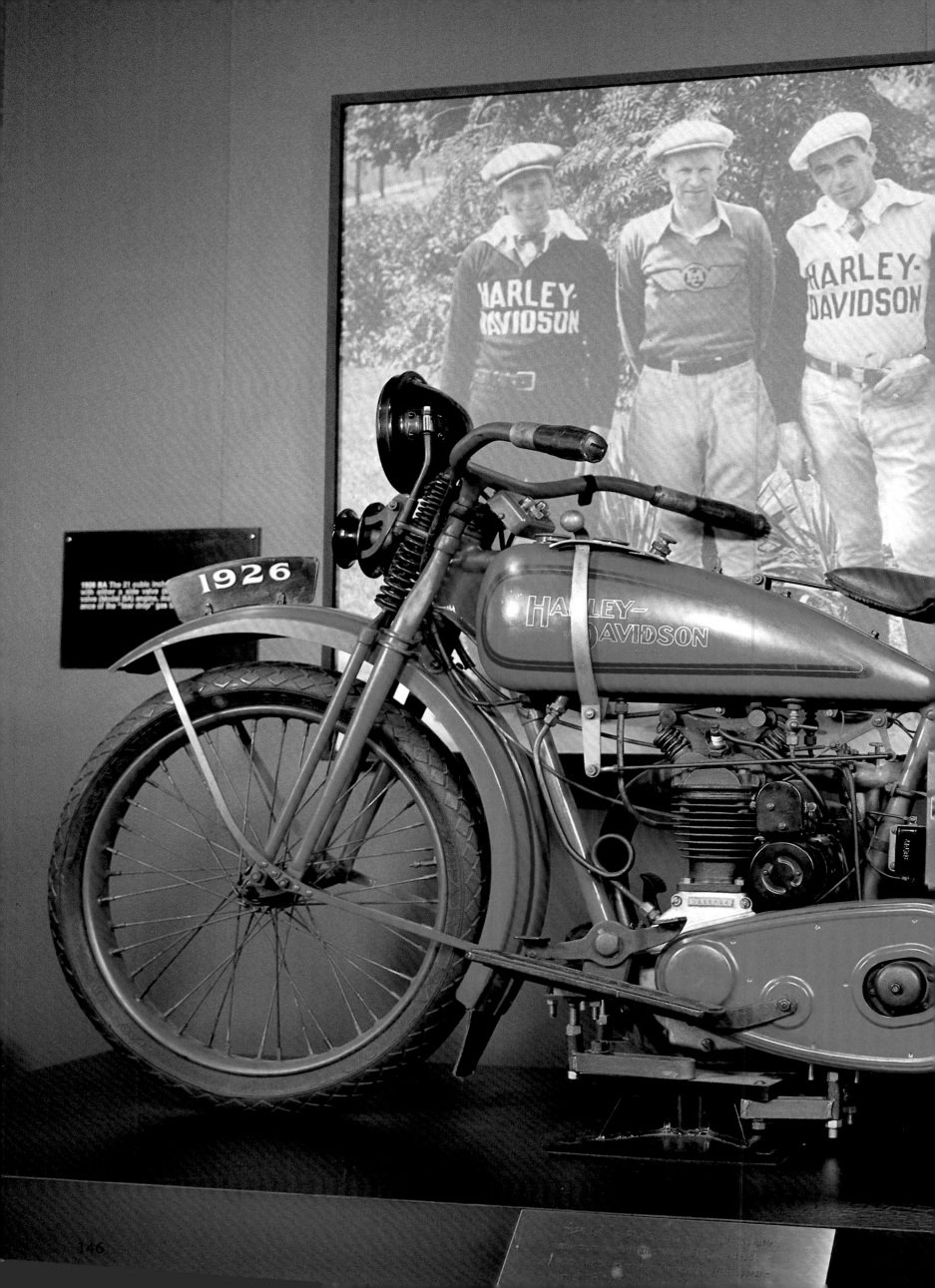

146-147 A new motorcycle came out in 1929, 23 years after the birth of the Silent Gray Fellow. Nicknamed the "Peashooter", it was lightweight and had a 21 cubic-inch (350 cc) displacement and a Schebler carburetor. The engine was lubricated by a mechanical oil pump. A rich mixture control, located on the right side, made starting easier. The wheels were 55 cm. This motorcycle was equipped with a tool kit, including tools for repairing tires. It was manufactured for ten years with two types of engines available: one with side valves and a capacity of eight horsepower, and the other with twelve-horsepower head valves, priced between $210 and $275. It could be fitted with either an electrical system or simply with a magneto. Like the 1919 Sport Twin Model, it became fairly successful in Europe, New Zealand, and Australia. In 1935 Joe Petrali (who, a few years later, was to establish a world record on a Harley-Davidson powered by a V-Twin) won several dirt-track races with this little machine. His thirteen victories prompted the American Motorcycling Association to create a new motorcycle competition category. During the last years of production, this motorcycle's power was increased, so that ultimately it could reach over 60 mph.

148 The 45 cubic-inch, three-speed Model D, produced from 1929 to 1931, was the first 750 cc displacement Flathead. This machine, fitted with a medium-displacement two-cylinder engine mounted on a frame like those of one-cylinder engines, was conceived to compete with Indian middle-of-the-range motorcycles. Its appearance was characterized by two headlights on the 1929 and 1930 models. Some motorcycles had a metal cylinder for a toolbox fixed under the lens. The 750 cc Flathead engine with side valves had cooling fins on each cylinder head cover. The W series faced a slight problem with the three-speed gearbox, which shifted into neutral between second and third gear. Despite this problem, the 45 cubic inch proved to be an excellent engine.

In 1931, starting with this machine, Harley-Davidson built a prototype called "Bullet" that could reach a speed of 85 mph. The strength of the low-compression 45 cubic-inch Flathead made it possible to run on both regular and super gasoline. Over 22 years this engine proved to be successful on all counts—from city roads, used by police departments to rough terrain, used by the Army during World War II. It was a solid, reliable engine that required little maintenance.

148-149 and 149 bottom The 1932 V and
VL models, produced for five years, had a
74 cubic-inch displacement (1200 cc) and were
integrated with the 80 cubic-inch (1340 cc)
model in 1935. Despite the introduction of
the Knucklehead, these side-valve machines
continued to be popular, renamed UL or ULH,
in 74 and 80 cubic inches respectively. These
were Harley-Davidson's most popular engines,
closely related to the 45 cubic-inch models
with which they shared some engine parts.
Their production ended with the introduction
of the Panhead in 1948. The tires on models
UL and ULH were identical. They were
designed to allow rapid disassembling.
Once the Knucklehead came on the market,
these machines adopted similar bodywork
and logos.

150-151 The 1930 V and VL models which became models U and UL in 1937, still used with 74 cubic-inch (1200 cc) Flathead engines. There was also an 80 cubic-inch UHS model, provided with a special trunk for sidecars. (This model had existed previously as a low-compression version, under the reference VSD). All these Harley-Davidson Big Twins fitted with Flathead engines look the same as those fitted with Knuckleheads. Only the engines help differentiate the motorcycles.

152-153 The Knucklehead, the first overhead valve V-Twin model, was called Model E when it first appeared in 1936. It had a 61 cubic-inch displacement (1000 cc), and the special shape of its cylinder head covers made it easy to recognize. Early on in production, it faced some lubrication problems. The oil didn't flow in the correct direction, flooding certain parts of the engine and leaving other gears without lubrication. Harley-Davidson corrected this flaw on the 1937—38 models. Three steel friction clutch discs were adapted on all models, followed by a larger air filter; a reinforced rear braking system (which increased braking power by 44 percent); better contact with the brake lever, no longer made of aluminum; and, especially, a new speedometer support inserted in the middle of the tank, which is still present in today's Harley-Davidsons. The gear-change lever and the clutch pedal were better positioned. The early lubrication problems kept the Knucklehead from selling at first. Sales dropped during the war, then afterwards started soaring.

154-155 The engine fitted on the WLA model, manufactured from 1940 to 1945, actually started as a V-Twin Flathead 45 cubic-inch side engine in 1929. During World War II, this model was called "Liberator," and it certainly appeared as such to the French. After the war, the V-Twin lasted for a long time, used for civilian purposes until 1951, when the K series replaced it. This engine proved to be comfortable, solid, reliable, never causing maintenance problems and always easy to adjust. This Flathead was available with 61 cubic-inch (1000 cc), 74 cubic-inch (1200 cc), or 80 cubic-inch (1340 cc) displacements. In 1929, the first Harley-

Davidson equipped with a 45 cubic-inch Flathead engine appeared: the three-speed Model D. In 1931, this engine was fitted on the Model D, and on the DL and DLD (both sport); it was called R from 1934 to 1936 and then W through 1951. Its toughest competitor was the 61 cubic-inch (1000 cc) Knucklehead, launched by Harley-Davidson in 1936 which sold with great success after the war, thanks to its overhead valves with rocker arms. When Harley-Davidson finally decided to stop manufacturing the 45 cubic-inch side engine, war had been declared. Americans involved this model in the conflict, where it served particularly well. By the

end of 1943, Harley-Davidson had produced some 40,000 WLAs for the U.S. Army. Originally, this motorcycle was fitted with an ammunition box and a submachine gun holster on each side of the front fork. The WLA cylinders were made of cast iron, with valves placed at the side, to the right of each cylinder. Valves were operated by four cams, one for each. A pump fixed at the end of the crankshaft ensured dry-sump lubrication; the exhaust system was a two-in-one. The fuel tank consisted of two sections, as do most Harley-Davidsons today. But at that time, if the left side contained fuel, the right contained oil.

The grip located on the right end of the large handlebar housed the timing advance control. (On the Harley-Davidson WLCs for the Canadian Army, the system was placed on the left.) The clutch was no longer controlled by a lever on the left of the handlebar; it was located next to the left footrest instead. The driver changed gears in the classic way, with a control to the left of the tank. A fairly simple dashboard included two odometers (one of them a trip odometer), an oil pressure warning indicator, a fuel level indicator, and on-off indicators for ignition and lighting. An engine guard protected the crankcase.

156 The 750 cc XA was produced for only one year (in 1942) at the request of the U.S. Army, which had been impressed by the performances of the German Army's Zündapps and BMWs. To manufacture this motorcycle, the Harley-Davidson company just copied a German machine with a flat two-cylinder engine, converting dimensions to inches. In fulfillment of its Army contract, Harley-Davidson manufactured one thousand machines, intended primarily for North Africa, where the shaft transmission, unlike the WLA chain transmission, could withstand the sand.

157 Just before the war, which slowed down production and sales of the Knucklehead, its displacement was increased up to 74 cubic inches (1200 cc). The bigger engine was called FL in 1941. Meanwhile, the EL (with 1000 cc) was thriving. In 1940, a combined total of 4,069 Knucklehead EL and ES models were sold; in 1941, 5,149 Knucklehead EL, ES, FL, and FS models were sold. In 1942, sales fell to 1,743, and to 200 in 1943. In 1944, the sales curves started up again, with the sale of 535 Knuckleheads, but truly positive figures (6,746 sales) only began in 1946. After that, ten thousand Knuckleheads were sold every year until 1948, when this model was replaced by the Panhead.

158-159 In 1948, the Panhead, a new generation of engines, replaced the Knucklehead, establishing itself firmly in one arm of the Harley-Davidson line with displacements of 61 cubic inches (1000 cc) and 74 cubic inches (1200 cc). From 1949, the Panhead equipped the new E Series called Hydra-Glide. This engine still had valves in the cylinder head, but they were made of aluminum, to ensure better cooling. In 1954, the 61 cubic-inch version disappeared. The Panhead was manufactured for 17 years as part of the Duo-Glide and then the Electra Glide lines. 1965 (the only year in which an Electra Glide was manufactured with a Panhead engine), was the last year of production for this engine. The Hydra-Glide, Duo-Glide, and Electra Glide were equipped with hydraulic telescopic forks. These models are still remembered for their harmoniously gentle and rounded features and their timeless look. Today, the Heritage Softail Classic and, even more so, the Springer Heritage aredevelopments of the Hydra-Glide and the Panhead, which may account for their commercial success. Besides aluminum rocker arm covers, the Panhead was fitted with hydraulic tappets for the rocker arm rods. Thanks to these aluminum parts, the cylinder heads dissipated heat more rapidly, reducing noise. A new camshaft was designed and a new oil pump was installed for better lubrication. In 1948, a few technical improvements were brought to this model, notably a corrosion-proofing painting, a more comfortable seat, and a pale blue color, unusual for a motorcycle. When a telescopic fork was added to the Hydra-Glide, the front drum-brake power increased by 34 percent. In 1952, the hand-operated gear change became a left-foot-operated gear change, with clutch disengagement on the handlebar. In 1953, the figures of the odometer, housed in the tank, appeared in miles, with the numerals 1 to 12 representing miles per hour from 10 to 120. It was an excellent year for this motorcycle and its V-Twin, highlighted by a golden V on the front mudguard, turned silvery the following year. In 1954, the Hydra-Glide was fitted with a chrome-plated chain guard, a horizontal taillight and, as an option, a couple of rigid bags on the back of the motorcycle.

160-161 After 1947, Harley-Davidson faced fearsome competition from English brands such as Triumph and Norton. The English motorcycles appealed to Americans, thanks to their sporty look and technical innovations. In 1952, Harley-Davidson adapted the English-style foot gear-changing system, incorporating it into the Model K. This bike, with its new 45 cubic-inch engine replacing the WL Flathead engine in 1952, was supposed to give Harley-Davidson an edge over the British competition. At first its structure required some improvement to become really reliable and efficient. Its WL heritage (side valves, identical bore, and stroke), its development over the years (55 cubic inches in 1954), and its variety of sport models allowed Harley-Davidson to accumulate victories for several years. On the front, it had a hydraulic telescopic fork at the level of the shock absorbers, and, with a weight of 450 pounds and a five-gallon gas tank its 30-horsepower engine provided good flexibility at low speed. A slightly improved racing model had a 40-horsepower engine. In 1954, the KH was presented with an 883 cc (55 cubic-inch) engine,

but this model was not very successful and disappeared after three years. Harley-Davidson built various specialty racing versions of the Model K, including: the 1953 KK, a specialty Model; the KHRM, which first appeared in 1954; the KRTT, another racer model with powerful brakes and reinforced shock absorbers; and the KR, a racing motorcycle manufactured for 17 years (1952—1969), which took part in C-class races. This model, in all its versions, represents an ancestor of the Sportster, first manufactured in 1957.

162-163 In 1957, American youths, put off by the problems of the 1952 Model K, were drawn by the superior performance of British motorcycles. So Harley-Davidson presented the XL, which kept the frame and low engine of the K models. The valves were no longer at the side but the engine was still cast iron. The exact displacement was 883 cc (54 cubic-inches), but was called 900 cc. Several options were offered the first year, including a double seat, a windshield, and saddlebags. During the first year, 1,983 Sportsters were manufactured, and by 1959, Sportster production jumped up to 2,053 machines, spurred by the success of Models XLH and XLCH, which were introduced in 1958. Some internal modifications were introduced, such as the adaptation of polished valves, but magneto lighting was maintained, resulting in rather poor reliability. Because of its small tank size, this model was called the "Peanut." At that time, California retailers urged factory managers to create a sport model based on the Sportster; as a result, the XLCH was launched in 1958 and became street-legal the following year, when Harley-Davidson manufactured 1,059 XLCHs. Sportster production nearly doubled by 1961.

During these years, new shock absorbers were added along with a new range of colors and a new streamlined look, called "jet-stream styling." Some parts were manufactured in aluminum. In 1964, the braking system was improved and a new 12-volt electrical system was developed. In 1965, the Harley-Davidson Motor Company signed its last contract with the U.S. Army, supplying 1000 XLAs (i.e. Sportsters) equipped to meet military needs. In 1967, an electric starter was fitted on the XLH, and a kick was all that was needed to start the XLCH.

1961
SPRINT

164 In 1958, the Hydra-Glide was replaced by the Duo-Glide, the motorbike of the 1960s. It was fitted with a rear hydraulic brake and a neutral point indicator light in the counter unit. In 1963, the front brake drums were made of aluminum. Little by little, the Duo-Glide was improved. It became a superb motorcycle, with features still found in some of today's models. Harley-Davidson first produced bikes with the Panhead in 1948 (the E Series). The last Harley-Davidson bike with a Panhead engine was the 1965 Electra Glide, in its first year of production. For the rest of its career, the Electra Glide had a Shovelhead engine. The Electra Glide, equipped with a push-button electric starter on the handlebar and a five-gallon gas tank, was exactly the type of motorcycle needed for highway driving, and it met consumer demand perfectly. Comfortable, reliable, and tough, it became the benchmark for those who liked to cover long distances on a prestigious motorcycle.

164-165 The Sprint Model C was a 250 cc machine developed in cooperation with Aermacchi. Produced from 1961 to 1974 with 250 cc, then from 1969 on with 350 cc, it was a Harley-Davidson by name only. In spite of being manufactured by Aermacchi with quite a dubious look for a Harley-Davidson, it became fairly successful within its market niche during the first ten years it was sold in the United States. Then its future became more uncertain, as Japanese manufacturing techniques invaded the market. Beginning in 1960, for five years, a scooter called the Topper was also produced, referred to as A and AU. In all, 5,246 such motorcycles came off production lines—not a large volume. A horizontal cylinder, a two-stroke engine, and a 1.7 gallon tank were its main features.

The Topper competed with the Italian Vespa, which, in the 1960s, was one of the most popular means of transport with certain drivers, such as students and artists. A small trunk under the seat of this small machine held books or other objects. In 1942, this model, with five to nine horsepower, sold for $445. Aermacchi and Harley-Davidson produced a 250 cc four-stroke Trial model, the Sprint H, in 1962, to allow race drivers to stand out in competition. Subsequently, Harley-Davidson provided it with a lighting system so that it could be driven in town.

The company continued developing the 250 cc Sprint C over the years. In 1964, it was fitted with an Italian carburetor, made by Dell'Orto. In 1967, its name changed to 250 Sprint SS, and, in 1969, it became the 350 cc Sprint SS. In 1972, it was finally called SX 350, manufactured until 1974.

166 Within the old Harley-Davidson range, there was a one-cylinder moped called the M 50, manufactured in cooperation with Aermacchi between 1965 and 1968. It was a carefully conceived and finely decorated two-stroke model, targeted at customers who were not particularly interested in the performance of the big Harley-Davidson models. One of the two models launched on the market had a character and look that recalled the excitement of competitions. The M 50 cost $250; the sport version, $275. To compete against companies supplying more modern models, in 1970 Harley-Davidson turned these models into the M 65 and the M 65 Sport, sold at more affordable prices. Between 1965 and 1972, AMF/Harley-Davidson produced 44,955 M-style mopeds, including the M 50, the M 50 S, the M 65, and the M 65 S. The last year of their production under these names was 1972; after that, the moped was renamed 65 cc Shortster and, from 1973 until the end of 1974, when production stopped, it was referred to as Z90 and X90.

167 In 1969, Harley-Davidson merged with AMF, an association that lasted for more than a decade. The Sportster benefited from the merger: production grew to 7,800 items in 1969, and to 10,775 in 1970. In 1970 and 1971, the Sportster came with an optional "boat-tail" back. This machine and the Super Glide, equipped with a similar back, were the first two customized motorcycles created by Harley-Davidson. Moderately successful in their own time, they are in great demand

today. At that time, customers could also opt for a front mudguard made of fiberglass rather than sheet metal or for a small "Peanut" tank, rather than a large one. Fiberglass boat tails were produced in Tomahawk, based on a design by Willie G. Davidson. But the line was not as successful as expected and fewer than 3,000 XLHs were manufactured, as compared with the 5,500 XLCHs produced that year. The majority of

these motorcycles were assembled with conventional mudguards, unlike the first Super Glide which, in 1971, was supplied exclusively with the boat tail.

The main mechanical changes on the 1971 Sportsters are easy to sum up. The clutch system was replaced by an oil-bath clutch and, since stronger pressure on the disks was then needed, the springs were adjusted more rigidly, making the hand control less flexible.

Platinum-plated screws and a condenser came in the timing case, to make the ignition system more damp-proof.

This machine was rare not only due to its boat tail, but also because it was the last cast-iron engine supplied with 900 cc.

In 1972, all Sportsters were supplied with 61 cubic-inch (1000 cc) engines in an attempt to become more like their Japanese and English competitors.

168-169 and 170-171 The Shovelhead engine appeared in 1966, replacing the Panhead on the Electra Glide. This engine provided about 15 percent more power, and it was hardly improved beyond that over the 18 years of its production. It became synonymous with Harley-Davidson's lack of brand reliability during the 1970s, in the period when AMF increased production and eroded product quality, which caused considerable economic difficulties for the company. The Shovelhead was developed due to the fight for survival against Japanese competition. A well-assembled Shovelhead, with quality components, was more reliable than the previous Harley-Davidson Big Twin models (the Knucklehead and the Panhead), even though it can't compare to today's Evolution models. The last Shovelheads were manufactured in 1983 and sold in 1984, when the Blockhead (Evolution) engine came onto the market. Besides the Electra Glide, the Shovelhead appeared on other renowned motorcycles, shaping styles that still appear today. The Wide Glides, the Low Riders, and the Super Glides—all were produced with this engine—which still has an important place in the spirit and history of Harley-Davidson.

172-173, 174-175 and 176-177 As a result of the merger between AMF and Harley-Davidson, Sportster production continued to grow, going from 8,560 motorcycles in 1970 to 10,325 in 1971 and 23,830 in 1974. Sportsters accounted for more than two-thirds of the overall company production, which included seven different models. Technical improvements on the Sportster or XLH came steadily. In 1970, Harley-Davidson replaced the electric kick-start with a battery-coil ignition. Purchasers could choose between a small and a large gas tank. In 1971, the oil bath clutch was replaced by a dry clutch, with the resulting greater plate pressure meaning stiffer springs and hand controls. Japanese competitors became all the more a threat, appealing to American customers in price, models, and technology. Sportster displacement went up to 1000 cc in 1972. In the same year, two other models in that line, the XLH and the XLCH, were equipped with a long, uncomfortable seat and a small tank. Factories produced 7,500 XLHs and 10,650 XLCHs. Before 1981, apart from rare exceptions like the Café Racer, Sportsters had only changed aesthetically. In that year, Harley-Davidson produced 41,606 motorcycles, 10,102 of which were Sportsters. In 1982, Harley-Davidson released a limited series of the Sportster to celebrate its 25th anniversary; in 1987, it did the same for its 30th. In 1983, two special models, equipped with an oval air filter, came out: the XR 1000, as a limited series, and the XLX. The XLX, a stripped-down, less expensive version of the Sporster, was their top-seller that year, with 4,892 sold. The XR 1000 was not as successful, selling a total of 1,018. Nevertheless, the following year, the company changed its design and reissued the same model, fitted with a lighter and more rigid frame, a four-gallon tank, a halogen light, and a new battery.

This extraordinary motorcycle kept evolving. In 1984, the front wheel was designed as a single disk of larger diameter, the clutch became more flexible on certain models, and an alternator replaced the generator. The Sportster preserves this look today.

178-179 Among the various models associated over 36 years with the important Sportster line, the XLCR Café Racer is a landmark in the history of the Harley-Davidson Motor Company. Released in 1977, a total of 3,124 of these bikes were manufactured, selling for $3595. Even though this model enjoyed modest commercial success, in aesthetic terms it was too advanced for its time. Now, collectors are constantly hunting for it, and its popularity has pushed its value much higher.

Further from ordinary motorcycles than most of the Harleys, this model, the product of Willie G. Davidson's creative imagination, was probably drawn from the famous English Café Racers of the 1960s, yet it is no mere imitation. The engine is that of an XLCH, slightly improved and mounted on a duplex cradle frame, which was derived from the famous racing model, XR 750. The same frame served other Sportster models from 1979 on. Its caster angle was 29.35°, and rear suspension was secured by three adjustable dampers. A classic telescopic fork supported two ten-inch disks, braked by new hydraulic calipers with simple pistons. The back drum, which still equipped the Sportster XLH and XLCH 1000 in 1977, was replaced with the same type of disk as in the front. Seven-spoke wheels made of a light alloy were meant to increase the Café Racer's sporty look. The position of the driver, determined by the small, flat handlebar; the controls, positioned further back; and the black elements in the chassis all highlighted this motorcycle's aggressive look. A small fork-head fairing, vaguely reminiscent of the Japanese style, ensured the rider's comfort. A tank solo-seat unit, with a four-gallon capacity, was added to the extension.

All mechanical parts were black, including the twin exhaust pipe with mufflers on each side. A Keihin throttle carburetor with a return pump ensured the fuel supply of this 500-pound machine. With the high 9-to-1 compression rate on the XL and XLCH 1000 engines, the bore and stroke remained unchanged and the rebore dimensions produced the exact displacement of 61 cubic-inches (997.5 cc). In 1977, this Café Racer, running 61 horsepower at 6200 revolutions per minute and reaching a manufacturer's top speed of 120 miles per hour, was fast enough. But the Café Racer was not a commercial success. In 1977, 1,923 Café Racers came out of the Milwaukee factory. In the following year, production dropped to 1,201. In 1979, only nine Café Racers were manufactured.

180-181 The year 1986 marked the debut of the Evolution engine in the XLH Sportster series, taking the place of the OHV V-Twin, which had powered the series since 1957. In 1988, the 1100 was replaced by a 74 cubic-inch (1200 cc) version. The 1986 Sportsters appeared in either a 883 or 1100 cc version. From then on, the Sportster Evolution has enjoyed a brilliant career. It is now available in two versions (883 and 1200 cc). Since 1986, it has undergone some interesting technical improvements, such as the addition of a fifth gear in 1991 and a standard toothed belt to replace the transmission chain, which had already been abandoned on the high-displacement motorcycles (1340 cc/80 ci). Now, in the middle of the 1990s, the Sportster family is aimed at two different customer niches: sportspeople and traditionalists. The Sportster XL 1200 has a new three-gallon tank, found also on the XL 883 Standard and XL 883 Hugger. The Hugger has remained the same for several years, despite modifications carried out on all the other Sportster models. The XLH 1200 S has features that make it even more sporty. The front and rear suspensions are entirely adjustable. Even the spring pre-load and the hydraulics can be adjusted. There is a cartridge front fork and the rear gas dampers have an attached tank. Floating double disks ensure front braking, and thirteen-spoke wheels, made of aluminum, are fitted with soft rubber tires. A flat track handlebar combines with a more sporty seat.

The XL 1200 C stands out with lots of chrome, notably a chrome-plated headlight without a cover. The handlebar fasteners, the risers, and other parts are also chrome-plated. The engine block is black and chrome, compared with the polished aluminum plating in other Sportster engines. The front wheel is a 21-inch model, as on the 1340 models with a chopper look; the rear wheel has a full rim, similar to that of the Bad Boy. The speedometer is electronic, the tank logo is made of metal, and the seat is about two inches lower than on the old Sportster 1200 cc. On this model, front braking is limited to a simple disk, floating back and forth, like that fitted on the Big Twin customs. This machine should satisfy the expectations of anyone searching for an easy-to-handle custom motorcycle.

184-185 The Evolution Softail marked the revival of the Harley-Davidson brand from late 1983 on. It was fitted with a modernized version of the traditional V-Twin engine, made of aluminum and mounted on a sprung frame that evoked the old rigid frame—just what tens of thousands of Harleyists deeply desired. In 1986, Harley-Davidson took an active role in the celebration of the 100th anniversary of the Statue of Liberty by organizing a marathon. The race started from numerous cities and ended at the foot of the statue, with profits dedicated to the statue restoration fund. The company also sold limited-series Liberty edition motorcycles, a total of 1,714 units in 1986, and for each motorcycle sold, $100 was allocated to the restoration fund.

arley-Davidson's emphasis
nological improvements is
by an emphasis on the rich
of the past. America's only
g motorcycle manufacturer
st sight of what it has taken
his far and p   keep
g into the

1986 FLHTC ELECTRA GLIDE
LIBERTY EDITION

HARLEY-DAVIDSON

Classic

186-187 When, in 1984, the Evolution engine, or Blockhead, appeared, they were fitted on all the FXRs, on two of the three FLs, and on the 1985 FXST. Only one Electra Glide and the Super Glide were still equipped with the Shovelhead engine, and that just for one more year. The FXR line, positioned as the most modern of motorcycles and the most futuristic made by Harley-Davidson, grew to include a light tourism version, the Sport Glide FXRT, in 1985. This machine was equipped with a profiled fork head, saddlebags, and even a small trunk on some models. It aimed at competing with the Gold Wing motorcycles, but it only managed to appeal to public servants, especially to the police. Harley-Davidson withdrew it from the catalog in 1993, after the public had neglected it for years. The FXR line, less popular with customers than the Softail, was also gradually abandoned during the first half of the 1990s, replaced by the more modern Dyna range, drawn directly from the 1991 Sturgis FXDB Dyna and commemorating the 50th anniversary of the show in 1990.

From the Chopper to the HARLEY-DAVIDSON Customization

Birth of the Chopper Concept

Initially, creating a chopper meant highlighting the engine and its performance, mainly by working on the finish, the paints, and then increasingly the frame. Over the years, the finishing work—accessory research and paint frenzies—gained importance until today they are an end in themselves.

But today, as a sort of return to the past, after an era of choppers based on all brands of motorcycle engines, Harley-Davidsons are back in the lead. At present, with the new cruisers fitted with V-Twin engines and impressive new Royal Star or FC6 machines, choppers can mean customization based on motorcycles of any brand.

A HIGH-PERFORMANCE CHOPPER

The name "chopper" originally described a motorcycle cut into pieces like a chunk of meat with a thick, sharp blade. At the end of the 1940s and the beginning of the 1950s, there was no efficient way to supercharge a road motorcycle. The only efficient parts were destined for the racetrack, in racing Harley-Davidsons and other motorcycles built specifically for racing; but they were too unreliable for the road. For someone who wanted racetrack performance on the road, the best solution was simply to adjust the weight. Since American motorcycles of that time had been adapted for touring over long distances and were equipped for comfort, they carried lots of extras, such as saddlebags, a windshield, huge exhaust systems, large wraparound mudguards, and huge seats, for example. One gained twenty or thirty pounds by eliminating all these accessories. A smaller seat was easy to find. You could remove the huge exhausts and replace them with parts developed for the competition sector or, even better, manufacture your own. You could take away the huge original tires, recovering the hubs or not, and fit smaller wheels in their place, both on the back and

the front (especially on the front).

At the same time, the too-large GT handlebar could be replaced, as could the huge tank. The name that emerged to describe the resulting bizarre motorcycles was "chopper."

By the 1960s this had been refined to an art. Here's how one contemporary article put it: "Apart from rare exceptions, the wild biker drives a Harley 74 which originally weighs 800 pounds and which can be brought down to 550, once it has been stripped, transformed, and made lighter. The chopper then consists of a massive frame, a tiny seat and a huge 1200 cc engine, twice the size of the English machines such as the Triumph Bonneville, the BSA Lightning Rocket, motorcycles whose speed approaches 120 mph. The original Harley-Davidsons were not up to such performances and needed to be

transformed to become competitive against their rivals, driven by standard riders, and against the souped-up cars and motorcycles used by policemen. In order to make a Harley 74 grant the same performance, the first priority is to change the power-to-weight ratio, which explains why the wild bikers strip their motorcycles as much as possible and only keep the essential parts, sometimes removing even the front brake. Once the motorcycle has been stripped it can already ensure completely different performance. But, since often this still isn't enough to leave the other motorcycles and the cops behind, the engines are also reworked, with performance camshafts, modified valves and a higher stroke-to-bore ratio. Only the compulsory accessories remain, such as the headlight, the taillight and the rear mirror, sometimes reduced to a simple dentist

mirror in compliance with the law. The weight advantage can still be increased by halving the tank, removing the front mudguard, truncating the rear mudguard at the top of the wheel, adapting a large-horn handlebar, reducing the seat, lengthening the forks, adding a clutch pedal called a 'suicide pedal,' adapting megaphone-like mufflers, a tiny cyclo-like front wheel, a front headlight reduced to the minimum, chrome plating and painting, etc.

"A chopper is often a veritable work of art with an impressive resale price, not taking the hours of work into account. Lighter, highly chrome-plated, and covered with complicated paintwork consisting of many overlapping coats, the chopper is a superb and distinguished machine, so mechanically perfect that it is difficult to imagine it on the highway, running at top speed, driven by a brute in a dubious state just before crashing against a tree or a car."

188-189 The chopper, idealized through its role in the film Easy Rider, was built from a Panhead engine and a rigid frame. Its look influenced generations to come.

189 At first, the traditional chopper was designed with a minimum number of elements, a big handlebar, a lengthened fork, and no front mudguard.

CHOPPER TRANSFORMATIONS

Nothing remains unchanged, especially in a field where creation prevails. Over the years, the chopper developed quickly, integrating many new ideas. The people riding and transforming their motorcycles were individuals with differing tastes and aspirations. Everybody started personalizing and modifying his machine in his own way, with each resulting motorcycle ending up far from the original.

It is worth remembering that only American machines developed in this way, as the Japanese were not yet present on the American market and the English machines, already simple and bare, did not yield to such radical transformations. It was a logical development, stemming from the need to make the large American motorcycles as efficient as the English ones. At that time, English motorcycles were agile, light, and powerful, due to their low weight. Their mechanical conception was also more modern than the big American machines. So, to counter the English and satisfy the chopper fans, Harley-Davidson put a more modern version of the side engine 750 on the market; it had a gearbox integrated in the engine sump, a double cradle frame, and a telescopic fork. But this engine was painfully lacking in power, compared with either English machines or the stripped-down big Harleys. This motorcycle was replaced by the KH 900 in 1954, an 883 cc engine with 38 horsepower, 5000 rpm, and a manufacturer's top speed of 100 mph. Those who liked performance and stripped-down machines finally had a motorcycle that lived up to their dreams.

Over the years, however, the big Harley-Davidson 74 machines were chopperized more often than other models. The Panhead lives on, now more than ever, synonymous with the chopper in bikers' minds. It was recognized as the best motorcycle of its time, not only by independent bikers but also by the Harleyists who belonged to official clubs and wanted a reliable, faithful motorcycle to cover long distances.

This phase of motorcycle evolution owed a lot to the media, too. The film *The Wild One*, starring Marlon Brando and Lee Marvin, brought American biker lore to Europe. This film retold, in romanticized Hollywood style, the story of Hollister, a little town in California (located more than fifty miles south of San Francisco, near Gilroy), where a biker revolt had taken place in 1947. During an Independence Day celebration, which included a motorcycle race, about four thousand motorcyclists, spectators and racers descended on Hollister. Some racers came with official teams but some were independents, competing even though they were not members of the American Motorcycle Association. The A.M.A., organizing the race, wanted to exclude the nonmembers. Between the numbers of bikers who had been let down and the quantity of alcohol consumed with meals (which actually dried up all the bars), the party deteriorated. The press, with nothing else to report at the time, jumped on the situation, quickly turning the motorcycle phenomenon into bands of terrible bikers roaring around on motorcycles and plundering the country. A few more meaningless episodes brought fresh interest, and the press embellished the stories, keeping up pressure in the biker-hooligan vein. The A.M.A. suddenly pronounced itself in favor of kind bikers—those who only used their motorcycle for sport or for the weekend family drive, whether associated with the A.M.A. or not. On the other hand, the association blamed wild bikers for all the scandal, identifying them as members of renegade clubs, not associated with the A.M.A., accounting for

only one percent of all motorcyclists . . . to which the birth of the phrase "one percent" is related.

The Wild One retold the Hollister story. After the release of the film in 1954, a number of wild biker clubs, issuing their own sets of rules, sprung up all over America. Rejected by conformist society as well as by other bikers, they decided to live their life according to their own aspirations, astride their choppers and stripped-down Harleys. The performance they got out of transformed motorcycles proved to be vital, but the aesthetic side of the chopper also started to take shape. With the passing years, the rush for performance gradually lost ground in favor of the quest for fashion. The chopper was finally tamed, and even turned into a real industry by certain dealers.

POLITE CHOPPER

Once choppers had their own specialized shops and custom motorcycle builders, the search for a different look began.

This occurred thanks to the gradual association between motorcycles and West Coast hippies. Performance—the original reason for creating these machines—was gradually forgotten and the look became vital. 1968 proved to be a particularly eventful year in the motorcycle world.

That year, Honda presented its four-cylinder CB 750 in the U.S. A little earlier in the same year, Triumph put the Trident on the market. And, also in 1968, Easy Rider came to the screen, starring Peter Fonda and Dennis Hopper in their search for freedom on two magnificent choppers.

Easy Rider inspired the motorcycle paintwork of a whole generation, and those styles still inspire certain customized paintwork today.

The Harley-Davidson motorcycle benefited most from this media attention because this motorcycle, always considered a comfortable machine, familiar by its association with policemen, now took on a new look. The Harley-Davidson police version did not disappear, but everybody became aware that it was possible to drive a Harley in a different way.

The brand was reborn, through stripped-down cycles and original choppers—machines now synonymous with freedom and rebellion. It was a fantastic feeling . . . even though much of the image was untrue. But that image took hold, and it is still alive today.

190 Today, the Evolution engine is most widely used for choppers. Harley-Davidson has been selling machines fitted with this engine since 1984. But the recipe for building a traditional chopper is still the same: rigid frame, long fork, big handlebar, and the minimum possible equipment.

190-191 Fairly new choppers, based on old Harley-Davidson Shovelhead engines, can even be found in Europe. They are particularly popular among purist enthusiasts.

THE DREAM AND THE MEDIA

192 top left and bottom The cult film Easy Rider made stars Peter Fonda and Dennis Hopper the idols of several generations of Harleyists.

192 top right ZZ Top took part in the ninetieth anniversary celebrations, leading the parade with their Harley-Davidson Hogzilla, their Cadillac Cadzilla, and a chopperized Harley-Davidson still under construction.

192-193 top The Wild One was the first film to put motorcycles center-stage. The motorcycles in the film were not all Harley-Davidsons, though, as shown in this photo of Marlon Brando on a Triumph Speed Twin.

192-193 bottom There are several exact replicas of the motorcycle driven by Peter Fonda in Easy Rider. At big meetings, one such replica escorts the truck from "Easyriders," an American retail shop.

It was not easy, though, for Harley-Davidson to counter the image held over from the 1947 events in Hollister, California. When the gathering erupted into a gang scene, the town became terrified and the situation which could have been solved calmly, escalated. Policemen from throughout the region were called in to restore order. *Life* magazine reported the event with a picture taken by Barney Petersen, portraying a drunk biker on a Harley-Davidson, towering over a stack of beer bottles, a bottle in each hand. The situation fanned the flames of polemic, and wild bikers and one percent clubs reacted, calling themselves the "Booze Fighters," "Satan's Slaves," "Satan's Sinners," "Satan's Daughters," and the "Winos." In July 1972, *Life* published another article, but by this time, many other magazines had run stories about the "wild bikers."

As a result of all this media attention,

the Harley-Davidson became a symbol of virility. Those who drove Harleys were terrifying tough guys with searing eyes. The films of the '60s portrayed this rather idiotic stereotype. Luckily, in 1969, *Easy Rider* revealed a different side of the Harley-Davidson. In it, the two lonely heros, travelling with an alcoholic lawyer (Jack Nicholson), discover the wide open spaces of America, as well as the hostility of some of its rural citizens. Their violent end evokes sympathy, not scorn.

The film combined hippies, drugs, and the chopper, opening new horizons for bikers and especially for future Harleyists of the time. The Harley-Davidson became an escapist motorcycle, not only on the road but also and mainly in one's head. It could be easily transformed, personalized, and made to represent just exactly the look that corresponded to one's desires. It could be driven on desert trails as well as on big

city avenues. A new generation of Harleyists was born.

A company such as Harley-Davidson must pay attention to such images. When public interest picks up again, as is happening at the moment, the company must keep the pace and counterbalance those images that do not correspond to its policies. Therefore, it must invest in image creation, arranging media events to convey a positive look. In Harley-Davidson's case, these efforts were accomplished through the company's association with the musical group ZZ Top.

In 1991, ZZ Top took part in the Bike Week at Daytona Beach, celebrating the 50th anniversary of the event. Special Harleys were of course on hand: two customized Fat Boys and the Cadzilla, a 1948 Cadillac with an entirely new body, designed to match the Harley-Davidson look. Peter Chapouris transformed the two motorcycles, taking three months to cover them completely in aluminum. He redesigned the whole look, fitting the headlight with a fork head and transforming the back of the two bikes to resemble a Cadillac. Billy Gibbons, guitar player and singer of ZZ Top, spoke of how their passions were motorcycles, cars, and good-looking girls. It all worked so well that afterwards, ZZ Top signed a contract with Harley-Davidson.

When the company celebrated its 90th anniversary, ZZ Top led the parade. Tens of thousands of Harleyists were there for the great event, all with their dream vehicles. The Hogzilla motorcycle, the Hogzilla car, and the Eliminator car all were there, plus new motorcycles, never before seen. Media efforts like these made people forget the films of the '60s . . . except for *Easy Rider*, which continues to thrive as a cult film, and is now a touchstone for several generations of Harleyists.

A WAY OF LIFE

An excerpt from *Male*, a paper from the 1960s that explored the spread of the chopper phenomenon throughout the United States, offers an idea of the image of bikers at that time, which irresistibly evokes the one with which we are familiar from films: "A very hot day in 1954, a tall, bearded, and tanned guy stops his Harley with a controlled sideslip in front of the bar favored by the bikers of an American city. His faded denim shirt, with sleeves cut in one whole piece, shows the colors of a club. Suddenly, with a turn of the grip, he tears the air of the road, on a quiet Sunday afternoon, steering his 5-feet high handlebar, disclosing his soaking sweaty armpits, before shutting off the gas.

"He leans his bike on its stand, polishes the glittering chrome of its forks, which are much longer than the standard ones, with a torn handkerchief. Then he gives a look around and nonchalantly dries his greasy hands on his jeans, encrusted with oil. This is the real thing." According to various sources, the choppers appeared most often in California after World War II. No other state combined so many favorable factors for the development of such an original vehicle — the permanent sun

shining on varied scenery, from the mountains to the desert, the large cultivated fields (instead of huge cities), the more than 600 miles of coast, the easy money, the challenge of heavy fines given for speeding by muscular cops riding huge Harley-Davidsons, and especially the constantly growing population, due not only to births but also and mainly to immigration from other states (and from abroad).

In the United States, as elsewhere in the world, young people began to distrust

adults, or worse yet, despise them as being powerless. Many teenagers felt that they were being forced to conform to a narrow-minded society with puritanical customs, and bred to conform politically. The protests and the reactions grew as the generation gap widened. Young people let off steam with cars, sometimes taking to violent entertainment. These games, such as being the last driver to jump out of a car running at full speed toward the edge of a cliff, could have fatal consequences. The concept of a gang increasingly came into play with these games. Not only is union strength, but also unusual and therefore disquieting actions — for example, wearing sunglasses and leather jackets with gang colors, and driving big noisy motorcycles — inspired fear in outsiders. These gangs gravitated naturally to the unique chopper look and the dissatisfaction with the status quo which it represented.

Today, the Harley-Davidson is still a way of life for an increasing number of people, but these ways of life have diversified. The number of people actually living as the original "wild bikers" is small in comparison with the number of Harley enthusiasts simply living with their passion for the wonderful mechanics of the Harley-Davidson.

The latter gather together with their friends or within Harley-Davidson clubs, H.O.G. or not. The Harley-Davidson clothes and accessories allow anybody to wear the colors of the company, whether or not they own a motorcycle, because fashion has become part of the Harley-Davidson phenomenon. As a result, many fans who do not yet own a Harley-Davidson still follow the rhythm of the "belle" of Milwaukee, waiting for the happy day when they will finally own the magic V-Twin; while others still simply wear all the clothes and accessories as a fashion statement. Unfortunately, the latter group will disappear as soon as the phenomenon fades . . . unless they become seduced by the machines themselves in the meantime.

194 top Whether based on a Panhead or on a Shovelhead engine, whether their frames are rigid or springy, whether they were simply derived from Softails with modified frames and a lengthened fork, choppers still symbolize the same spirit of freedom.

194 center and bottom New custom styles and new choppers have continued to appear over time. Some of them evoke the old machines. Others have been simply stripped to enhance their performances. Always, care for detail has been the priority.

194-195 and 195 top Beginning as rough, stripped, and lightened machines, designed simply to increase performance, choppers have gradually developed a look which is as sophisticated as ever.

CHOPPER EVOLUTIONS

In the United States, mail order of chopper parts grew, allowing everybody to build his own personalized motorcycle at home. This industry, which began in the mid-'60s, has thrived over the years. But as the bikers' aesthetic quest became increasingly specific, mail order alone no longer sufficed. A real industry with stores and workshops has developed for manufacturing and marketing parts, not only for motorcycle transformations but, gradually, for their entire manufacture as well.

The chopper underwent a spectacular development but preserved an image connected with its troubled past: newspaper articles continued to promptly report any accident involving one. Subsequently, certain states passed laws

designed to limit chopper eccentricity. The best example is the laws enacted in Florida, which regulated the maximum distance between the handlebar grips and the gas tank, and called for exhaust systems of a certain shape. These laws were passed in the '70s, when the competition and the search for originality made manufacturers build increasingly souped-up machines, which sometimes became dangerous to drive. The Show-Bikes — motorcycles just for exhibition — made their first appearance at the same time. Only the engine worked, so that the machine could cover the few yards needed to be classified as a motorcycle. The Show-Bike never ventured onto the road, not only because of complete law infringement, but mainly

because the machine simply could not be driven. As a result of these laws and the settlement of dealers, individual D.I.Y., which often proved dangerous due to lack of knowledge disappeared in favor of safer and more reliable work. (It must be admitted that accidents arising from unskilled, amateur work were the impetus which led to the enacting of the most restrictive laws.) Of course, not every individual initiative disappeared, but those who did not feel able to perform adjustments to their frame or fork appealed to dealers or to friends who had the necessary knowledge, instead of risking their lives on machines that might thereby endanger the chopper phenomenon. In the '70s, the Harley-Davidson was gradually

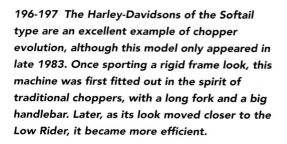

surpassed by the Japanese machines, not only on the road but also in the chopper field. Japanese four-cylinder engines increasingly replaced the big V-Twin in frames specifically designed to house them, or in original frames, such as those with rigid backs, which had been suitably modified. The multitude of available possibilities made it necessary for the choppers to be classified into categories, but these were not fixed and overlapped according to the modifications implemented on each model. In general, the Street-Racers can be defined as stripped, slender, thin choppers offering good performance and aimed mostly at attaining this goal. It is from this type of chopper that the Café Racer, a name which

was even adopted by standard motorcycle manufacturers, later differentiated itself. At present, the traditional chopper can be defined as a Chop fitted with a mainly rigid, long and slender frame, but with a big enough caster angle to house a fork which is longer than the original, a small tank, a flat and small or backward and long or raised handlebar, a seat which suits the spirit of the machine, and a sissy bar. There is great freedom concerning the Chop, as the very principle at the basis of this machine implies. Then there is the Low Rider, a long, low machine, with or without an inclined steering stem and with an original or shortened fork. The Low Rider is the result of extensive work on details and on engine performance, and it is more

compact. The Street-Drag, on the other hand, appeared with the shape of a Street-Racer towards the end of the '70s and the beginning of the '80s. It is a machine designed for high performance, with a modified engine, low and compact lines, and sometimes the addition of N.O.S. in order to improve its starting efficiency after stopping at traffic lights. The Show-Bike is a motorcycle built for exhibition, not for driving. The Oldies are recent machines that try to resemble the old models. The chopper has a bright future, as it is supported by the custom field, where crazy transformations are more and more applied to original Harley-Davidsons. This original approach looks to the chopper.

THE OLD DREAM MODELS

The ancestors are pampered, restored, and often customized according to the rules of the time. These ancient motorcycles, which are either the products of American brands which have disappeared or of Harley-Davidson, make up part of America's cultural heritage.

The Harley-Davidsons are those which most often seduce the collectors, but it is also true that they are easier to restore than the majority of the other, vanished brands. It is possible to find parts for old Harley-Davidsons in the catalogs of some big companies that specialize in supplying parts which can be adapted to modern bikes. This is not the case for other brands.

198 Although a few Flatheads still exist together with the few remaining Knuckleheads, discovering an XA of this type is exceptional. Not only are the military versions of this machine very rare, since only a thousand units were built, but it is practically impossible to find a machine of this type that was transformed for civil uses.

199 *The Sportster can be adapted for customization in a variety of ways. Whether it becomes a rigid-frame chopper or a performance model, it is equally popular as both the old models and the recent Evolution versions.*

SPORTSTER

The work of customizing and transforming Sportsters grows, both in the United States and in Europe. The choice of the Big Twins as a base for transformation prevails, but the Sportster, which sometimes becomes the second motorcycle for Big Twin owners, benefits from the advantage of time. In other words, not only are there an increasing number of elements which can be used for modifying the Sportster, but because many Sportster owners also own another bike, they don't hesitate to put it out of operation for a while, during which they can create something remarkable.

The Sportster's classic lines are often changed radically, and it is possible to come across Custom Sportsters with a Big Twin line, or even a Low Rider or a Softail one, with a Fat Boy tank, or suitable mudguards—not to mention the growing use of Softail frames manufactured by specialized factories. However, motorcycles with the look of old machines, of choppers, and of touring models, which still show a quest for performance, are also very common.

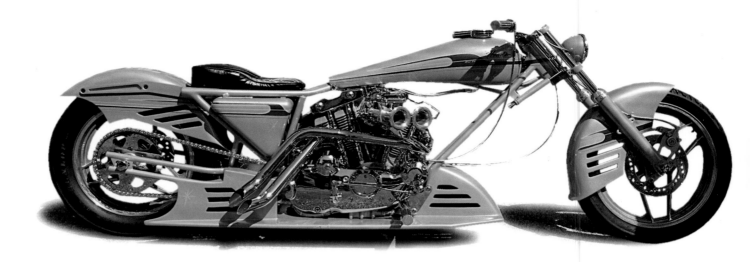

SPORTSTER AND PERFORMANCE

For Americans, Sportsters are the ideal base for building very sporty motorcycles. The Buells are the best example of this idea, but they are not the only ones to occupy this performance niche. There are both mechanical and aesthetic preparation kits. They can generally be found at shows and, on rare occasions, on the road. According to the owners, this engine is full of potential and unexploited possibilities and requires a minimum amount of work to grant the better performances than the Harley-Davidson Big Twins.

200 These machines, based on modified Sportsters, have a sleek look even though they are intended mainly for shows. In the dragster performance field, old engines are also very popular.

The beautiful choppers of the past, whether they come from radically transformed machines or from machines that have simply been stripped and fitted with personalized parts, always elicit a nostalgic sigh. These machines, unlike others from the same era which have simply been restored, have a special soul. They are the owners' unique creations and, even more, they represent the first steps towards the chopper and towards customization. It was these bikes which were first modified by Harley enthusiasts who desired more efficient and aesthetically unique machines. The more restrained chopper option uses a Knucklehead or Panhead

201 From an aesthetic point of view, choppers based on Knucklehead engines provide the best design, but they are difficult to find. The Panhead, also quite elegant, is more common and has been customized as well.

engine on a rigid frame, with a long fork of the "oldstyle." Panheads are also good for mounting in the Low Rider style, to increase performance. Beyond their technological suitability, both engines are also suited aesthetically to this type of transformation. Certain people have even tried to fit out Evolution engines to make them look like Panhead or Knucklehead engines, by using cylinder head covers and an X-Zotic crankshaft cover.

The Shovelhead engine has a past which is rich in history, though this is not always to its advantage. It is possible today to drive a Harley-Davidson equipped with a perfectly restored Shovelhead engine. Of course, this engine will never be as reliable as an Evolution model or reach similar levels of performance, but there is still pleasure to be taken from this fantastically souped-up, die-cast engine.

The Shovelhead is always present at the shows that take place during the great meetings. The many types of transformations on display are the result of research aimed either at improving performance or finding the Harley-Davidson look of the future.

Luckily, the traditional chopper category with a rigid frame has a very strong presence as well, but it is no longer the only category in which motorcycles equipped with Shovelhead engines take prizes.

202 top and bottom The Shovelhead engine appeals to many Harleyists as a motorcycle that reconciles reliability, performance, and a look which is both different from the Blockhead engine and return to the always fashionable retro motorcycle look.

202 center Some Shovelheads are turned into high-performance models by being fitted with compressors and internal parts taken directly from dragster racing bikes. Several bikes with engines of this type still take part in races against modern aluminum engines.

HARLEY-DAVIDSON RATS

Shows mainly include Harley-Davidsons that have been customized or chopperized, but other types of vehicles are also welcome. They may be Harley-Davidsons or a different brand, and may be equipped with two, three, or occasionally even more wheels. Among the many categories, the most peculiar may be the one including motorcycles referred to as "Rats." A "Rat" is a machine that looks like a motorcycle which has not been maintained: it is dirty and covered in all sorts of accessories, some of which are only for decoration. Although some "Rats" are well enough maintained to be able to cover a fair number of miles without hitches, despite the numerous oil leaks which are intentionally left unrepaired, some are real rolling wrecks.

"Rats" like those of Big Daddy Rat have a strong presence at the shows they attend, where they generally appear laden with accessories, gadgets and, obviously, the oil and dirt which they have accumulated over the years, honing their look little by little.

203 The most well-known owner of a Rat motorcycle fitted with a Harley-Davidson engine is Smithy. He travels and regularly wins races on his Rat Knucklehead.

LOW RIDER AND DYNA GLIDE

Low Riders and Dyna Glides are very often used as bases for customization, as they were the first machines to benefit from the initial transformations carried out by dealers.

Low Rider engines were isolated from the frames and consequently spread fewer destructive vibrations than the Softails. Even so, the original look of the Low Rider did not appeal to the public, and so it was less appreciated than the Softtail. This explains why bargain Low Riders are much cheaper to buy than the Softails. Because

the Low Rider Evolution frame was deemed aesthetically unappealing, Arlen Ness decided to create a more refined one, returning slightly to the design of Low Rider frames which were equipped with old Shovelheads. In the end, Ness's line prevailed.

Later, other types of transformations appeared which led to today's mature version: performance is still always a priority, as the Low Rider frame can house any improvement designed to produce more efficient machines which also hold

the road well. But the quest for modern version of the chopper is also a recurring feature.

Thus, there is a growing trend towards unique, sophisticated models, where the Low Rider frame is hard to see.

After the new Dyna Glide range replaced this type of frame, the approach remained the same, and the work carried out has had fairly similar aesthetic results, apart from an oil tank integrated around the gearbox. This development should permit much more adventurous research.

204 Low Riders were still largely present at shows, even after the arrival of the Dyna Glide. Dynas rapidly replaced them because of the greater possibilities for customization that they offered.

SOFTAILS

The Softail frame provides the widest range of possible transformations. Originality and aesthetic research prevail, but technical detail is never left aside. There are many kinds of V-Twin engine blocks mounted on Softail frames, whether they are Harley-Davidson originals or not. Similarly, there are many Softail frame manufactures for Big Twin Evolution engines, in which it is possible to adapt non-Evolution engines, such as the Shovelheads, the Panheads and the Sportsters engines, and everything may either be fitted as rigid on the frame or on Silentblocs.

As for the style, many different looks are popular. There is the nostalgic look of the old Duo Glide, which is very popular because it is easy to obtain from Softail Heritages; there is the radical chopper look obtained through a modified and lengthened frame and an outsize fork; there are the customized machines which are obtained through chrome plating and Hi-Tech parts, sometimes flabby, or fitted out; and finally, there are motorcycles which have a look aimed at reaching high performances. In short, the Softail is suitable for any kind of customization and chopperization.

205 Softails were customized in the old chopper style, then transformed into efficient, aggressive, and tightly packed models. Later, their lines were lengthened for a more modern look.

206-207 The frames of the Softtail motorcycles have been modified by lengthening and refining the frame, or even almost completely replacing it with parts available on the market; the end result bears little resemblance to the original.

206 bottom This Canadian Softail is decorated with paintwork over tinted chrome: a new technique which allows paint to adhere to the chrome and offers new possibilities to the fans of customization.

207 bottom This Softail represents a streamlined modification. The tank is longer and sleeker, and the body, including the articulated front of the oscillating arm, is thinner, for an overall high-performance look.

ROAD KING

The Road King is a touring machine which has only been available in the United States since the end of 1994; nevertheless, it is often modified and benefits from rather daring customizing. A craze for this motorcycle has been developing amongst Harley-Davidson enthusiasts, and the trend towards customization is reinforcing the phenomenon. Although a certain amount of personalizing is obtained through paintwork, this is not always the case. Accessories are also used and radical transformations are done on frames, tanks, and even saddlebags. Once the saddlebags have been modified, plates are sometimes integrated, and then the motorcycle is lowered. The result is a touring motorcycle, which has been personalized, but retains the advantages linked to its original purpose: comfort over long distances. Owners refine the line of the motorcycle, but not at the expense of losing its practical attributes; in other words, it keeps certain pieces of equipment which, in another time, would have been removed to achieve radical transformation.

208 top Despite modern aluminum parts, this classic Road King customization has a nostalgic character, thanks especially to the fringes.

208 center and bottom The Coca-Cola Road King represents the quintessential customized look. Every bit of bodywork, down to the tiniest detail, has been modified to evoke the look of the Coca-Cola logo. This motorcycle called "Secret Formula," represents the harmonious efforts of Skip Hoagland's team.

ELECTRA GLIDES

Although the Electra Glides are beautiful machines for travelling and have always attended all the Harley-Davidson meetings in large numbers, they do not have a comparatively strong presence at custom shows. This is due to the fact that, as this motorcycle is mainly intended for tourism, it is customized less frequently.

Customization is often confined to specialized paintwork, chrome plating, and accessories. It is very difficult to implement more radical transformations on a motorcycle of this type and preserve its functional character at the same time. Luckily, this fact does not stop many very beautiful versions from being produced and it has the advantage of making them stand out among a crowd of other Electra Glides. The most current transformations are the lowering of the motorcycle, the integration of the saddlebag into the overall look of the machine, and the reduction of the fairing; the picture is completed by the addition of details softening the general line of the vehicle. The result speaks for itself, and Electra Glides of this type are the stuff of dreams, even if they do function less well.

209 Since the Electra Glide is a popular touring machine for families, its customization often involves just adding accessories. Some people push further, though, entirely disassembling the machine to add a personal touch.

A Unique Motorcycle for Everybody

Specialized Companies

The companies specializing in supplying parts and accessories for the Harley-Davidson motorcycles have multiplied, reaching amazing international sizes with yearly turnovers of several million dollars. This success has been achieved by devoting themselves to selling parts for a single motorcycle brand: Harley-Davidson. After a modest start for most of them during the '70s and the opening of a few others during the '80s and the '90s, they began building a good reputation amongst specialist customizers, as well as Harley-Davidson dealers.

Custom Chrome Incorporation, Drag Specialties, Chrome Specialties, Nempco, Mid U.S.A., and dozens of others distribute parts for these legendary motorcycles. These companies are so successful that many of them now manufacture their own parts for Harley-Davidsons as well, and promote them exclusively in their catalogs. Since the middle of the '90s, the Harley-Davidson company has reacted strongly, hoping to gradually regain their share of this lucrative market.

Custom Chrome

The biggest company among those specializing in aftermarket parts is called Custom Chrome and has a financial statement showing an increase of 16.2% over the first 4 months in 1995. The Custom Chrome company was founded in 1970 and it has become the most important distributor of parts for Harley-Davidson motorcycles in the world, with a general headquarters in Morgan Hill, California and distribution offices in Visalia, California, in Louisville, Kentucky and in Harrisburg, Pennsylvania. Custom Chrome Incorporation perfectly illustrates the above-mentioned phenomenon concerning the distributor who starts manufacturing his own parts, which he sells in addition to all the official products and parts for Harley-Davidsons listed in most of its catalogs.

These parts are manufactured by companies owned, in this case, by C.C.I., such as RevTech, Premium, Dyno Power, and C.C. Rider. Every year, Custom Chrome presents new motorcycles customized with its unique parts and proposes styles which are sophisticated enough to make Harley owners feel like transforming their motorcycles.

This policy has spread among big distributors, but the people who increasingly work this way — that is to say, who present the largest number of motorcycles with radically different styles — are called Drag Specialties.

210 top This special commemorative machine was built by John Reed, who managed the Custom Chrome research and development department. This Softail, a lottery prize at Sturgis' fiftieth anniversary party in 1990, was later bought back by C.C.I. from the happy winner.

211 top This Custom Chrome Softail's tank is decorated with paintwork portraying the company truck used during the mid-1990s for special events and showroom appearances.

211 center The considerable number of elements available means Evolution, Shovelhead, or even Panhead engines may be used.

211 bottom The old-style chopper, based on Softail models, is still in demand among Harley-Davidson aficionadoes. Because of its popularity, many parts are available for those who want to modify the cycles themselves.

210-211 This is a typical Custom Chrome machine, built with parts from the C.C.I. catalog and decorated with the C.C.I. logo. The parts, signed "RevTech," come from a special series of performance elements and can be found on C.C.I. machines.

Drag Specialties, another specialized company, regularly presents its special machines during the big meetings at Daytona and Sturgis. The range of products displayed is developing gradually, and the same is true for the work carried out on motorcycles. In addition, the quest for originality prompts the experts such as Arlen Ness and Don Hotop, to indulge their imagination on an ever-wider series of bikes.

The specialist Don Hotop has already manufactured many parts and motorcycles for Drag Specialties, and over the years, these have been presented as exhibition machines in the company's catalog. They are generally manufactured on a Low Rider base; however, since Drag Specialties distributes parts for all types of Harley-Davidsons, other models of the brand are also customized and presented every year. The Softails bzcame more used and popular thanks to Drag Specialties. Thanks to the new ideas for transformations that have been unveiled and the production of new original parts for the Softail, its

transformation has been made easier.

Touring machines, such as the Electra Glide, are particularly popular in the U.S., a country of vast open spaces where comfortable travel is particularly valued. Unfortunately, these motorcycles are too heavy and, above all, too high for small people. The Drag Specialties Research & Development department decided to take over the Electra Glide Classic case as well. The result was a motorcycle lowered to the minimum, using a tire several inches lower than on the original Electra Glide.

The modifications made to the frame to lower the motorcycle were based on techniques previously used on chopperized machines. For the front: a bigger caster angle and a Withe Bros kit allowed the fork to be lowered; and for the back, which was lowered to the same extent as the front: a reversed rocker arm, (the right arm was placed on the left with its head down and short dampers were adopted) — original solutions which reflect the expertise of the people who manufacture these very special motorcycles for Drag Specialties.

212 and 213 bottom Every year, Drag Specialties uses Low Riders and Dyna Glides in their catalog to demonstrate and promote new parts.

212-213 and 213 top Softails offer a variety of options for transformation. The frame permits aesthetic creations of unquestionable quality.

HARLEY-DAVIDSON AND THE AFTERMARKET

From the middle of the '90s, Harley-Davidson became seriously involved in the marketing of parts and accessories for the motorcycles it manufactured. The department dealing with this sector was established within the company a long time ago, but this proactive approach is relatively new. In the time immediately after the brand and AMF had split up, exploiting this market was not the highest priority. At the beginning it was necessary to reinstate the range of motorcycles based on the Evolution engine, reassert control over and develop the dealerships, fight the illegal use of the Harley-Davidson name and logos, increase motorcycle production in order to meet the user demand, and so on, the result being that the parts and accessory market, although it was part of the Harley-Davidson Company's activities, were left to the competition. The parent company could not put up any resistance because it was unable to cope with all the problems at the same

of this sector. During the '80s, Clyde Fessler had worked as sales manager for Harley-Davidson, then as the marketing manager. Subsequently he became the head of the "Rider Accessories Division," which then became "Motorclothes," and which he managed with a completely different approach. Success was just around the corner, and now he hopes for similar success in the accessory department. He began by studying the success of Harley-Davidson's competitors in this market and found out that not only do they do good work, but most of them concentrate solely on that sector and therefore are able to manufacture most of the parts much more rapidly than Harley-Davidson. Additionally, Harley-Davidson is bound by certain constraints. The company has committed itself to producing only

time; as a result, the aftermarket sector developed rapidly, to the advantage of companies such as Custom Chrome, Drag Specialties, Chrome Specialties, and others. From the beginning of the '90s, Harley-Davidson geared up, starting a successful clothing line which was eventually called Motorclothes. Then, in the middle of the '90s, a man named Clyde Fessler took charge of the Harley-Davidson accessories, grouping them as G.M.A. (General Motor Accessories), thereby linking his name inextricably to the growth

parts which are legally fit for use on the road. This means abiding by regulations concerning noise, the size of headlights and indicators, etc. Fessler concluded, therefore, that Harley-Davidson should not compete directly with the independents, but should instead look to the future, where the company had a distinct advantage. Only the company knows what new developments are in the pipeline; the G.M.A. department, as part of Harley-Davidson, can work on a range of accessories intended for the machines

of the future, thereby having a ready-made range of accessories as soon as the new bikes are launched. Such accessories made their first appearance at the 1995 Sturgis meeting, where a new, "detachable" range of products —sissy bars, luggage racks, saddlebags, a windshield that could be assembled and removed without tools in a few seconds, etc.—was presented. But there is much more room for growth as ranges develop around such sectors as Performance, Custom, and New models, and Fixed parts.

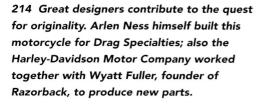

214 *Great designers contribute to the quest for originality. Arlen Ness himself built this motorcycle for Drag Specialties; also the Harley-Davidson Motor Company worked together with Wyatt Fuller, founder of Razorback, to produce new parts.*

Harley-Davidson is aware that its parts are not as widely distributed as those of its competitors; there are about 4,500 stores specializing in products for Harley-Davidsons in the United States, but the number of official dealers, where G.M.A. products are sold, is only 600. In addition, G.M.A. put 280 new products on the market in 1996. By contrast, the number of new parts and accessories produced by two of Harley-Davidson's main competitors in this market in 1996 exceeds 2,800—and there are about one hundred of these companies, of different sizes, manufacturing new parts for Harley-Davidson motorcycles.

On the up side, the Harley-Davidson Company has a strong hold in the franchising, gadget, and clothing sectors, as the brand benefits from a worldwide reputation.

215 top *Electra Glides, for a while overlooked by designers, have increasingly benefited from a specialist's touch, as with this motorbike by Drag Specialties, customized beyond the usual chrome plating and luminous arrays.*

215 bottom *Sometimes, for special meetings, Harley-Davidson will recall its glorious past by positioning an old machine in a period setting or working one into a party, as here for the celebration of the eightieth anniversary of the magazine The Enthusiast.*

THE AMERICAN TRANSFORMATION EXPERTS

216-217 top A 1992 Harley-Davidson FLHS, entirely revised and corrected by Downtown Harley-Davidson of Seattle, Washington. All the bodywork was shaped by hand.

216 bottom This machine, with distinctly radical bodywork, is based on an FXST in principle and conception. Its fork prolongs the line of its engine block, which rises up to cover the frame.

216-217 bottom Certain technical solutions proved to be original, such as the rear shock-absorbing system, aided by a torsion bar. But it is the personality of this motorcycle that is particularly impressive; the unusually voluminous exhaust outlet highlights an aggressive animal look.

CUSTOMIZATION IN SEATTLE

These two motorcycles opened up new possibilities for customizing and transforming Harley-Davidsons, as they set themselves free from the limitations established by the parts made available by great designers.

Russ Tom, from Downtown Harley-Davidson, a dealership located in Seattle, Washington, decided to create two totally different motorcycles. It is worth pointing out that he was a long-time friend of Arlen Ness and that he had literally swooned after seeing Arlen's Nesstalgia, a motorcycle that convinced Tom to go even further with motorcycle customization.

Working with an FLHS — or at least on what was left of it after its complete disassembly — a new frame was created that was over three inches longer and increased the caster angle by about six degrees.

Weeks were spent hammering and shaping the mudguards and tank. At the end of the work, it was realized that the rear mudguard was a bit too wide so, for this very simple reason, the feature was extended even more in order to house the rear exhaust outlet.

The motorcycle tank was lengthened and modified as Terry, an aluminum worker at Downtown Harley-Davidson, had spent time shaping the mudguard and tank. He was open to all possibilities and did not hold back, pushing his creation even further. Air-scoop style body work underlined the exhaust pipes on both sides of the motorcycle, which ended in two huge megaphones, the biggest ever seen on a Harley-Davidson. A small fork head and a profiled mudguard gave a look redolent of Japanese motorcycles, an effect that is promptly forgotten as soon as the machine is considered as a whole; its aesthetic is unique.

218 left Sbarro hubless wheels and steering linked into a hydraulic system are solutions which may be used on production motorcycles in the near future.

218 To obtain the expected aesthetic result, even the engine is fitted out with elements to make it look as if it comes from the future.

218-219 The futuristic lines of this prototype mirror the motorcycle's state-of-the-art technical solutions as well.

APACHE WARRIOR

The Apache Warrior, presented during the 1995 Bike Week at Daytona Beach, was a revolutionary machine, conceived around a Harley-Davidson engine block. Styled as a state-of-the-art motorcycle, it was manufactured by Next World Design and was fuel injected to obtain 110 horsepower from the big V-Twin which they had carefully fitted out. Other advanced techniques used here included Sbarro wheels (without hubs) and power steering, with the whole machine weighing 570 pounds. This is a motorcycle which has effectively passed to the production phase, as more than twenty were ordered as soon as it appeared in public.

ARLEN NESS: MASTER OF MOTORCYCLE DESIGN

Arlen Ness: more than just a name, he is a guru for the fans of beautiful motorcycles. His machines, carrying the Harley-Davidson label, are sculpted, evolve, and become real works of art in the hands of this international design specialist.

Arlen Ness has been a professional creator and manufacturer of exceptional motorcycles since the beginning of the '70s; he created a new style of chopper and modified motorcycle that gradually prevailed among many other creators, and eventually was referred to as the "Ness Style"—a considerable success for the young truck driver who began this paint and transformation work on Harley-Davidson models as a hobby at the end of the '60s. But this restless spirit was not content with simply manufacturing identical motorcycles to meet customer demand. He continued to question his work, pushing the limits of feasibility further and further.

Ness quickly moved away from the "Frisco Style" shaping the development of choppers to create his own style of low, lengthened, and slender motorcycles, which irresistibly conjured up the Dragsters. This is how the "digger style" of the '70s took shape.

In 1979, his creativity reached a frenzied pitch when he coupled two Sportster engines, thus creating a 2000 cc motorcycle with a semi-supporting engine, with a positive displacement blower and two double-cases grazing the ground. The suspension was based on torsion bars and the steering was from a car. "Two Bad" won all the shows it took part in.

Throughout the '80s, Ness monopolized the trophies in all the motorcycle shows, always surprising his fans with new and ever more daring transformations; he pursued his quest for originality, fitting a turbocharger on one machine, producing another with a "retro" look, creating a futuristic motorcycle on a third — and, of course, he always travelled behind the wheel of his newest creation. The Low Riders replaced the Sportsters little by little as Arlen Ness's favorite bases for transformations. The FXR Police models, fitted with Evolution engines, rapidly became his forte during the second half of the '80s.

In this period, through meetings and motorcycle shows, he discovered Europe. He appreciated the continent, and, as soon as he could spare some time, he returned. At the beginning of the '90s, he revisited the countries to which he had traveled for some shows, such as Germany, Great Britain, and Sweden, but he also discovered Italy and France, two countries he particularly liked. He went back for a journey on motorcycle over the Alps, then visited the Pyrenees, the Languedoc region, and Spain, and took part in a trip around Corsica in 1996.

As Arlen Ness's company started to grow, Arlen's son, Cory Ness, followed his father's example more and more closely. Arlen consequently had more free time both for travelling and for creating motorcycles with increasingly original designs. A lover of beautiful cars, his designs often paid homage to exceptional models. In 1990, he unveiled his "Nessrossa," a red and chrome-plated

2000 cc V-Twin motorcycle, with rear side covers replicating the design of the Ferrari Testarossa. Various other vehicles followed, based on the concept of "dressed" motorcycles, with or without detachable body, which grew closer to the idea of the car body. At the end of 1994, he put this concept definitively into practice, by presenting his "Nesstalgia," a Harley-Davidson evoking a '57 Chevrolet. Then in January 1996, he unveiled his incredible "Bugatti-Ness," which epitomized the

220 center and 221 top The Ness Convertible Harley-Davidson has two facets, one of the touring motorcycle type with enveloping mudguards and a big tank, the other is a performance Street Racer with mudguards and other bodywork removed, and has a lighter line.

221 bottom There are two examples of "Mona Lisa," with the rear wheel entirely unveiled when viewed from the back. This design appealed to a Spanish Harleyist, who ordered an exact replica of Arlen Ness's original creation.

220 top Arlen Ness presents one of his fabulous machines, this one fitted out with bodywork that he designed to pay homage to the Bugatti.

220-221 This classic Ness creation reuses elements well-known in his production line.

concept, both in terms of aesthetics and quality of designs, and allowed Ness to pay tribute to two of the machines he loves the most.

Today, thanks to his work and his broadmindedness, Arlen Ness is even accepted by the Harley-Davidson Motor Company, which considers him an ingenious designer, a positive force for Harley-Davidson, and not a competitor. Arlen Ness, whose many transformations based on Harley-Davidson motorcycles are already displayed in American museums, now has a worldwide reputation, thanks especially to his recent spectacular success in Japan. After first being recognized in California, then in the whole United States, before spreading over the North American continent and creating unprecedented excitement, both in Europe and in Indonesia, Arlen Ness has been fascinating the Japanese with his products for Harley-Davidsons for more than a year.

Interestingly, Japan, itself the top motorcycle manufacturer in the world, is conspicuous for its large consumption of Harley-Davidsons. Arlen Ness has estimated that it will be his principal export market before 2000. Arlen Ness, a man of exceptional talent and character, who continually renews his ideas and puts into practice the inspiration of the day before, deserves all the success he has received. His most recent forays into the far Eastern market must be a thrilling development for the man who could only receive customers at his first small shop in the evening, because during the day, he still had to work as a truck driver to support his family.

222 bottom FXR bases like this one, of the Low Rider type, often come from Sport Glide motorcycles once owned by police forces, who sold them after renewing the stock. In these cases, various frame elements have often been modified.

222-223 These classic lines correspond to those of motorcycles built regularly in Arlen Ness's shop, where he adds touches designed to meet the requirements of customers, friends, and aficionadoes, all of whom want to ride a motorcycle signed by Arlen Ness.

223 center The line of low, long machines, originally based on the FXR frames of old Low Riders, is now based on Dyna Glides.

223 bottom This machine, based on an old Sportster engine, perfectly corresponds to the exceptional creations that Arlen Ness has made popular, building his reputation as an extraordinary designer.

224 bottom Machines coming out of Arlen Ness's shop prove to be easy to date, since he signs their engine parts. Here, the air filter and the rocker arm push rod covers are the most visible Ness elements. On a more recent machine, the gearbox and ignition covers and the cylinder head covers would signify the Arlen Ness touch.

224-225 This Sportster engine, fixed on a rigid frame, has lines that evoke the look of old Harley-Davidsons. It is an original creation utilizing a Springer fork, a tank design of the 1920s, and a handlebar that sweeps back. The whole thing has then been painted bright red, to turn the machine from a fake old bike into an ageless motorcycle.

225 top The third Royale, built by Bob Dron, is much lighter in line. With its whole bodywork finished in colorless metallic paint, it proves to the most skeptical that it is not made of plastic.

225 center Bob Dron and his wife, Tracey, are the official Harley-Davidson dealers in Oakland, California.

Whether on two wheels or four, Bob Dron knows how to attract attention! After working in the car field and then branching out into choppers and custom manufacturing, he has become one of the most important dealers in the world.

Faithful to the brand since 1981, he has, on five different occasions, been awarded trophies by the company, among them, in 1991, the highest Harley-Davidson decoration: the Bar and Shield with special mention.

Since the release of his red and chrome-plated Heritage Royale, fitted with aluminum body work evoking the fineries of the elegant European car brands of the '30s, Bob Dron has been considered an unquestionable world master in the art of customization. The heritage Royale was followed by the Heritage II model, fitted out with aluminum body work and painted in royal purple, in 1994.

These motorcycles are the result of the combination of Bob Dron's two passions: the customization of cars and Hot Rods and that of motorcycles. This attraction for original cars can be traced back to the very beginning of the '60s, when he used to polish cars and boats for exhibition just before their admission to the famous Oakland Roadster Show. In the '70s, this passion developed into a profession when, after leaving his home town, he founded the American Choppers Enterprise (A.C.E.), a company which specialized in designing and manufacturing custom motorcycles, show bikes, street choppers, and sidecars. Bob became gloriously successful in his field and one of his machines was even on the cover of the first issue of *Chopper Magazine*. He met Arlen Ness, who opened a new view of the chopper world to him, as Ness had just created the Californian "digger look". Bob immediately realized that Arlen was both diligent and passionate, and in Bob's view, he is a master of innovation.

The Royal Heritage 3 is based on the same principles as the previous versions, but with its "body art" pushed even further.

Its forms are more profiled and less massive, and highlight the mechanical parts by further reveiling them. The aluminum forms are further modified and state-of-the-art technology is present in terms of the engine development and of the frame, which uses a Buell reversed fork. Nonetheless, this kind of body work is usually the product of automobile professionals rather than motorcycle professionals and this customization has proved to be closer, in aesthetic terms, to conventional machines than the previous Royale models.

CYRIL HUZE

Cyril Huze is a Frenchman who moved to America more than ten years ago to live out his American dream.Cyril: "There was nothing original in a French teenager at the end of the '50s dreaming of America with all its stereotypes: rock 'n' roll, cowboys, the open spaces, jeans, the films, the hot rods, and obviously the Harley-Davidsons running along Main Street. Similarly, there was nothing original in becoming one of James Dean's fans. He was young enough to be close to all the world's teenagers . . . and old enough when he died to become a hero. By contrast, the fact that I could not content myself with simply watching the three cult films *East of Eden, Rebel Without a Cause*, and *Giant* was rather original. Like all young people, I was happy believing that the characters interpreted by Dean were not simply film roles. Thus, even before examining his life, I was convinced that this angel-faced guy, who behaved like a rebel in the films, was also a rebel in real life. But

I also wanted to know why.

My youth was difficult and agitated. Was this also the case with his? The hardest thing was to find out information because all the interesting things which might concern him were written in English — a language I could not yet speak. As Christmas was approaching, I explained my problem to my grandmother. She understood the problem perfectly and gave me two autobiographies by James Dean with . . . an English-French dictionary. So I started learning English at the age of eleven, through James Dean's life. Thank you, Jimmy."Cyril emigrated to the United States in 1986; years of work had finally allowed him to make many of his American dreams come true. One of these dreams was that of building a Show-Bike dedicated to James Dean and, logically, its name "Deanager" gave it a nostalgic note, its blue was that of Jimmy's eyes and its tires had white walls.

"Deanager" was built from an Evolution

226-227 Cyril Huze created this "Road Star," a modification of the Road King, for everyday travel. It is a motorcycle which is good-looking, practical, and full of personality.

226 bottom Reminiscent of James Dean, the "Deanager" was painted by Chris Cruz, an exceptionally talented artist from Florida. Cruz's work focused on a thorough finishing, an oscillating arm, and some engraving work in a modern design, repeated on all the metal parts.

engine, but Cyril opted for a Shovelhead block for his other exceptional bike, "Miami Nice," which was fitted with an exhaust pipe with closed ends. (Cyril had the pipes cut at the sides so that the gas could escape from there.) The dampers were also quite original: they were hidden, but still existed and fulfilled their function perfectly. These elements, together with the saddlebags and many other details, were his brainchild. Thus, he was among the first to conceive the growing trend in customization, in which the work is shared among the designer, the manufacturer, and the machine assembler.

Cyril considers himself a designer, and he maintains that, at the present time, there is a sort of rivalry between those who assemble customized motorcycles and those who design them. Up until recently, mechanics used to assemble motorcycles without following real plans; today, designers design machines from start to finish and submit the related plans to the professional mechanics. Now, there is a shortage of designers on the market, and, in their rivalry with "bolt assemblers," they are likely to win, because they always seek new inspiration.

According to Cyril, a Harley must remain a Harley, and all the motorcycles he designs have the Harley-Davidson look. They are the expression of his personality; he transfers his emotions to them,

gives them a name and, from there, he decides which colors are suitable to characterize the chosen themes. The aesthetic is then drawn from the chosen theme and name, and underlines and emphasizes the form, greatly influencing the final result. The engraving, too, reflects the theme. The theme for the motorcycle "Miami Nice" is Art Deco, a style that was invented by the French and modified by the Americans, and is so prevalent in Miami.

227 top With this motorcycle, Cyril Huze was awarded many prizes over the course of several exhibitions.

227 bottom Although this "Deanager" Softail is not the first creation by Cyril Huze, this motorcycle brought him public attention and professional recognition as an exceptional designer.

227

CORBIN BODIES

Ron Simms, from Bay Area Custom Cycles, produced the first bike based on body work elements which had been created by Mike Corbin. Corbin worked regularly with designers and transformation specialists, who focused on the particularly interesting possibilities offered by the Corbin body to those working in the customization field. Thus the "Warlady," whose design is based on the "Warbird" kit by Corbin, is a motorcycle with performance worthy of road and even sport qualifications.

In building the Warlady, Ron Simms was allowed total freedom—except for modifying the Warbird kit, for which the machine was supposed to act as a promotion tool. It is worth remembering that the purpose of the Corbin monocoque kit was primarily to allow anybody to transform the look of his motorcycle by bolting the parts together, with no need to change anything on the machine.

Ron Simms chose an aviation theme, in particular to a World War II fighter plane. The fairing was decorated with a pin-up in the style of Vargas, the famous *Playboy* magazine illustrator whose drawings had decorated all young American males' bedrooms and vehicles for decades. To further emphasize the aviation look, the upper part of the motorcycle, which was visible from above, had desert-camouflage paintwork, while the bottom part was pale blue so that the vehicle would blend with the sky during its flights.

After this creation, many Harley-Davidsons were decorated with Corbin Warbird kits, which were often combined with saddlebags also designed by Corbin; the motorcycle personalized in this way by Arlin Fatland from Two Wheelers proved undeniably successful.

228 top Warbird bodies give a performance look to Big Twins and Harley-Davidson Sportsters.

228 center Corbin's "Warlady," based on his "Warbird" body, is a creation by Ron Simms aimed at promoting this new design for Harley-Davidson.

228 bottom By completing Corbin's "Warbird" body with polyester saddlebags, a Harley-Davidson can be fitted out in an original way. The result proves to be quite successful, particularly if the machine is customized by a professional like Arlin Fatland.

CYCLE SAVAGE WORKS

Cycle Savage Works has evolved, improved, and diversified its work thanks to Lonnie Cantrell and his partner Anthony Verdibello, who form a top customization team in Florida. Lonnie started working in a small windowless room on Pompano Beach that was originally a goods store which had been turned into a workshop. Now he is employed in a real store and, above all, he has enough room to meet his customers' growing demands. Although most of his customers are based in Florida, orders are coming in from further afield, thanks to the renown gradually achieved by Cycle Savage Works throughout the United States.

229 top All types of Harley-Davidsons benefit from some work, such as this Dyna, whose final look only vaguely resembles its original appearance.

229 center The classic reconstruction performed on this Softail was requested by a German customer who rode the motorcycle in Florida before taking it home to Europe.

Lonnie is used to modifying all the original parts of the motorcycle he works on. This white machine is a Dyna Glide whose components have all been modified, reworked, or replaced. The wrapping mudguards have been obtained by assembling and modifying two Dyna Glide rear mudguards for the front and by doing the same thing for the rear — a total of four mudguards to create two unique models.

The dampers, placed well back, are of chrome-plated metal; they slide inside metal tubes, even though they retain total freedom of operation.

These tubes were originally exhaust pipes and have been capped with the old FLH damper covers. It's a technique that required extensive research and many tests to perfect, but now it is possible for the machine to run as reliably as an original motorcycle.

229 bottom Cycle Savage Works, a fairly recent Harley-Davidson customization company, has grown rapidly, producing models based on a variety of themes, including this personalized Softail.

DONNIE SMITH

Donnie Smith is one of the most renowned bike builders in America, but he is less popular abroad than most of his counterparts. This may be due to the fact that he takes the time to personally build the machines; he does not try to produce huge quantities. As a result, he manages to maintain a constant quality level in his products.

This approach stems from his wealth of experience and his love for metal and good work. Always in search of new custom fields to develop, he has explored all the present trends, leaving his personal mark each time.

Donnie Smith was born in a small town in Minnesota and later moved to Minneapolis. He was educated at a farming school, but as a youth spent most of his free time with his friends, exploring their mutual love of metal working.

Subsequently, he worked for Honeywell and took an interest in drag racing, and spent every weekend on the tracks with Willys Gasser's team. During the week, Donnie and his teammates manufactured parts for other drivers, and this rapidly turned into a full-time occupation. Soon they decided to open "Smith Bros. and Fetrow," a store opened with the purpose of financing a dragster while they built it. All the work was focused on dragster cars — until the day they were asked for motorcycle parts.

The parts were for some friends, but, as demand grew, the related accessory activity rapidly became the main occupation for the store, which in the end, turned into a workshop specializing in repairing and manufacturing motorcycles.

"Smith Bros. and Fetrow," had become a chopper specialist and was among the most famous for the quality of its work. Donnie manufactured numerous original parts, such as frames and forks, until the day the demand for chopper parts calmed down, at which time Donnie and his friends closed the store and decided to go their different ways. Donnie took the opportunity to travel and even thought about retraining; but he loved that type of work too much, and soon encouraged by the level of demand from customers who wanted to have a machine built especially

230

230 top *Donnie Smith poses on his Road King during Bike Week at Daytona Beach, enjoying an overdose of sun, far from Minnesota's winter snows.*

230-231 *The Road King models appeal to an increasing number of designers. They offer practicality, with their saddlebags and removable wind-screen, but they also offer improved lines, filling in the empty space between the saddlebags and the rear mud guard.*

by him, he settled down by himself in a new shop. In this new workshop, he not only manufactures custom motorcycles, but he takes his time to discover new facets of the field; he even loves explaining the modifications he carries out, the procedure he applies, or why it is necessary to reinforce a certain part at a particular point. He is a real technician who knows his field inside and out, which explains his present success and international recognition he has garnered as a master of the subject in the manner of Arlen Ness and Dave Perewitz, just to mention the best known of the Hamsters.

230 bottom *Before developing an interest in the Road King, Donnie Smith applied his skills to the Electra Glide and other Harley-Davidson models.*

231 bottom *Donnie Smith is most famous for this motorcycle, which he derived from an FLHT. Its thin wheel nuts and the handlebar with a speedometer, are particularly popular.*

HARDLY CIVILIZED

Every year, at the great American meetings, and in particular at the Daytona Bike Week, the bike shows act as springboards for launching fantastic new creations. Here, both amateur and professional designers unveil their masterpieces, which may be finished or may still be works in progress.

In 1995, two men named Eddie and Simon, who had formed a partnership called "Hardly Civilized" Incorporated, stood out from the crowd when they exhibited two highly original Harley-Davidsons, on which their owners travelled everyday.

These machines had been assembled in Liberty, South Carolina and had been fitted with a unique exhaust system. This impressive innovation was built from a single pipe connecting the two cylinders, without a baffle, and cut sideways in the middle. Contrary to expectation, the noise is kept within

232 *Hardly Civilized immediately stood out from other customization specialists, offering particularly original exhaust systems on Harley-Davidsons.*

acceptable limits, and more importantly, the engine works perfectly and performances have been increased.

But these are other innovations as well. Hardly Civilized focuses on each specific motorcycle they transform. They rarely use parts which are widely available on the market, and when they do, they transform and personalize the parts before using them in their creations. One example of this is a handlebar which is fixed under the tee, thus obviating the need for a linking bar between the arms.

Since their debut in 1995, Hardly Civilized have presented their innovations and their creations at every big American meeting, consistently pushing the limits of design.

232-233 This exhaust system connects the two cylinder outlets to obtain a deep but moderate sound and improved performance, according to designers.

233 top left Few customized machines and even fewer road motorcycles have adopted this type of exhaust. Nevertheless, its aesthetics draw attention at shows.

233 top right A Harley-Davidson decorated to match the label design of Jack Daniels—definitely a "Biker" look.

BAY AREA CUSTOM CYCLES

Ron Simms's history as a designer began a long time ago, when he purchased a dismantled Sportster belonging to one of his neighbors. He wanted to reassemble that machine for his own use, adding a few personal modifications, which then multiplied as the work went forward. When the motorcycle was finished, he was offered a much higher sum of money than what he had paid. This gave Ron the idea of doing it as more than a hobby. He constructed several machines in his own garage and later, in the '70s, decided to open Bay Area Custom Cycles. The shop he found in Hayward, California had originally been built in 1956 for a Harley-Davidson dealer, who was now just closing his doors. Ron Simms moved in and has never left the place. He carries out work of acknowledged quality, endowed with personal style. It's a look that he alone can provide and which has fascinated an increasing number of people, including stars such as Neil Young, Greg Allman,

and Boz Scaggs. His approach to motorcycles is focused on both the aesthetic and the technical.

This approach dates back to the time when Ron Simms opened his shop, and decided to create a look that was different from that of the local choppers. He created a customization aesthetic which was entirely new for the time. He built motorcycles with a different steering stem angle and a shortened fork, thus implementing his first low and imposing motorcycles. The real B.A.C.C. style was refined with the passing years; and, at the beginning of the '80s, Ron Simms increasingly engaged himself in the manufacture of the elements used in composing his motorcycles. Since then, he has kept the same policy; and when the parts do not come from his workshop, he always selects models which he thinks are produced by the best manufacturers so as to produce motorcycles of unquestionable quality.

234 top and 235 bottom Using many custom-manufactured elements, Ron Simms of Bay Area Custom Cycles builds Softail Harley-Davidsons, mounting huge rear tires and preserving a belt-type secondary transmission.

234 bottom The "Fandango," with which Ron Simms won the Oakland Show in 1993, was initially a Softail. A radically different motorcycle from Simms's other creations, this cycle took part in many subsequent events.

RICK DOSS

Rick Doss, the Harley-Davidson parts specialist based mostly on the East Coast for C.C.I., regularly produces machines for Custom Chrome in addition to his personal parts. Doss deserves to be recognized because he is living evidence that anybody with a bit of taste and, above all, ideas can impose himself on the market of transformed Harley-Davidsons.

Rick, who designs and manufactures his own parts to transform and customize motorcycles, is also, like John Reed who works in the Custom Chrome research and development department, a designer-manufacturer of new products for Morgan

236 The Softail has been the Harley-Davidson most widely customized, following many themes and interpreted by many designers.

237 Rick Doss, a renowned designer who creates parts for Custom Chrome Incorporated, shows the motorcycles he builds in a variety of American shows. They can also be found on the pages of C.C.I.'s catalog.

Hill. Every motorcycle that Rick Doss builds, using parts which he designs specifically for that machine, allows him to test the market during big shows like Daytona and Sturgis.

The bike is exhibited, and depending on the reactions of Harley enthusiasts, its parts may be launched into production. Thus, the motorcycles act as showcases for the new parts which will to be available in the C.C.I. catalog.

Initially, Rick owned a service and repair workshop for cars and trucks. However, being very fond of motorcycles, every time

he bought a Harley he could not help modifying it, first changing the color and then some of its parts, such as the tank.

At first, his work was mostly carried out at home in his leisure time; then it gradually encroached on his working hours, because he was always looking for new ideas that went against the various standard concepts of the time.

(For instance, when everybody wanted chrome plating and polished parts, he painted them black.) Then, more than twenty years ago, he decided to sell his car and truck workshop and settle down in a

new place to work on Harley-Davidsons. Today, he is still in the same place and still works in the same way, acting on impulse according to what he feels like doing with the motorcycle he is about to build.

He is capable of spending hours on a component and then abandoning it when he realizes that its final line is not suitable for that particular motorcycle. He always aims to design machines which are both good to look at and easy to ride. His greatest pleasure is when a Harley enthusiast admires one of his motorcycles and imagines himself at its wheel.

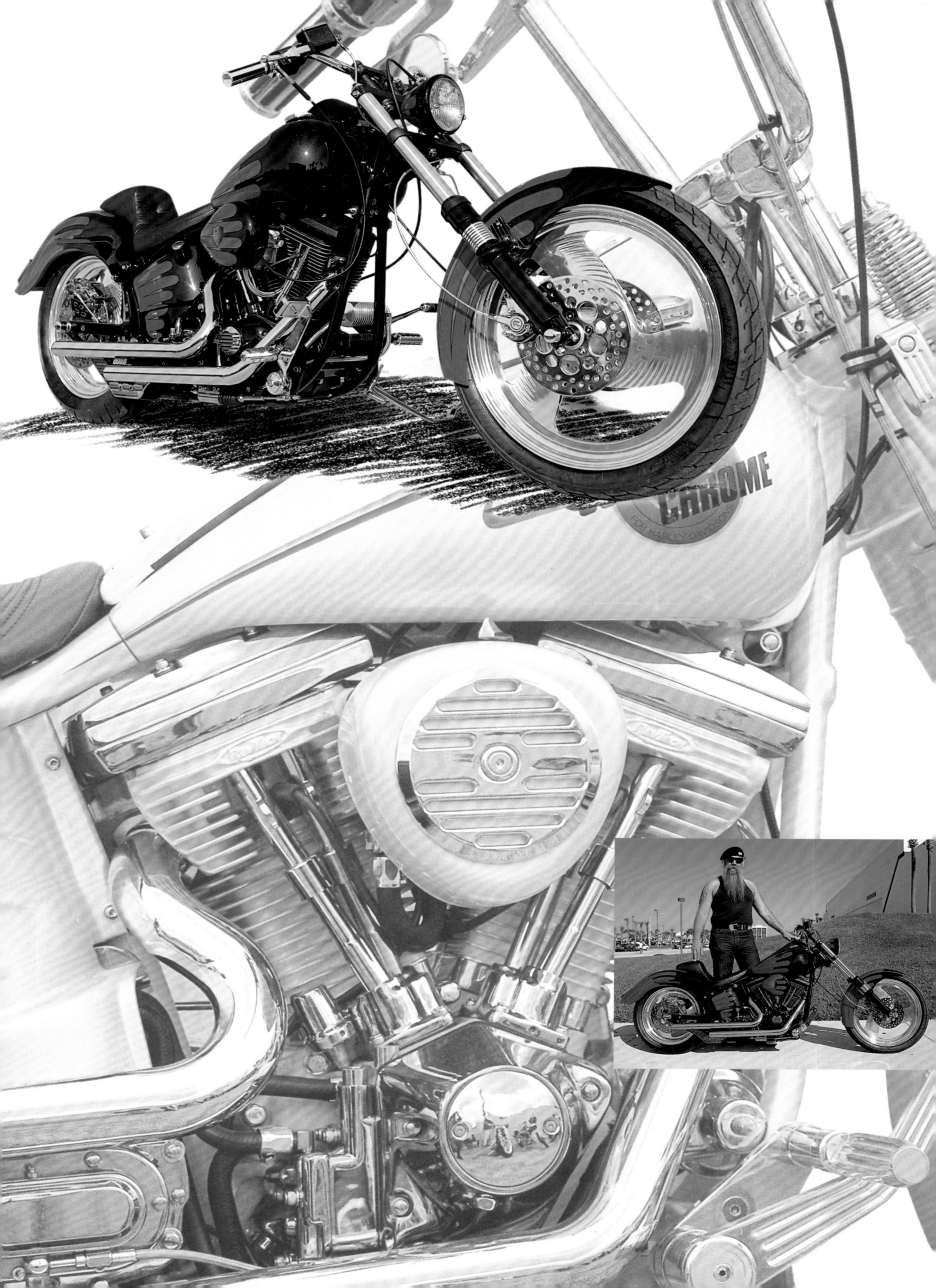

238-239 The "Nightmare" model, by Jay Brake, unveiled state-of-the-art technical solutions. The fork prevents all bolts and axles from showing.

Jay Brake is a famous company specializing in braking systems and controls which are placed well forward. It likes to unveil its exceptional and thoroughly researched motorcycles, such as the famous "Originator" and "Nightmare," during the big American shows.

The Originator is a motorcycle designed by Jay Brake, whose brake calipers do not act on the central brake disks but directly on the rims and whose fork hides the front wheel axle completely.

The Nightmare adopts the same type of fork, a very similar design for the frame, and practically the same front. But the back of the motorcycle is much more tapered and integrated into the general line of the motorcycle, whereas the Originator has a more truncated back line.

The name "Originator" was derived from the new braking system adopted, whereas

"Nightmare" is related to the huge amount of work that the design and implementation of this motorcycle required and, above all, to the need for finding solutions to problems which at first appeared impossible to untangle — as is usually the case when an exceptional motorcycle is being built, maintains Jay Brainard, the owner and eminence grise of Jay Brake Enterprise.

Motorcycles have always been a passion for him and working in a field related to Harley-Davidsons is an ideal opportunity for manufacturing fantastic motorcycles.

239 bottom Jay Brake's first exceptional creation was this "Originator," equipped with brake calipers, clamping a disk on the perimeter of the rim.

J.P. Poland has become well-known in the field of transformation by manufacturing a Harley-Davidson called "El Tigre," which was the product of his encounter with Dan Meyer, a styling specialist and one of the designers of the Absolut vodka bottle. Dan Meyer understands the requirements of creating a design which will appeal to a large audience, and thus, beyond castings reinforced by the addition of metal in certain points of the mudguards, he suggested tiger-striped paintwork. It was very successful. After being displayed in the window of a cafe in Florida, this motorcycle appeared on the *Regis and Kathie Lee Show*, after which it was invited to the Harley-Davidson Café inauguration in New York City. As a result of the success of the first El Tigre, the Café ordered a similar machine on a Sportster base.

Then J.P. decided to undertake a new project, which would be based on the same principle but would focus on another theme. He and Dan Meyer purchased a new FLHTC 94 and started transforming it into a dragon. As they had more time now, they were even more painstaking and built a motorcycle which was trimmed and decorated in every detail according to the dragon theme. The bike was fitted out with polyester and resin and the casting, assembly, and molding work, as well as the aluminum parts, were by J.P. and Dan, who also carried out the tapping and setup, with a final result of spectacular aesthetic effect.

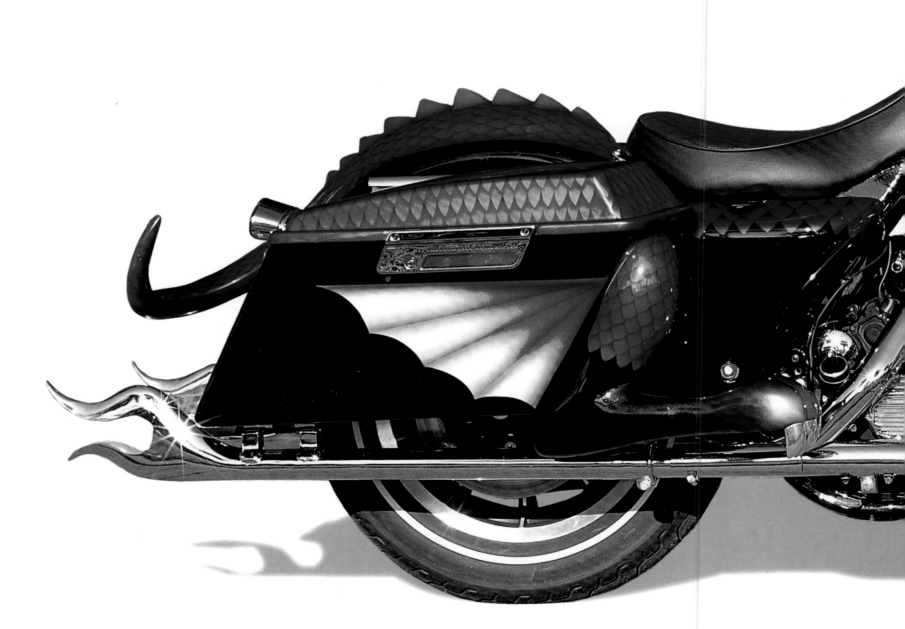

240–241 The "Dragon" motorcycle is a 1994 FLHTC with bodywork in polyester and resin. This motorcycle could be ridden, but J.P. Poland decided to reserve it for shows and promotional display.

242

242-243 *J.P. Poland first built "El Tigre" and presented it during Bike Week at Daytona Beach. Built on a FL base fitted with a Shovelhead engine, the body is composed of reinforced polyester elements.*

243

244 bottom Here, Bob Lowe used a Jay Brake fork, disguising both axle and bolts.

Bob Lowe first entered the custom motorcycle field with a 1993 Fat Boy. This first motorcycle was built when Bob Lowe already had several customized cars; he used it to extrapolate the styles existing in the automotive sector and adapt them to motorcycles. After the success of this first machine, which was rewarded with prizes during various shows, he undertook the creation of a second motorcycle on an FXR base, as few people had done such extensive work on this base. On this machine, as on the previous one, everything was made of metal and no parts were built in plastic or polyester. His friend Ron Englert, who had already built three cars for Bob, took over the task, and not a single element was left in its original state. Everything was modified, reworked,

replaced, or adapted.

This FXR won the first prize at the Oakland Show in 1995 and stimulated Bob Lowe's creativity; with his third motorcycle, called "Evil Twin," he pushed the limits of feasibility even further. He wanted to design a machine that abandoned the usual and allegedly compulsory central headlight, which appeared on all creations, even the craziest. By replacing the headlight with two stylized lights sunk in the front of the tank, not only did he achieve his goal but he also created an original front line that shaped the whole motorcycle by giving it the look of a shark muzzle.

All Bob Lowe's motorcycles are built on a theme and the design is thought through from the beginning. Those who

245 top This light belongs to Bob Lowe's first creation, presented at the celebration of the 90th anniversary of the Harley-Davidson Motor Company.

245 bottom The first motorcycle Bob Lowe built on a Softail base was so successful, it encouraged him to continue his aesthetic flights of fancy.

manufacture the technical parts are given strict instructions. The aesthetic part is up to Ron Englert, who uses a traditional method to shape all the metal parts: the hammer. He certainly has the necessary experience for this type of work, thanks to many years of practice in the car customization sector. As for the details, all parts are unique and are specially constructed for each machine. Moreover, since Bob knows a great deal about customizing cars, he can adapt these parts, or at least the ideas behind them, to achieve perfect motorcycles.

246-247 After Bob Lowe's FXR won first place at the Oakland Show, his Softail (called "Evil Twin") won first place again—a unique performance for a motorcycle designer.

246 bottom All the elements composing this machine are arranged to evoke the contours of a shark.

247 bottom left The tank and the fork head form one single piece on this motorcycle.

247 bottom right Bob Lowe's initial idea was to build a motorcycle that abandoned the traditional single central headlight. The result: a complete success in both looks and efficiency.

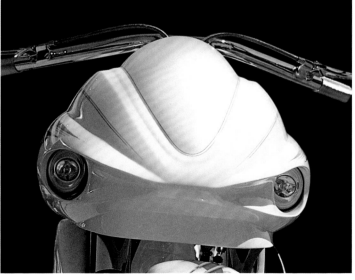

248 top A gentle line characterizes the rigid frame of this motorcycle. Its Evolution engine and a secondary transmission are covered by a finned Milwaukee Iron case reminiscent of old machines.

248 bottom This Evolution engine was equipped with a distinctive old-style crankcase cover and a gearbox.

249 top A Harley-Davidson fitted with a Shovelhead engine and refined to the max, for the look of an old racing motorcycle.

249 bottom This Knucklehead engine has been adapted to a motorcycle with a traditional chopper look, but special parts transform it into a modern machine.

MILWAUKEE IRON

The Milwaukee Iron company, already renowned in the United States for the quality of its work, has become increasingly popular in Europe for the same reason. Milwaukee Iron has deliberately chosen to do things differently from the others, thus creating its own style.

Milwaukee Iron manufactures parts and builds whole motorcycles.

Their original projects generally keep the Harley-Davidson frame, transmission, and original engine. Sometimes, though, a frame, for instance, will be descreetly and carefully modified. In doing so, Milwaukee Iron tries to equal the quality of other professionals, but does so in a more modest way. Even when doing more radical transformations, though, they take

the same approach.

This, combined with their use of computer-driven lasers and machine tools, means that they can give their parts an irreproachable finish.

This technique allows Milwaukee Iron to create unique parts, such as their famous air filter, which are then marketed through the catalogs of major distributors. The parts supplied by Milwaukee Iron are of exceptional quality, the best that American production can provide.

Their success is fully deserved: it has been achieved through an original method of working which looks to the future, and combines new techniques with outstanding craftsmanship to create truly world-class parts and unique motorcycles.

250-251 *This Knucklehead with a rigid frame, shaped as a modern chopper, has a line that breaks radically from the style that ordinarily characterized it.*

251 top *This Knucklehead engine has been fitted out with Milwaukee Iron elements to improve its looks and with an air filter cover, which reproduces an old Harley-Davidson siren.*

PARAGON LOCOMOTION

252 top Based on a Softail, this classic personalization combines the comfort of a good ride with the pleasure of an original motorcycle.

252 center This Softail was customized with an eye to preserving original elements: engine, frame, fork, etc.

252 bottom Thomas E. Worrell, Jr., head of Paragon Locomotion, a company specializing in the customization of Harley-Davidsons.

252-253 "Dragula", a Harley-Davidson with a body inspired by the vampire Dracula, built for a Florida customer.

253 top The lines of this FLH have been improved for the exclusive use of Paragon.

253 bottom This motorcycle may look like a restoration of an old Harley-Davidson, but it is in fact a modern machine, fitted with an Evolution engine and redesigned for a really retro look.

The story of Paragon Locomotion, a company based in Florida, officially started in 1991, but its specialists have been working since 1984 within Angless Automobile Restoration, at the same address. At that time they only worked on cars, transforming some into rods and restoring others for collections. Nevertheless, they were keen on motorcycles, and using the skills and knowledge at their disposal, they personalized their own Harley-Davidsons. These were such a success, soon their friends asked for transformations as well. The phenomenon grew gradually, as the car market shrank slightly and the demand for customized motorcycles grew. This culminated in the creation of Paragon Locomotion, which specialized in the modification of Harley-Davidson engines.

The Paragon Locomotion team consisted of several people working in the workshop, an artist/designer, and a saddler specializing in leather. The saddler, a professional artisan, worked mainly on La Pera saddles, which he chose for their quality and their metal saddle base, and which he radically personalized every time. He also produced bike leathers, belts, clothes, and tank panels, as well as leather clothing for restored or personalized cars.

Regarding motorcycle manufacturing, the Paragon Locomotion method is always the same: the customer places his order, and two or three months later, he receives his motorcycle. All the personnel engage themselves on the project, with everyone giving his input, improving on other people's suggestions, and developing a detailed plan on paper of the final model, before any work starts in the shop.

The customers are people from all backgrounds, and whether they are doctors, police officers, or lawyers, they are selected customers: Paragon Locomotion manufactures only ten to twelve motorcycles per year. Given the number of employees, this provides the best possible rhythm for Paragon to carry out thorough work that is truly personalized and of top quality. It is true that they also execute additional small jobs on machines which have already been customized and whose owners merely wish to improve them in keeping with the new styles. On request, they carry out all imaginable styles of work, whether involving a modification of the frame or something simpler. On average, about 65% of the parts they use are unique, specifically created or modified for each motorcycle — a method which corresponds for the most part to the one adopted by the other customization professionals presented in this book.

254 top Paragon Locomotion modified this fuel tank to match the long line of this motorcycle.

254 bottom left All parts are engraved, even the tiniest: hence this brake caliper and disk, engraved to the same extent as the Springer fork.

254 bottom right The quest for quality finishing is pushed to the extreme. Even the least accessible part is decorated.

255 All mechanical elements and chrome-plated parts are engraved. Look at this engine in detail, for its sweep of arabesques.

256 top and 256-257 bottom The Springer theme, reminiscent of old Harley-Davidsons, appears here, but with Western-style paintwork.

256-257 top A Softail modified according to the retro theme, with mud guards on a Springer fork and rear wheel.

258 This machine shows an Indian theme on a Softail Springer FXSTS base—a look entirely based on finishing and decor.

259 Chrome-plated and painted parts are combined in these exhaust outlets to create an Indian look. The cylinders are painted, the edges polished, and lower engine fins removed, and with space left free, the cylinder bases could be painted, too, according to the Indian theme. Although the air filter was an old S&S chrome-plated model which had not been modified, it was partly covered in embossed leather to match the motorcycle's paintwork.

260-261 This motorcycle was completely dismantled so that all its parts could be polished or painted. During the job, the steering shaft was modified to obtain an overall lower line.

DAVE PEREWITZ

Cycle fabrication can be summed up by one name: Dave Perewitz. Dave Perewitz's relationship with motorcycles started in 1964, when he bought a Sportster. He was only sixteen years old, but he became interested in custom fabrication as soon as he started to work in a shop after school, sandblasting parts and doing simple paintwork. He got better, and then he dared to paint his Sportster by himself.

Friends recognized his talent and asked him to paint their motorcycles, too. What started as just an after-school job was turning into a profession. He studied mechanics, and later, he started working as a mechanic for a Chevrolet garage, still modifying motorcycles in his spare time. He took a crucial step in the early 1970s, when he opened his own shop to repair and personalize motorcycles. A few years later, he also opened a store, selling parts and accessories. But it was in 1975 that his career took the biggest turn. Dave Perewitz

met Arlen Ness, who introduced him to the world of engine builders and, ultimately, helped Perewitz stand out among them.

By the early 1980s, Dave Perewitz had expanded his business and moved into his present workshop. Like every engine builder, he follows his own work methods. He starts with ideas, gathering and organizing them into a single design. Then his hands start moving, and finally he works directly on the concrete implementation of his project. Whether it is going to be an exclusive motorcycle or simply some flame paintwork—one of his favorite touches—he works with equal spontaneity.

As his business has grown, he has gathered together a select team who work to support his visions. Every year, Dave Perewitz unveils whole lines of stylized motorcycles, as well as machines built for certain customers, with paintwork that bears the distinctive Perewitz touch.

262-263 This type of FXR made Dave Perewitz known. He had been working for a long time, but he was known mainly on the East Coast until he started taking part in big meetings, presenting motorcycles with his kind of sophisticated paintwork. He then gained nationwide notoriety.

264 top The Harley-Davidson Road King also interested Dave Perewitz. This first model, used by his son, was stripped and fitted with a new exhaust system and a few other modifications aimed to improve its performance.

264 bottom This more classic Road King customization preserves the elements of the machine while providing new paintwork and lightening the front, next to the fork.

264-265 bottom With this elegant figure, refined frame, and a look that evokes the Hamsters, the hand of Dave Perewitz on this Softail cannot be denied.

265 bottom *The Softail is one of Dave Perewitz's favorite frames. His paintwork always stands out from the rest of the machine. When he's finished, you can tell that he has designed a motorcycle for riding.*

WYATT FULLER, EX-RAZORBACK

Wyatt Fuller is a name long associated with customized motorcycles, created for years by Fuller's own Razorback Motor Works. Today, Razorback no longer exists, and Wyatt Fuller works for Harley-Davidson. Still, it is worth remembering the full history behind this king of customization from Florida.

Fuller was the founder, owner, and creative genius behind Razorback Motor Works in Pompano Beach, Florida. Early in 1991, his business began as a one-man custom shop in his home, but it quickly grew into the larger Razorback Motor Works.

266 top Known for machines with angular, massive forms, Razorback's custom work stands out. This full-bodied Softail epitomizes his creations.

266 center Despite conventional lines, this Low Rider is a Razorback creation, customized to order with respect for classic design.

266 bottom These machines, although less spectacular than others Wyatt Fuller has built, drew the attention of Harley-Davidson executives, making them decide to bring Fuller into the firm.

267 top Characterized by less massive lines, this Softail shows elements that single it out as a Razorback motorcycle, especially the signed parts and the rear mud guard decorated with a spoiler.

266-267 Razorback transformed Softails by replacing original body elements with Wyatt Fuller parts. They weren't radical frame transformations, but they were exactly what Harley-Davidson looked for in products intended for the aftermarket.

In its short independent lifespan, Razorback racked up a good reputation and a strong hold in the custom field, first in Florida then in the rest of the U.S. and even in Europe, where some of its motorcycles still circulate today. In 1992, Razorback increased its custom and show market shares, thanks above all to customized Harley-Davidson models. Razorback style was distinctive: lines were more aggressive and gave the impression of controlled power. Razorback imposed a new style, which answered customer taste, and pushed Wyatt Fuller to the forefront in the field of customization. Never trained as a designer, still Fuller managed to envision new ideas and to make the most of state-of-the-art materials and techniques and excellent professional skills.

By 1994, Razorback's work was so highly acclaimed that Harley-Davidson bought the company and all of its assets. Harley-Davidson's Jerry Wilke, vice president of marketing for motorcycles and accessories, explained that the company snatched up Fuller, wanting his design work for its own.

While building custom masterpieces, Fuller didn't forget the prospect of building a business based on deluxe accessories. "We've now got about 22 custom components on the market under the Razorback name," he explained to *Big Twin*, the online Harley magazine, "and we're always working on more. We also do custom work on Fat Boy solid-disc wheels. People either send their wheels to us to have different slot patterns machined in them, or they can buy ones that we've already machined and plated. A lot of the bikes we build—including that white '92 Fat Boy—have wheels that have been modified."

Today, Wyatt Fuller contributes to the field of accessories and parts for Harley-Davidsons, through work that shows up in the official catalog. His Biker Blues, for instance, was originally a Harley-Davidson Fat Boy, entirely personalized and customized along the new jeans theme—an original customization that proves that the company from Milwaukee knows the commercial potential of such work on its motorcycles.

268-269 Abstract and futuristic paintwork take Harley-Davidsons far from earlier paintwork styles.

X-Zotic

X-Zotic specialized in Evolution engine transformations, first with a kit that made the engine look like a Panhead, then by expanding on this look with bodywork parts. X-Zotic's biggest accomplishment, in 1995, was to reproduce a Knucklehead, using a Harley-Davidson Evolution. Engine and bodywork replicated that of an old Harley-Davidson, at least in aesthetic terms.

With its Evo-Indian kit, X-Zotic pushed the limits of feasibility even further, creating a machine with a pronounced Indian look on a Softail base. This model included all sorts of features that looked like those in Indian engines: cylinder head covers and a cam-cover with distributor, for example.

The kit added exhaust pipes, metal mudguards, and footrests. It included either a front fork with headlight or the original fork bodywork, for those who preferred to economize. The carburetor pipe ran down the left side of the motorcycle with an Indian air filter and two Indian front and rear lights. In other words, the X-Zotic kit provided the elements that permitted a Softail to be turned into an Evo-Indian so well that it deceived a great number of amateurs.

270 top X-Zotic supplies elements that emphasize an old-style look, such as a crankcase cover or fork front bodywork, modern elements with a deceptively antique look.

270 center and 270-271 Many Harley-Davidsons are fitted with these Panhead cylinder head covers, with no other retro transformation, simply to obtain a different engine look.

270 bottom X-Zotic produces parts kits to transform an Evolution engine into an old Panhead or Knucklehead, as is the case here.

271 bottom A Softail motorcycle, personalized with cylinder head covers made by X-Zotic to evoke the America of the 1950s.

Battistinis, based in Great Britain, supplies Ness, Performance Machine, and Battistinis parts to several other European countries, adopting the American policy of building motorcycles as showcases. These motorcycles show a quest for aesthetic effects evoking the Arlen Ness style, but they also reveal Battistinis' mark. Company professionals work in total cooperation with Arlen Ness, and they always take into consideration that their motorcycles must cover several hundreds of miles. Of course, this is the best possible promotion for the parts and products their company supplies. Battistinis workshop is integrated with its distribution unit, which explains why all members of the company have a comprehensive knowledge of the products they sell and can continue to unveil the endless creative solutions to problems of motorcycle manufacture.

272-273 At first, Battistinis presented motorcycles either created by Ness or based on Ness lines, with parts coming from Ness' catalog.

274 top This Sportster, revised by Battistinis, typifies the harmonious forms designed to evoke a bigger Harley-Davidson than the original.

274-275 top *Battistinis rapidly adopted the policy of manufacturing new motorcycles each year to promote company products, in particular those by Arlen Ness. Like this FXR, they use Ness parts, but are built in England.*

OMP AND CARBON DREAM

OMP, an Italian parts manufacturer, makes items for Harley-Davidson such as risers, handlebar grips and controls, air filters, fork tees, rear-view mirrors, covers, pulleys, belt guards, and even wheels. The company has developed a following, especially in Europe, thanks to its high-quality parts, which have a special look which is different from American products. Motorcycles presented by OMP often include carbon elements, built by Carbon Dream, another Italian manufacturer that produces items for sport motorcycles, not only Harley-Davidsons but other brands as well. Cross-fertilization between the brands has meant that the ideas coming out of these companies are multiplied and adapted to Harley-Davidsons with very interesting results.

ZODIAC

Based in Holland, Zodiac advertises that it builds parts for Harley-Davidsons, and it was actually the first European company offering parts for Harley-Davidsons on the European market. Its market plan was to supply both high-performance and custom parts for performance cycles and dragsters.

In the mid-1990s, Zodiac started to showcase custom parts used to personalize Harley-Davidsons. The company thus showed to what extent these machines could be transformed using parts produced in Europe and Asia in addition to those imported from the United States.

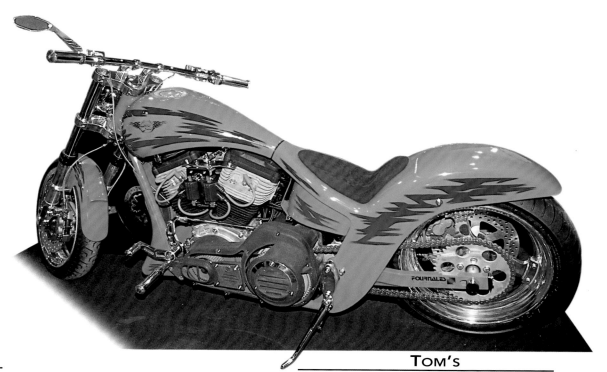

277 top Zodiac, a Dutch company distributing parts built for Harley-Davidsons, also supplies custom and performance elements, thanks to a thorough understanding of dragster competition.

277 bottom Tom's, a large German company, builds motorcycles to highlight the quality of the accessories and parts offered through its catalog.

TECHNOPLUS

TechnoPlus is a French company specializing in precision parts, which dedicates its knowledge, techniques, and equipment to the service of the belle from Milwaukee.

The courtship has proven fruitful. Company owner Claude Babot spurs on the development of new products, continually coming up with new parts instead of modifying those that already exist. Aluminum creations combine with original lines to provide parts which, once assembled, radically transform the Harley-Davidson aesthetic into something new. This philosophy, with its ever-new vision of possibilities for Harley-Davidsons, appeals not only to Europeans, but to Americans, as well.

TOM'S

A special Softail was made for Tom's, a German company distributing products for Harley-Davidsons in Europe. It was built entirely with parts advertised in its catalog, and represents a promotional strategy similar to those adopted by American distribution companies. The basic idea for the machine came from the art department of Tom's. The machine itself was built by a customizing shop in Germany called Bike Schmiede, and it was designed to highlight the growing importance of the Asian parts market. The quality of products manufactured in Asia is constantly being improved, competing more and more strongly with other parts available from other countries. Built to match models conceived by great American designers, Asian manufacturing can reduce costs. In this case, the result is a clever combination of American state-of-the-art technology, German know-how, and Asian manufacturing expertise.

Photos courtesy Tom's

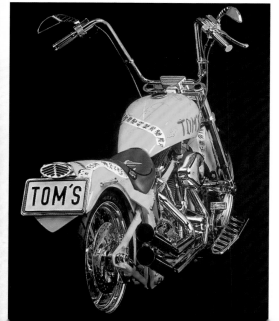

CANADIAN HARLEY-DAVIDSON

278 top This Softail is more classic in feel: a sophisticated look for a motorcycle intended for riding on the road.

278 bottom The frame is fitted with a metal skirt similar to a spoiler; the rear mud guard consists of three metal parts molded to the frame, fitting out a "Hexco" oscillating arm with lightened lines. Engine cylinder heads and cylinders have been machined to the vertical, with three fins removed at the base of each cylinder. The result is an exceptional Canadian motorcycle.

278-279 A traditional rigid chopper, but fitted with an Evolution engine, built entirely in Canada.

279 top A Canadian Softail, built with parts manufactured by the French company TechnoPlus: body, fork, oscillating arm, brakes, etc.

Canada includes a good population of Harley-Davidson aficionados, and they are particularly keen on cycle transformations. Canadians are currently customizing the Harley-Davidson Low Rider and the Sportster, and several Canadian professionals produce such work. By contrast, the modifications carried out on FLH bases, whether they are Electra Glides, Electra Sports, or Road Kings, are still quite rare in Canada, except when a specialist like the painter simply known as "Bob," renowned in Quebec, becomes interested.

In spite of its proximity to the United States, Canada has developed its own particular line of transformed motorcycles. Whether they are massive machines or machines with slender, feline lines, they always suggest power—but they are never directly copied from the great American specialists. Canada's own sophisticated customization phenomenon has recently appeared at Bike Week in Daytona Beach.

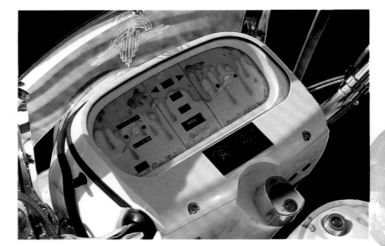

280 top left and center A 1993 FLHS, entirely customized in Canada. Its owner, Michel Ethier, enlisted Deshaies Cycles' Bob and Sylvain Beliveau to build the machine. All the elements are painted according to the theme, even the inside of the dashboard.

280 top center The dampers are disguised under metal covers hand-built by Daniel Laugon.

280 top right The original motorcycle saddlebags are preserved, but their look is modified by extending the splashes of paint so as not to load the rear line.

280 bottom The original front fork is chrome-plated, while the motorcycle wheels are powder-coated.

281 Before being painted, this fuel tank was entirely molded so its line harmonized with that part of the frame on which its back was fixed. As a result, the tank seems to be one piece with the frame.

282-283 This Harley-Davidson FLHS, modified
by Michel Ethier and his American friends,
won some prizes during shows at Daytona
Beach in 1995.

V-Twin Engines and Harley-Davidson Models

V-Twin Engines and Custom

Motorcycles that are not Harley-Davidsons but look like Harley-Davidsons are increasingly frequent. First of all, several U.S. companies are building V-Twin motorcycles with aftermarket parts produced especially for Harley-Davidsons—parts such as frames, engines, gearboxes, or certain types of bodywork. Many Japanese motorcycles reflect the Harley-Davidson spirit, too, built as they are on the basis of V-Twin engines. As customer enthusiasm grows, and if customer demand remains unfulfilled, this sort of copycat growth will continue to happen. Thus, the Harley-Davidson Motor Company has conceived a huge expansion plan, which should allow it to exceed an annual manufacturing quota of 200,000 machines by its 100th anniversary, in 2003. However, such success may only continue to generate copies, as other manufacturers exploit the same touring custom motorcycle trend. There are certainly other great displacement machines, built with power and torque and an aesthetic that shows a strong personality, such as the Honda Walkyrie, equipped with a flat six-cylinder engine, and the Yamaha Royal Star, provided with the old Venture engine of the same brand. All these machines take their look from the custom-style, grand-touring conception, but they also provide an alternative to the Harley-Davidson, which has been a benchmark in this niche and has been monopolizing the market for years. These developments may threaten Harley-Davidson, since these motorcycles, unlike V-Twin imitations, may prove to have their own winning personalities. Luckily, the company from Milwaukee seems to be responding positively to the competition, thanks to the possibilities offered by customization and transformation.

The Prototypes

Today, other manufacturers copy Harley-Davidsons, but a few decades ago, exactly the opposite went on. At first, the Harley-Davidson look did not develop as much as did the spirit of the machines and a certain conception of their driving capabilities. Mechanics had to be reviewed and, at the beginning of the 1950s, the major preoccupation was the range diversification. Besides the big V-Twins, Harley-Davidson focused on the production of medium-displacement engines. Many sketches of small models similar to the British ones were drawn, and the company even thought of reintroducing the Harley-Davidson one-cylinder engines of the 1930s.

While slowly developing the Big Twins, Harley-Davidson contented itself with replacing the 750 WL with the K, then with the KH, and developing the 750 KL at the same time. The 750 KL, which had 150 cc less than the 900 KH, proved to be more efficient thanks to its carburetors, its chain distribution with overhead valves, and its aluminum engine, a concept completely new to Harley-Davidson. This motorcycle was not mass-produced, since marketing the K and the KH was already proving very expensive. Subsequently, in view of the huge success obtained by the first Sportster in 1957, the KL project remained practically stillborn. Nine years later, the Harley-Davidson research and development department produced a scale model of a motorcycle called the X1000, with a four-cylinder engine and double overhead camshaft.

However, the X1000 required a huge investment, in terms of new buildings and

machine tools, which made for slow progress. This was just as well, because the first Honda 750 soon appeared on the market. It was much nicer than the X1000, and if Harley-Davidson had tried to compete directly, the Honda could have struck a fatal blow.

At about the same time, the Harley-Davidson Motor Company was taken over by AMF. In 1971, the new company made an attempt to replace the Sportster with a 55-degree V-Twin 750 whose frame and tank were inspired by the XR, with exhaust pipes on both sides, an electric starter, overhead camshafts, and front and rear disk brakes. The new model was poised to compete against English and Japanese motorcycles, but Triumph and BSA stopped production and Japan's Kawasaki and Honda fought it out with each other, armed with the 900 Kawa and the 750 Four. Since that battle was already lost for Harley-Davidson, the 750 Overhead Cam was abandoned.

At the beginning of the 1980s, a new range of Harley-Davidson motorcycles appeared. Porsche engineers in Weissach (RFA) were charged with implementing a liquid-cooled V engine, whose displacement ranged from 500 cc to 1200 cc, divided between two, four, or six cylinders, according to the model.

Each engine had to be built with a double overhead camshaft, while still preserving the image of a traditional Harley-Davidson. The starting contract amounted to only $10 million, and as American engineers travelled back and forth to Germany, their discouragement grew. They ended up with a mediocre product, so disappointing that it was never even tuned up. They needed another $20 million to obtain a worthwhile result, so this project was also abandoned.

The only diversification that enjoyed commercial success, thanks to the company's help, was the association with the Buell Motorcycle Company, of which the Milwaukee company is now the main shareholder.

284 top To evoke the old Panhead machines, this Heritage Springer is fitted with fringed saddle gear and a double exhaust system.

284 bottom The Heritage Springer fork is fitted with a passing lamp, located above an imposing horn, which nicely covers the modern front damper.

285 A classic Evolution engine with a tank logo on top, which adds to the retro line of the machine, emphasizes the old style of the Heritage Springer line.

286 top The Harley-Davidson VR 1000, presented in 1994, is a racing machine decorated black on the left side and orange on the right, the colors of the Harley-Davidson racing team.

286 bottom left Buell models came on the market slowly, but sales were always uncertain until Harley-Davidson invested in the company.

BUELL AND VR 1000

While other motorcycle builders used different bases for their sport cycles, Erik Buell, the founder of the Buell Motorcycle Company, only used Harley-Davidsons. An engineer with a strong taste for sport machines, in 1987 he founded the Buell Motorcycle Company, which had 11 employees and was located in Mukwonago, Wisconsin, 20 minutes away from Milwaukee. Buell planned to create his own motorcycle, the RR 1000, entirely streamlined and equipped with an XR 1000 engine. Since it was lighter and more efficient than any the Harley Owners Group had seen, they decided to equip themselves with Buells.

The Buell is built with a molybdenum chrome tubular trellis frame under which the engine is fixed, thanks to a Uniplaner system, patented by Buell. Silentblocs and adjustable axles allow the engine to be centered on a rocking arm, which isolates the driver from vibrations. In 1989, Buell launched the RR 1200, using the Uniplaner system with a more modern engine, bought directly from Harley-Davidson. The major drawback was that although Buell created and built high-quality frames, the company chose to use the original engines.

In 1990, Buell launched the RS 1200, which had technical improvements for greater comfort and practicality. Also, the hinged saddle went from a solo- to a twin-seat, with a raised rear contoured to fit the passenger's back.

The Buell saga continued for a few years until recapitalization was needed. At that point, Harley-Davidson injected capital and took over the company. Buell, which had practically stopped operations, once again began adapting Sportsters and soon diversified even further. The line ranged from roadster-style Buells to sport Buells, equipped with polyester saddlebags and a touring base (similar to the Japanese sport motorcycles which pretended to be touring motorcycles). The idea of these machines, hybrids of sport and tourism cycles, has never been fully appreciated, perhaps because they proved to be very fast but uncomfortable over long distances.

Nevertheless, the decision on the part of the company from Milwaukee to engage in competition with a real racing motorcycle, the VR 1000, proved salutary. As races are the best possible laboratory for developing motorcycles, the VR 1000 allowed Harley-Davidson to implement new techniques that could then be applied

to touring machines, without altering the spirit which animated them and their success.

The VR 1000, with a frame made entirely in the U.S.A., used a transmission integrated with the engine, as in the Sportsters. But the most original thing was the 60° V-Twin engine, which had crankcases fitted with planes of horizontal joints. The engine weighed 73 kg and achieved 140 horsepower at the maximum speed of 10,850 rpm. This motorcycle, which ran in various American races, has improved over the years. It will surely take its place in championships, as soon as Harley-Davidson decides to win.

Harley Davidson Evolution
from 1984 to 1997

EVOLUTION BIG TWIN

In 1984, the 1340 cc Evolution engine appeared on some models. This machine represented a completely original conception, the Softail. The study of this new engine and its different designs started at the end of the 1970s, but the Sportster engine development program was rapidly upstaged by Harley-Davidson's preferred study on the new Big Twin engine, which it hoped to sell as soon as possible.

The Evolution engine included a newly designed combustion chamber, engineered in compliance with new government regulations aimed at reducing exhaust emissions. These new regulations came into force on January 1, 1984. The Shovelhead could not adapt to them, so the new Evolution engine proved to be vital. The same regulations pushed Harley-Davidson into manufacturing all its 1984 Shovelhead models in 1983.

The Evolution engine was a huge step forward for Harley-Davidson engineering. Not only did engineers create an engine in compliance with very strict regulations;

they also achieved a level of reliability and performance unknown until then, also running on unleaded gasoline. Neither the valves nor the valve seats of the earlier Shovelhead could withstand unleaded gas. Given the new regulations, Harley-Davidson would not have survived without the Evolution engine. In the Evolution engine, or the Blockhead, Harley-Davidson had an engine that could be easily adapted to all uses. It could fit on Softails with a chopperized look, like the Custom

or the Springer; it could look as if it had come from the past, with the Heritage or the Nostalgia; it could be adapted to sport use on the road, closer to conventional motorcycles like Low Riders and Super Glides; and it would do the job required for deluxe touring with Electra Glides.

In 1991, Dyna Glide models emerged, built with a futuristic design generated by computer . . . but, luckily, they were still based on the V2 Evolution.

288 top The Electra Glide was the first standard machine provided with electronic injection. It was tested in a limited version for a year before becoming an option on Harley-Davidson grand touring models.

Future demands seem still to be answered by this engine, thanks to Harley-Davidson's effective study and research department. Since 1995, they have also brilliantly adapted Harley-Davidson engines to use electronic injection systems, in an Electra Glide limited series not yet available in Europe. New designs seem to be answering consumer taste as well, whether it's the 1995 Bad Boy or the 1997 Heritage Springer.

EVOLUTION SPORTSTER

In the middle of 1985, the 1986 Sportster with an aluminum engine appeared at a very low price—lower than the price of Sportsters with cast-iron engines. As Harley-Davidson had not produced any Sportsters in 1985, the concessionaires had no old stock to sell off and could therefore concentrate on selling the new bikes. The new Sportster allowed Harley-Davidson to recover financially. With this model, Harley-Davidson offered a machine at a lower price than the Big Twins, which appealed to new customers. The plan was to generate future customers for the Big Twins, on the assumption that someone purchasing a Sportster now would be a future Big Twin customer.

Unlike the machines of other brands, Harley-Davidsons do not die; they are often reconditioned or transformed and continue to run or remain part of a collection, even when they become old. At first the Sportster was only available with 883 cc. Then, in 1986, a 1100 cc model came out to complete the range. These were not common displacement values for Harley-Davidson and the difference did not justify a higher price, according to the customers. Sales were moderate. Harley-Davidson reacted immediately. In 1988, the 1100 cc became a 1200 cc, which has been successful to this day. In 1992, all Sportsters were fitted with a secondary transmission by belt and, in 1996, two new models came out, the Custom 1200 and the Sport 1200, each targeting a very special group of customers. Both new Sportsters have bigger capacity tanks—12.5 liter—, which have now been adopted across the 1997 Sportster line.

288 bottom When it appeared, the Softail Fat Boy was amazingly successful, prompting Harley-Davidson to try other variations on the Softail to differentiate them from existing models.

289 top The Evolution Sportsters developed rapidly, thanks to an attractive price and a good promotional campaign. Furthermore, new technology ensured reliability and higher performance.

289 bottom Sportsters are often transformed into racing machines and used by official riders of the brand.

The Harley-Davidson Evolution: A gradual fade-out between 1998 and 2000

THE BIRTH OF THE HARLEY-DAVIDSON TWIN-CAM 88 IN 1999

The 1998 Harley-Davidson range was marked by the appearance of a new power plant for the Big Twin Harley-Davidsons of the future. 1998 also marked the 95th anniversary of the Milwaukee company and this event was celebrated with the appearance of new bikes while certain models were decorated with particular scripts and special two-tone colors – Midnight and Champagne Pearl – and with '95th Anniversary' written on the tank. The models covered the entire range and were

the Sportster 1200 Custom, the Dyna Wide Glide, the Fat Boy and Heritage Springer Softails, the Electra Glide Classic Injection and Ultra Classic, the Road King Classic and the Road Glide.

The appearance of the Softail Night Train in 1998 should be underlined. Based on a Softail Custom, painted black all over for the European market and attractively priced, this bike met with such immediate success that it was incorporated into the Harley-Davidson range from 1999. Its success is an indication of future Harley-Davidson Softail models, and it also provoked the reintroduction of the Softail Standard into the range in 1999.

Apart from some minor modifications on certain Big Twins, in 1998 only the Sportster XL 1200 S Sport showed a real mechanical improvement, with dual ignition, a head capable of taking two sparkplugs per cylinder and new camshafts. 1998 was also the year the Sportster XL 53 C appeared, with a great deal of chrome, a two-seat saddle and a solid rear wheel like the Softail Night Train,

with which it shared this development.

The real innovation in 1998 came during the summer: it was the new Twin Cam 88 engine that was to be mounted on the 1999 Dyna and Electra Big Twins, even if they became available in autumn 1998. Officially, therefore, it was from 1999 that Harley-Davidson equipped part of the Big Twin fleet with the new Twin Cam 88 engine block that was nicknamed 'Fathead.' Although this new 1450 cc motor (88 cubic inches) looked like a more massive version of the Evolution, its internal architecture and technology were

290 top New Twin Cam 88 motor. Available in two versions: aluminum tone or black paint.

290-291 Sportster 883 Custom XL 53C, also designed for the European market and later incorporated into the Harley-Davidson American range.

291 top First version of the Softail Night Train with the 1340 cc Evolution motor. Originally to be sold only in Europe, it has now been incorporated into the Harley-Davidson American range.

completely new. The data tell the story eloquently: with a torque of 106 Nm at 3500 rpm (greater than that of the Evolution) and 14% more power (63 hp), the engine was more responsive, more reliable and more silent. In line with Harley-Davidson tradition, the V-Twin is positioned at 45°; it was used exclusively on the Dyna Glide and Electra Glide in 1999 but a version was produced for the Softails for the 2000 models.

This new version was called the Twin Cam 88B and was fitted with dual rocker arms to reduce the vibration and allow it to be fitted on the new Softail frames.

1999 was the last year that the 1340 cc Evolution engines were produced. A new bike, based on the Twin Cam 88, appeared in 1999: it was the Dyna Super Glide Sport. In 2000 the mounting of the Twin Cam 88B on the Softail range was accompanied by the presentation of the elegant Softail Deuce, with a modified tank, saddle and fenders, and a solid rear wheel. The year 2001 saw the Softail Fat Boy, Deuce and Heritage Classic available in carburetor or injection versions and the Super Glide Sport in a new model, the Super Glide T-Sport. This bike was easily customized to suit the rider's needs and was fitted,

originally, with nylon bags and an adjustable sport fairing. These small modifications heralded a new future for Harley-Davidson and, above all, demonstrated that its centenary year was approaching.

Summer 2001 marked the presentation of the 2002 range and the appearance of the new Sportster XL 883 R (R stands for Racing). This bike was painted in the colors of the mythical XR 750 Dirt Track and had a new two-into-one exhaust. The real novelty, though, lay at the heart of the Harley-Davidson marque: the new family of V-Rods.

291 bottom The following year, the Twin Cam 88B appeared on new Softail frames.

HARLEY-DAVIDSON V-ROD
FROM 2002

2002 will pass into history as Harley-Davidson's most surprising year, owing to the novelties the company presented to its public or, rather, the entire motor-cycling fraternity. In particular, the V-Rod was aimed at a new type of customer as well as being the Motor Company's response to the increasingly strict standards applied to air and noise pollution. Yet the engine is a high-performer and boasts a particularly modern architecture. The bike can be described simply as a Harley-Davidson with the look of a Custom but the character of a Dragster. The engine has been named Revolution which sits well with the fact that it has made a complete break with Harley-Davidson's past engines.

The looks and design of the V-Rod were worked on by the Studio and Design offices in Harley-Davidson from 1996. Aesthetically it resembles a Low Rider with its aggressive appearance, but the nature of the powerful engine transforms the beast into a dragster. The first V-Rod suggests there will be a family created around the Revolution motor, which may be given a more conventional appearance.

All it would need to make it suitable for a 'touring' (or retro) bike would be some generous finning and a lick of black paint. To complement the Twin Cam 88 and Sportster engines, a V-Rod family might therefore be developed without limitations being imposed by excessive closure of the exhaust owing to reasons of noise or for the emission of hydrocarbons. This would therefore provide Harley-Davidson with a third family.

292-293 and 293 top The V-Rod was presented in the middle of summer 2001 and figured in the 2002 Harley-Davidson catalog. It is a unique engine with revolutionary features for a Harley-Davidson and is aimed at winning the Motor Company new customers.

V-TWIN HARLEY-DAVIDSON PRACTICE

The Harley-Davidson V-Twin engines have a long and complicated history. They can easily be identified by certain distinguishing characteristics. The names of the various Harley-Davidson V-Twins refer primarily to the shape of the cylinder head covers.

In order not to confuse them, it is necessary to consider the top part of the engine to establish its name and period.

FLATHEAD

The Flathead, with its finned and relatively flat cylinder-head cover, is available with a complete range of displacements: 750 cc, 900 cc, 1200 cc, and 1340 cc.

The most widespread model in Europe and particularly in France is the WLA 750, which arrived with the Americans during the Second World War. Built from 1929 to 1951, this 750 cc Flathead was a standard model with side valves, from which arose its common name, Lateral.

The official names for this machine were DL for the standard, DLD for the high-compression version, and simply D for the version with sidecar, until 1936. In 1936, the military versions of this famous 750 cc standard gained the reference tags WL and WLA. A sport version called WLD and a racing version called WLDR were also derived from the same model.

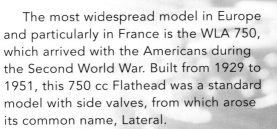

As can be observed, the Flathead 750 was used in all imaginable ways. From 1932 to 1974, it was used to equip Servi-cars, three-wheeled vehicles built by Harley-Davidson primarily for garage owners to repair or tow cars. Later, the Servi-cars were produced for the American government. There were various versions available: model G was the standard; GL was a more sophisticated version; GA was designed for the Army; and GE was fitted with an electric starter. They were like normal solo-machine engines with a gearbox that added a reverse gear.

The 1200 cc engines were also produced in various versions: V for the standard, VL with high compression, and VS and VC for those fitted with gearboxes especially intended for sidecars. The first versions of these motorcycles were quite disappointing, but Harley-Davidson rapidly solved the problems by increasing resistance. Finally, the reliability of this model made it the most successful among customers.

The Flathead 1340 was produced from 1936 to 1944 in two versions: the standard UL and the ULH, to be combined with sidecars. This highly reliable machine appealed to many users, but the Knucklehead and the Flathead 1200 surpassed it. The Model K, an ancestor of the Sportster manufactured from 1952 to 1956, also had side valves, putting it too in the Flathead category. At first the available models were the 750 K and the KR, the sport version. Various racing motorcycles were built on the KR base. In 1954 the K series was completed with a KH 900 and, in 1955, with a more sporty KHK.

KNUCKLEHEAD

The Knucklehead is easily recognized by the aluminum covers, shaped like clenched fists, which decorate the cylinder head. The first model of this engine appeared with a 1000 cc displacement, in a standard version E, a sports version EL, and a version with a special side-car gearbox, ES, in 1936. In 1941, the Knucklehead 1200 was created with a standard version called F, a sports version FL, and a special sidecar gearbox version FS. The Knucklehead faced a few reliability problems at the beginning of its career, but they disappeared once the lubrication system was modified. Then its performance became very impressive for the time. Its career came to a rapid end in 1947, however, when it was abandoned and replaced by the Panhead, whose internal works were more straightforward.

PANHEAD

The Panhead, with cylinder head covers shaped like an upside-down saucepan, appeared in 1948. It offered the technical advantage of being much lighter than the Knucklehead, since many of its elements were made of aluminum. Its internal lubrication system was less complex, and thus more reliable. A standard 1000 cc model was available, referred to as E, a sports model EL, and a special sidecar model ES. The 1200 cc version offered the same three basic models: F, FL, and FS. The Harley-Davidson Police developed on a Panhead base, and when the Duo Glide turned into an Electra Glide in 1965 the Panhead gradually took on a GT machine aesthetic. Over the years, as the FLH, FLHF, FLE, FLF, and FLHB models emerged, the line became quite extensive, which explains the great number of Panheads still in circulation today.

294 and 295 Throughout the life of the Panhead engine, transformations and technical innovations kept evolving. The Panhead first appeared in 1948 on Harley-Davidson bikes fitted with Springer forks. It equipped the Hydra-Glide models provided with telescopic forks from 1949 to 1957. From 1958, *these Harley-Davidsons were called Duo-Glides, until, in 1964, the Big Twins adopted a rear suspension system. The Panhead's career ended in 1965, with a motorcycle called the Electra Glide, although its lower engine was incorporated into the first Shovelhead engines.*

SHOVELHEAD

The Shovelhead, named for the flat, shovellike shape of its cylinder-head covers, appeared in 1966. Early models—later unofficially called Early Shovelheads—did not have the same look as the modern Shovelhead, since they were fitted with an engine base similar to that of the Panhead. Available with 1200 cc, it modified its engine base at the end of 1969, adopting the typical look of today's Evolution engine and losing any resemblance to the Panhead. The Electra came out with 1340 cc only in 1978, followed by the whole Big Twin line from 1979 on. The Shovelhead was produced until 1983 and sold until 1984, when it was replaced by the new Evolution engine, made entirely of aluminum.

BLOCKHEAD

The Blockhead 1340 cc engine, named for its massive look and for the way its engine seemed cut out on top, was first sold in 1983 under the name Evolution. By then, the cast iron of the old engines had disappeared, making way for the advantage of an engine made completely of aluminum. Harley-Davidson really wanted to break from its past and mark its revival with a completely new, infallibly reliable engine. As a result, marketing emphasized the name Evolution, not the less-futuristic name Blockhead.

Today, the company from Milwaukee is still developing this engine. Engineers continue to face greater challenges along that path, responding to increasingly draconian requirements for pollution and noise control, put upon them by certain states and also by European Union countries. The future seems too difficult to predict. An injection system was introduced in 1996 on several models, so now the purchaser can choose between classic carburetion and electronic injection.

THE FATHEAD, OR TWIN-CAM 88

The Twin-Cam 88 was designed on the computer and then tested over 2.5 million miles before being made available to the public.

This approach has made it the most reliable, long-lasting and powerful engine in the company's history; it is characterized by an increase in the piston displacement (with a modified combustion chamber), a new design of the valve ducts and exhaust, a sequential ignition system, and increased air intake due to a new front-entry air-box. The bore/stroke ratio has also been altered from the Evolution's 88.8 x 108 mm to the Twin-Cam 88's 92.25 x 101.6 mm. Harley-Davidson has therefore moved away from the long stroke engine toward a squarer ratio for greater reliability and a higher engine speed.

But the most surprising modification is the replacement of the single camshaft used till now with dual camshafts that work in harmony with short, silent transmission chains.

Another change is that the tappets are no longer visible as they have been placed inside cases. These improvements lower the bike's running noise. In addition, the 50% larger cooling finning makes the engine more reliable, the engine casing is sturdier and the flywheel has a larger diameter, thereby benefiting rotation, and the integrated oil pump has a new circulation system for better lubrication of critical points. Fundamentally, this Twin-Cam only uses 18 of the 450 components used by the Evolution, from which it is further distinguished by the more voluminous head covers (which is why it is called Fathead), the greater capacity of the air filter and the more extensive finning.

297 top Thanks to Electra Glides fitted with Shovelhead engines, the Harley-Davidson Motor Company stood out for its deluxe grand touring motorcycles at a time when no other manufacturer had penetrated this market.

297 bottom The old-style Sportster engine, fitted on Harley-Davidsons from the 1970s, was supposed to counter the invasion of Japanese engines. The Big Twin belonged to a different market niche, with well-defined customers.

SPORTSTER

The first real Sportsters, which followed the Flathead K series, were called XL. They were built between 1957 and 1985. The power of the first 883 cc engines allowed them to compete against Triumph, which had been invading the U.S. market and taking a bite out of the Harley-Davidson market share. The Sportster 900 came out in 1971, under the basic name of XL, and was available in different versions: standard, with electric starter, and with various other ignition systems. In 1972, the XL 1000 cc replaced the XL, and various versions evolved from it over the years, of which the two most outstanding were the Café Racer and the XR.

At the end of 1985, Harley-Davidson abandoned the cast-iron engine and replaced it with the Evolution, made entirely of aluminum. The success of that machine has been growing ever since. It was first made available in 883 cc; then, in 1986, with 1100 cc; and later replaced by a 1200 cc model in 1988, which resulted in a clearer differentiation of the 883 cc, thus encouraging sales. In 1992, all the Sportsters abandoned the chain secondary transmission for the toothed belt transmission, which had already been fitted successfully on all the Big Twin models.

THE V-ROD AND ITS REVOLUTION ENGINE

As has already been described, the V-Rod is a Custom Harley-Davidson in appearance with the character of a dragster. The motor has been named Revolution in tribute to its radically different nature to previous Harley-Davidson power units.

The engine is not made in the Big Twin assembly plant in York but in the new factory in Kansas City where the Sportsters and Buells are produced. The Revolution motor is the first to make use of liquid cooling on a series Harley-Davidson. It is a 60° V-Twin with dual camshafts, 4 valves per cylinder and a fixed magnetic alternator.

This revolutionary motor was the outcome of the collaboration between Harley-Davidson and Porsche Engineering, as well as a direct result of the VR 1000 Superbike program. The new propulsion unit is operated by a drive shaft forged from a single piece of metal; it displaces 1130 cc, develops 115 hp at 8250 rpm and has a torque of 100 Nm at 7000 rpm. The dual overhead camshafts are moved by hydraulically tensioned chains and control 4-valve high-compression heads; the fuel supply is provided by sequential port system.

Other innovations are the wet sump lubrication, which implies the absence of an external tank, and the gearbox which is hydraulically controled. The exhaust is a large two-into-one-into-two that successfully meets gas and noise emission strictures but without sacrificing the characteristic Harley-Davidson sound. A system of counter-rocker arms and a rubber-mounted motor contribute to a reduction in the vibration transmitted to the silver perimeter frame (a novelty for Harley-Davidson). This type of frame provides greater rigidity and, as looks are a key element to this particular make of bike, it has been created by die-casting rather than welding. The fuel tank is placed beneath the saddle to bring the mass of the machine lower to the ground and to improve the fuel supply.

The two induction pipes and the large-volume air filter are placed above the middle of the engine where the fuel tank usually sits; this allows a direct intake of the air, beneficial to the engine block. At the front of the bike, the sculpted headlamp is crowned by the new shell-shaped instrumentation that includes the tachymeter, rev counter, fuel gauge, temperature gauge and diagnostics display. This is a completely new concept compared to the traditional Big Twins and it takes the V-Rod closer to the spirit of the Harley-Davidson Sportster.

The numbers 45, 74, 80 or 88 (the commonest) refer to the size of the engine and not the date of construction.

45 cu. inches = 750 cc
54 cu. inches = 883 cc
55 cu. inches = 900 cc
61 cu. inches = 1000 cc
74 cu. inches = 1200 cc
80 cu. inches = 1340 cc
88 cu. inches = 1450 cc

The equivalents are not exact but represent numbers most commonly used by Harley-Davidson to indicate the engine size of their motor-cycles.

298 Not just the motor of the V-Rod is a surprise. The perimeter frame too is an unusual design, similar to those used by its competitors.

299 The V-Rod engine (partially derived from the competition VR 1000) was named 'Revolution' for its innovative characteristics. It is liquid cooled, has 4 valves per cylinder and is a 60° V-Twin.

A new century and a new era for Harley-Davidson: this seems to be the underlying theme for the Motor Company from Milwaukee, even though its hundredth anniversary to be celebrated in 2003 already seems to have set the neurons buzzing.

The end of the last century brought the advent of the new Twin-Cam 88, and the year 2001 saw the presentation of the revolutionary V-Rod, a completely new concept for Harley-Davidson but one that

and criticized by the competition, the Softail immediately seduced a new swathe of fans, as well as the majority of the established Harley-lovers. It rapidly established itself as a standard Harley and generated a family of models. The Softail's unusual lines were copied by many builders who wanted to produce their own V-Twin custom bike. The Softail technology, it must be pointed out, was also used by most of the custom or cruiser bikes made by other manufacturers.

not to ride a bike considered so different from the others on the road, not only by the motor-cycling world but also by the profane. With the new V-Rod, whose commercial success seems confirmed despite the high sales price, Harley-Davidson will be able to develop a range of engines that will complement the Big Twins and Sportsters. Based on the V-Rod engine, the not-too-distant future may bring Buells fitted with a variant of this modern, high-performing power plant.

remains faithful to the spirit of the brand. In yet another innovation, Erik Buell presented the surprising XB 9R in 2002, a bike designed around an original concept and a revolutionary frame, yet still based on the traditional mechanics of the Sportster. In short, 2003 will be the year that marks the Milwaukee company as the manufacturer of bikes that are living legends.

Even the most inexperienced motor-cycling enthusiast will recognize that the V-Rod is a Harley-Davidson different from any other bike the company has produced. Though still a Harley-Davidson – as the logo on the tank confirms – it does not resemble the usual HD products at all. This design of the machine is so particular that it has shaken off the tradition of the Customs and Cruisers on the market. It is long and very low, has a modern V-Twin engine and already seems a bike that has been customized for its owner … and this is exactly where Harley-Davidson's strength lies. With the V-Rod, the company from Milwaukee has created a new standard that stands out.

A moment is all that is required to recognize that a similar event occurred when the aesthetics of the Softail progressively became a reference point for custom bikes with its new, modern aluminum 'Evolution' motor. Denigrated

Harley-Davidson's success at the start of the third millennium is clearly underlined by the company's mid-90s target of producing 200,000 bikes before the year 2003, which has already been achieved and well exceeded: the number of bikes forecast for 2002 alone is 258,000! Compare this figure to that of 1985, when the company almost had to close down: its worldwide sales figures were less than 35,000. Harley-Davidson kitted itself out with the tools needed to satisfy the new production policy by opening a new factory in Kansas City, Missouri in 1998 that has a surface area of 323,000 square feet. This is where the Sportsters and Buells began to appear and where the V-Rods will also be built.

The Harley-Davidsons in the Big Twin family – the Softail, Dyna Glide and Electra Glide – with the family of Sportsters, provide a regular and constant increase in sales to their established clientele.

The aim of the V-Rod is to repeat the Softail's success and to bring attention to the current Harley-Davidson models with a new generation of aluminum engines. It is with this propulsion block – equipped with modern technology, liquid cooled and with four valves per cylinder – that Harley-Davidson will try to win new customers, the kind who in the past have hesitated to cross the showroom threshold and decided

300 top left The Softail Standard, which disappeared from the Harley-Davidson catalog in the early 1990s, returned successfully to the Softail family in 1999.

300 top right The Softail Heritage Classic, built on a basic Softail and fitted with a Twin-Cam 88B engine, met with instant and constant success after its appearance in the Harley-Davidson catalog at the end of the 1980s.

BIKES FOR EVERY KIND OF CUSTOMER

Any biker can find the Harley-Davidson that corresponds to personal character and aspirations. The question of age no longer has any relevance given that the sporty Buells and Sportsters are more attractive to a young clientele for their livelier performance than the Big Twins. As for the new V-Rod, this was aimed at a slice of the Harley-Davidson clientele unsatisfied with the company's range.

A more detailed test of each large category – Electra, Softail, Sportster, Dyna, Buell and V-Rod – allows one to appreciate the diversity of the Harley-Davidson range.
Their differences lie in the performance of the individual bikes and the use of them made by the riders, yet each one remains faithful to the spirit and philosophy of the brand.

300-301 The Dyna Glide Low Rider: a constant seller for the Motor Company and the basic model from which the Sport and T-Sport models for fast road use were derived.

301 top left The Buell Lightning X1 was built around a Sportster engine yet remains a traditional model with good performance. It was built for sports bike fans and to attract more customers indirectly to the Harley-Davidson range.

301 top right The Buell XB 9R is an exercise in style and a technical prodigy. It is the Buell of the future and at some stage its frame will probably accommodate a variant of the V-Rod engine.

301

HARLEY-DAVIDSON ROAD KING

The Road King, a simple but practical bike, was presented to the public in 1994. Equipped with a chrome streamlined nacelle, a removable windshield, a removable passenger seat and instrumentation traditionally placed on the tank, the Road King is immediately associated with the classic image of the large American Custom Touring bikes. Aesthetically it is a materialization of the dreams and aspirations of many current and future Harley riders. Good-looking and powerful, solid and provocative, it symbolizes the image of the easy-to-ride touring bike free of superfluous features.

Whereas the Softail family provides the Harley-Davidson range with a note of nostalgia, the Electra family (to which the Road King belongs) is aimed at customers looking for a good touring bike with a certain touch of tradition. This is the equivalent of a large Electra Glide stripped of its fairing and top-box, and transformed into a bike that is more agile and easier to ride in all circumstances. This concept had already convinced many adepts before the appearance of the Road King and explains the model's success. Whereas the beauty of this Harley-Davidson is worthy of reflection, its overall mass impresses the future rider: with its large streamlined fork topped by a headlamp surrounded by smaller lights and indicators, its wide handlebar, the footrests, leg and bag protectors, the bike is undeniably impressive. Its design appears traditional, unchanged over decades, but objectively

it is a modern bike camouflaged by traditional bodywork. The engine, in fact, is the Twin-Cam 88. The particular maneuverability of the Road King – despite having a 1450 cc engine – is due to the intelligent distribution of the weight. This is the result of a very low center of gravity and the reduced height of the saddle. The motor responds to the lightest touch on the throttle and the engine speed remains regular, whether in

the city or out on the highway. The bike's considerable and ever-present torque facilitates manageability and allows the rider not to have to worry too much about the gear when coming out of a curve, and the power produced by the engine is sufficient to be appreciated. Faithful to the Harley-Davidson spirit, the Road King eats up the miles and need not blush at its arrogant name: the road is its kingdom.

HARLEY DAVIDSON SOFTAIL NIGHT TRAIN

The Harley-Davidson Softail Night Train, all dressed up in black, is in practice a Softail Custom that has been slightly modified aesthetically to produce a bike at a specially interesting price.

This was a shrewd commercial decision as the modifications bring freshness to the Standard model and endow it with a touch of aggressiveness. The all black and chrome Night Train is perfectly integrated into the large Harley-Davidson family and the legend that the bikes represent. Its name refers to the nickname given to the 1971 FX model, the first, authentic Custom Harley-Davidson, created by the famous Willie G. Davidson.

The riders of this bike find themselves low and sitting in a position typical of the innumerable drawings of custom Harley-Davidsons. Sitting in the saddle of a Night Train, you enter fully into the Harley-Davidson myth, and one suited ideally to the modern American cavalcade of bikers across North America. Perfectly designed to slip through city traffic and avoid the jams because of its ease of handling and excellent low distribution of weight, the Night Train is equally pleasing to ride out on wide straight roads or on narrow, more demanding routes: just like the Softail whose philosophy it inherited.

Given its touring capabilities, it is a bike just right for long trips, and is happier cruising at low revs than at speed. It offers comfort to its rider though it is quite capable of pulling sharply away from the lights.

As with all Harley-Davidsons of this type, all you need do is customize and improve it to suit yourself and this, as we have seen, is one of the strengths of Harley-Davidsons, bikes that stand out from the motor-cycling crowd. The Night Train wishes only to be customized to suit the tastes of its owner – to become a unique and unmatchable Harley-Davidson.

302 top Road King Classic.

302-303 Softail Night Train.

HARLEY-DAVIDSON
DYNA SUPER GLIDE T-SPORT

This Harley-Davidson was aimed particularly at the European market of travelers. Lighter and more manageable than an Electra Glide, fitted with side bags and a sport fairing, and given the performance of a street bike, it bears some resemblance to European touring bikes. Although the range of Dyna Glides does not include the best known Harley-Davidson models, in recompense it is more innovative in terms of modernity. This demonstrates that the Milwaukee company, having now passed its sports bikes over to Buell (built round Sportster engines), is attempting to widen its range in the touring sector starting from this base.

The Dyna Super Glide T-Sport is therefore a touring bike rather than a sports bike, despite its name. It is perfect for a trip with two-up and side bags strapped on and offers real dynamic qualities; tending to place performance above looks, it has a rather traditional sport fairing and side bags. Its riding position is akin to that of traditional touring bikes to conform to the expectations of new customers who have always wanted to ride a Harley-Davidson but in the form of a European tourer: the rider's legs do not point forward, the torso remains upright and, in consequence, the arms are not held tense and the posture is not tiring. In any case, this is not a Harley-Davidson that forgets its personality and spirit, just riding it will tell you that. Agility and torque provide no unpleasant vibration, and the belt-driven transmission is not noticeable. In front of the rider, a sport fairing with a windshield that can be simply regulated for height and

inclination protects the rider from the wind and rain. There is an easily read fuel indicator on the 4.75 gallon tank and the two-seater saddle is low and comfortable. At the rear there are two extendable bags that can be quickly and easily removed, and which are fitted with integrated covers in the event of heavy rain. The dual front brake disk is sufficient for touring and the rear shocks, traditional in appearance, can be regulated even under compression.

This is also the case with the fork, which is an important fact as it allows the bike to be regulated to suit the load and riding style. Easy to handle and ride, the T-Sport tackles bends in a comfortable, relaxed manner. Its preferred riding style is touring but even when pushed it performs impeccably. In short, this is not a sports bike but a genuine and effective road bike which, when the gas is opened, will give just a little, plenty of fun.

HARLEY-DAVIDSON SPORTSTER XL 883 R

An XR Replica Sportster in the original Harley-Davidson version was a strategic move that allowed the XL 883 R to return to the limelight without any innovations.

The Harley-Davidson XR 750 for dirt track competitions continues, as it will for a long time yet, to give competition loving Harley-Davidson fans something to get excited about. The 'Racing' colors of the inimitable 750 XR Dirt Track ridden by the famous Jay Springsteen can be seen regularly on custom Harley-Davidsons, but in this case it was the Milwaukee company that offered a replica of the XR. It was a breath of fresh air for the Sportster 883s although the improvements were minimal and the basic model did not change. The surprising XL 883 R therefore offers an innovation thanks to its old Racing logo: this is the Harley-Davidson paradox but, at the end of the day, it works: after admiring its appearance it is enough to climb on to the beast to be won over.

This model harks back to a certain classic image of the sports models, from which it borrows a 45° V-Twin and the same double-cradle steel tubular frame. Evidently this is not an exact replica of the XR 750 but a simple customization of the non-fundamental elements of the basic Sportster. The magic is created by

the racing orange paintwork, the logo on the tank, the two-into-one exhaust, the wide, black handlebar like the one on the Dirt Track bikes, by the matte black metallic paint on the motor, the satin black paint on the oil tank and air filter, and by the dual front disk that underlines the bike's sporty image.

The elegance is completed by a heavily profiled two-seat saddle, short mirror rods, sculpted indicators and sexy wheel rims. Riding the Sportster XL 883 R will not amaze anyone who knows this type of bike; the enjoyment is experienced from the first

turns of the wheels and continues on narrow, twisting roads. Just a minimal flick of the throttle pulls you out of a curve to the lovely growl of the V-Twin.

The rider feels these sensations immediately and tends to forget what the bike offers at higher engine speeds; moreover, the bike's behavior on the road offers gratification in any situation. The riding position is not tiring, despite the width of the handlebar, and the bike can be maneuvered with ease. You feel at home immediately as a result of a solid frame and the bike's rather unsophisticated handling.

304 top, bottom and 305 bottom Dyna Super Glide T-Sport.

305 top Sportster 883 Racing XLH0 883R.

HARLEY-DAVIDSON V-ROD:
A NEW GENERATION IS BORN

In the summer of 2001 Harley-Davidson presented its new V-Rod and, shortly after, announced its intention of temporarily halting high-level competition and the VR 1000 program. The development of this racing bike and the competitions it was involved in were the testing ground for new technologies, some of which filtered down to current road models. However, even if Harley-Davidson really abandons racing and the VR 1000 project, the technology and development of this bike formed the starting point for the creation of the V-Rod. When the bike was presented to the public, the Harley-Davidson spokesman declared, 'It is time to challenge preconceived ideas and the status quo. The latest Harley-Davidson is ready to enter the scene and minimize all previous conceptions held about Harley-Davidson Customs and Custom Cruisers in general....' This was a declaration that seemed to suggest the abandonment of the air-cooled, 45° V-Twins with two valves per cylinder. Fortunately, this was not the case – at least not for the moment – as they remain the most important source of income to Harley-Davidson.

So the V-Rod was a response to increasingly strict norms on road traffic and an attempt to win over another slice of the public, with the incorporation of decidedly modern technologies and the rejection of some traditional ones. This was a decision that should be more advantageous to the company than the earlier weak attempts at aesthetic and technical modernization represented by the Low Rider Evolutions and Dyna Glides. With the V-Rod, Harley-Davidson has maintained the spirit of the brand and succeeded in attracting the attention of those members of the biking public who are resistant to buying a Harley.

The fairly fashionable appearance of this Dragster type bike was partly responsible for the change of opinion and behavior of many motor-cyclists. The saddle is only 26 inches from the ground and provides the rider with a comfortable seat even if the footrests and handlebar are slightly distant for shorter riders. However, that is a problem that can be resolved as Harley-Davidson has provided an optional seat whose design allows the rider to sit about 1 inch closer to the footrests.

Once on the road, the sound of the V-Rod is pure Harley-Davidson as its twin cylinders rise and fall together, though without transmitting vibration to the rider. The flexible Revolution motor offers constant torque and generous increases in engine speed, allowing it to pull away at only 2000 rpm in 5th gear, to pick up vigorously around 4000 rpm, and to provide a good kick in the backside at over 6000. The power of the ponies and the pick-up are so evident that they give the V-Rod the behavior of a drag bike.

This engine provides many possibilities for development and will undoubtedly appear on different bikes and in different sizes. The commercial success of the V-Rod is reflected by the impatience of the dealers, who have to wait as Harley-Davidson is unable to put more than 1703 on the market before the end of 2001.

306 Customization, personalization or transformation of the V-Rod does not hide the fact that the bike is at heart a traditional Harley-Davidson.

307 The V-Rod has a high-performing engine which requires a third disk in the brake system, but the bike does not lose either its dragster-like character or appearance.

BUELL: BLAST AND XB9R
DIFFERENT HARLEY-DAVIDSONS

On 19 February 1998, Erik Buell announced he had sold almost all his shareholding in the Buell Motorcycle Company to Harley-Davidson Inc., which had already been a minor partner for five years. Erik Buell was made Managing Director and Technical Director while Jerry Wilke was made President of the new organization. During the Harley-Davidson press conference held in Daytona Beach in March 1998, Erik Buell stressed the fact that the buy-out by Harley-Davidson showed the commitment of the older company to invest in the development of Buell bikes in their own right: 'Now, thanks to the support offered to us by Harley-Davidson, we have the possibility to attain the growth I have always dreamed about. This new start is a demonstration of faith by Harley-Davidson in myself and the entire Buell team. And whereas our business is strongly expanding, I can tell you now that you ain't see nothing yet!'

In 1999, the opening of a 65,000 square foot research and development center near the factory in East Troy, Wisconsin, ensured modern internal growth to both Harley-Davidson and Buell. For Erik Buell, 'That is where the future of Buell will be developed.'

To general surprise in 2000, Buell presented a small and low bike that is easy to use in the city. After having produced a range of two-cylinder bikes, Buell brought out its first single cylinder. It was called the Buell Blast and has a 492 cc motor. The Blast is an ideal bike for a new public in America (it is available only in the United States) and it has received wide praise for its innovative features. Based on a Sportster engine, from which a cylinder was removed, it is fairly light and simple to handle which makes it ideal for novice motor-cyclists or for short daily journeys.

Buell's specialty is sports bikes, however, as is demonstrated by the XB 9R Firebolt, a bike with a very special configuration. With such a futuristic name, the Buell XB 9R had to be innovative: in fact, though it uses the traditional power plant derived from the Harley-Davidson Sportster type V-Twin, it produces 72 hp and a torque of 9.37 mkg at 7200 rpm. It is probable that, in the future, some Buells will make use of the V-Rod's Revolution motor since the company now belongs to

Harley-Davidson, although any supposition is valid since the Buell bikes now have a revolutionary frame like the KB 9R available to them.

The mechanical aspect of Buell bikes is not obsolete either, as the engine was entirely redesigned and now has a bore/stroke of 88.9 x 79.38 mm (3.5 x 3.125 in); these are figures that are more akin to a super square motor than a long stroke like the Harley-Davidson. The

engine in question develops 92 horsepower and has electronic injection, and the pin of the rear fork is anchored to the guards, thus making the XB 9R a modern bike despite remaining faithful to the V-Twin tradition from which it was developed.

Aesthetically, the XB 9R is a break with the other Buells as its huge air filter is no longer present on the left side and the frame has a highly visible, double aluminum beam, a fact which also allows it to act as a fuel tank. The fuel circulates freely in the

two side-members and around the steering column, thus lowering the center of gravity and freeing up the space necessary for the air-box, which is fed by an intake measuring 1.8 inches in diameter.

Then there are other new features: the XB 9R also has a larger exhaust than other Buells as the rear shock absorber no longer sits below the motor thanks to recent alterations to the frame. The Buell V-Twin Sportster has separate lubrication and,

whereas till now the oil tank has sat beneath the saddle, on the XB 9R it is the swingarm that acts as the tank. The space freed by the removal of the old oil tank means that the rear cantilever shock absorber can be positioned more conventionally as in the majority of modern sports bikes.

A closer look at the XB 9R brings to light even more specific innovations, for example, the front brake system – which uses a simple perimeter floating disk on which a 6-piston caliper operates – and the final transmission which combines a tension pulley with the traditional toothed chain. On this bike, the goal was not simply to provide the rear wheel with more power but to improve the effectiveness of all the low engine speeds to provide the rider with a truly pleasurable sporty ride and a new engine that can be exploited in any situation.

308 The Buell XB 9R represents the future of the company's bikes. It contains surprising but effective concepts in the frame and promises, in the short term, to do the same for the power plant.

309 The false fuel tank hides the air-box. The fuel is held in the beams of the frame and the oil in the rear fork!

Harley-Davidson Models

Since 2000, Harley-Davidson models have no longer been fitted with the 1340 cc Big Twin Evolution motor and are now divided into three distinct families based on three different types of V-Twin engines and sizes.

The main family is that of the 1450 cc Big Twins with a separate gearbox. These bikes are fitted with Twin-Cam 88 motors on the Dyna and Electra Glides, and with Twin-Cam 88B motors on the Softails. The bikes that have Evolution V-Twin engines fitted, with the engine casing where the gearbox is mounted, are the Sportsters: these have two engine sizes, 883 cc and 1200 cc. These two large families break down into different models, categorized by frame function for the Big Twins and by engine size and finishings for the Sportsters.

The third family of Harley-Davidson bike is the V-Rod, which currently comprises a single model but which is rapidly inspiring new ideas that will eventually form a range parallel to the other two families. Looking like a Low Rider Custom, the V-Rod is fitted with a Revolution engine that marks a new departure for the Milwaukee company. It is liquid cooled, with overhead camshafts and four valves per cylinder; it is no longer a long-stroke motor.

The engine unit meets the production criteria for modern, high performance V-Twins and matches the technical refinements on models produced by the competition, yet without sacrificing the Harley-Davidson spirit. This was the challenge that the company had to face, and it seems that it has won because the bike meets the expectations of a new slice of the motor-cycling public.

The Softail models include the Softail Standard, Night Train, Deuce, Fat Boy, Springer, Heritage Springer and Heritage Classic, all of which are reminiscent of bikes of the past but are fitted with modern technology.

The Dyna Glide family numbers the Dyna Super Glide, Dyna Low Rider, Dyna Convertible and Dyna Wide Glide.

The group of Touring Bikes comprises the Road King, Electra Glide Standard, Electra Glide Classic and Ultra Classic Electra Glide.

The 883 Sportsters are available in the Standard, Hugger (a lowered Standard), Racing and Custom 53 C versions. The Custom 53 C has a solid rear wheel.

The 1200 Sportsters are available in the Custom and Sport models.

The V-Rod, built around the Revolution engine, is the head of a new family. It is innovative mechanically, technically and aesthetically: low like a dragster, it is a perfect expression of the new, revolutionary power plant.

Harley-Davidson Nomenclature

FL/Electra Glide: full dresser, low compression, 4 gears, non-rubber mounted motor.

FLH/Electra Glide: full dresser, high compression, 4 gears, non-rubber mounted motor.

FLF/Electra Glide: with pedal gear change.

FLHS/Sport Solo: Electra stripped of its fairing, 4 or 5 gears.

FLHT/Electra Glide: full dresser, rubber mounted motor, 5 gears, fairing on fork.

FLHT/Electra Glide Standard: a basic Electra Glide but without the box and with minimal instrumentation to keep the price low, available since 1996.

FLT/Tour Glide: ditto, with fairing fixed to the frame.

FLTC/Electra/Tour: ditto, with two-tone paintwork.

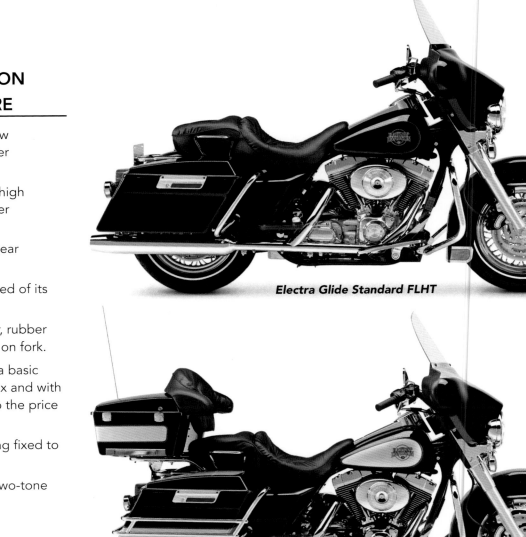

Electra Glide Standard FLHT

Electra Glide Classic FLHTC

Road King FLHR

Road King Classic FLHRCI

Ultra Classic Electra Glide FLHTCUI

FLHTC/FLHTCI/Glide Classic: Tour Pack, radio as optional extra. Available with carburetor or fuel injection since 1996.

FLHR/FLHRI/Road King: light Electra Glide, fitted with a removable windshield and side bags for a manageable touring bike. Available with carburetor or fuel injection since 1996.

FLHRCI/Road King Classic: fuel injection Road King with spoked wheels and leather a traditional old-fashioned look.

FLHTCU/FLHTCUI/Ultra Classic Electra Glide: Tour Pack, radio, electronic overdrive, CB, intercom. Available with carburetor or fuel injection since 1996.

FLTR/FLTRI/Road Glide: Electra Glide Standard with audio system and fairing fixed to the steering column. Available with carburetor or fuel injection.

FX/Super Glide: smaller fenders, narrower fork, 4 gears.

FXE/Super Glide: ditto, with electric starting.

FXEF/Super Glide: ditto, with dual tank.

FXS/Low Rider: the first Low Rider (with chain in 1977).

FXB/Sturgis: production Custom, belt-driven transmission. (1980-1982).

FXSB/Low Ride: ditto, but only secondary transmission was belt driven.

FXWG/Wide Glide: production Chopper, wide fork, 21" front wheel, Fat Bob fender.

FXEF/Low Rider: electric start and Fat Bob tank.

FXFB/Low Rider: basic Low Rider with kick start and Fat Bob.

FXDG/ Low Rider: rear wheel with disk brake (Disc Glide in 1982).

Road Glide FLTRI

Softail Standard FXST

Springer Softail FXSTS

FXST/Softail: rigid frame with shock absorber, 4 or 5 gears. New name: Softail Standard.

FXSTC/Softail Custom: ditto, customized version.

FXSTS/Softail Springer: Softail with Springer fork.

FLST/Softail Heritage: Softail Hydra Glide type fork.

FLSTC/FLSTCI Heritage Classic: Softail Heritage, 60s style. Available with carburetor or fuel injection.

FLSTF/FLSTFI Softail Fat Boy: Softail with solid wheels. Available with carburetor or fuel injection.

FLSTN/Heritage Nostalgia: Softail Heritage with saddle lined with cowhide.

Softail Deuce FXSTD

Softail Fat Boy

Softail Night Train FXSTB

FXSTSB/Bad Boy: Softail Springer that combines nostalgia with a contemporary look, painted entirely black.

FXSTB/Night Train: Softail Custom (telescopic fork), painted entirely black.

FXSTD/FXSTDI/ Softail Deuce: Softail with elegant lines and solid rear wheel. Available with carburetor or fuel injection.

FLSTS/Heritage Springer: Softail Springer with vintage appearance, inspired by a 1948 Panhead.

Heritage Softail Springer FLSTS

Heritage Softail Classic FLSTC

313

FXR/Super Glide: new frame, 5 gears, rubber-mounted motor, no accessories, (the name was Super Glide II, but the "II" quickly disappeared).

FXRS/Low Glide: ditto, with different Low Rider options and now called Low Rider.

FXRS-Sp/Sport Edition: ditto, suspension higher by 2 inches.

FXRS-CONV/Low Rider: ditto, with sport fairing and bags.

FXLR/Low Rider Custom: Low Rider customized with leather strip tank cover and counters on the handlebar.

FXRC/Low Rider: 1985 Low Rider Custom with candy-colored paint and a chrome engine.

FXRT/Sport Glide: Low Rider with fairing and touring bags made from glass-fiber.

FXRD/Sport Glide: ditto, with radio and Grand Touring options.

FXDL/Dyna Low Rider: Low Rider with new frame, rubber-mounted motor, gearbox casing adapted to the oil tank (model preceded by the Dyna Sturgis and Dyna Daytona versions).

FXDWG/Dyna Wide Glide: ditto, with wide fork.

FXD/Dyna Super Glide: Super Glide on a basic Dyna.

FXDS-CONV/Dyna Convertible: Low Rider on a basic Dyna with sport fairing and bags.

FXDX/Dyna Super Glide Sport: Dyna Super Glide fitted with a Twin-Cam 88 motor, dual front disks, low saddle and long stroke suspension.

FXDXT/Dyna Super Glide T-Sport: Dyna Super Glide fitted with a sport fairing, removable nylon bags, wide saddle and suspension suited to fast touring.

Dyna Low Rider FXDL

Dyna Super Glide FXD

Dyna Super Glide FXDX Sport

Dyna Super Glide T-Sport FXDXT

Dyna Wide Glide FXDWG

315

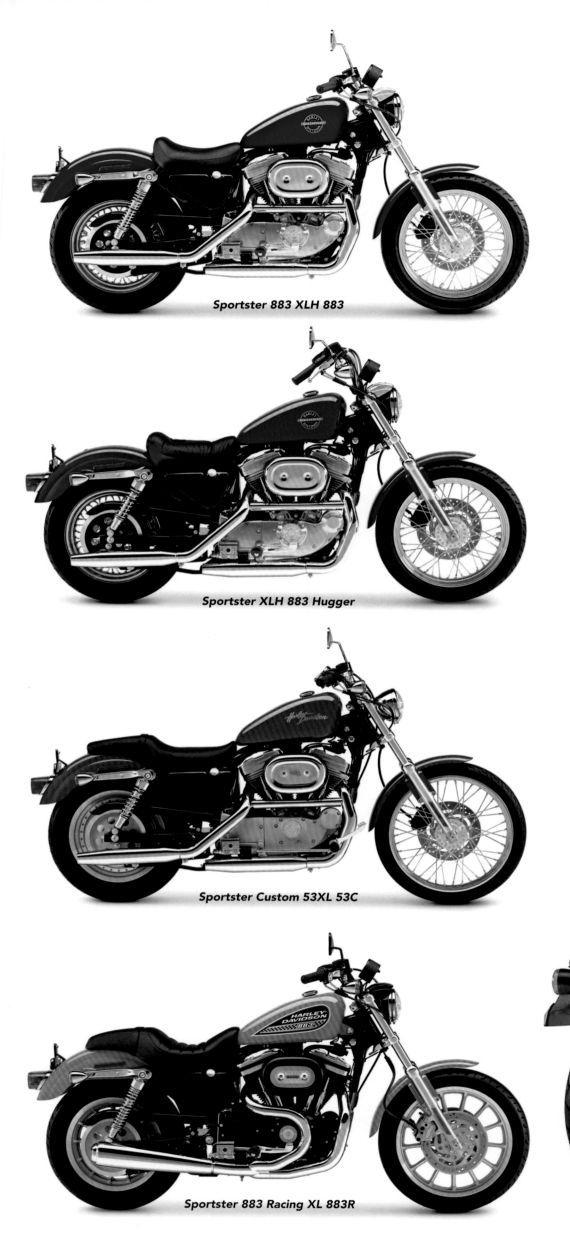

Sportster 883 XLH 883

Sportster XLH 883 Hugger

Sportster Custom 53XL 53C

Sportster 883 Racing XL 883R

XL/Sportster: the first Sportster, from 1957, followed by all the other Sportsters.

XLCH/Sportster: first high-performance Sportster, kick start.

XLH/Sportster: ditto, with electric start. The Evolution version of the basic Sportster was given this name.

XLH 883/Sportster: Standard version.

XLH-DLX 883/Sportster: De Luxe version.

XLH-HUG 883/Sportster: low version of the Sportster.

XLS/Roadster: customized version of the Sportster.

XL 53 C/Sportster Custom 53: custom Sportster 883 cc with solid rear wheel.

XL 883R/Sportster 883 Racing: Sportster with two-into-one exhaust, motor painted black and given XR 750 type racing decals.

XLH 1200/Sportster: Standard version.

XL 1200 S/Sportster: Sportster 1200 Sport.

XL 1200 C/Sportster: Sportster 1200 Custom.

XLT/Sportster: with touring equipment.

XLCR/Café Racer: the first and only Harley-Davidson Café Racer.

XLX/Sportster: entirely black version of the Sportster, cast iron motor, very low price.

XR 1000/Sportster: sports version inspired by the racing XR 750.

VRSCA V-ROD/V-Rod: new Harley-Davidson with a 1130 cc, 60° V-Twin engine, dual overhead cams, 4 valves per cylinder, liquid cooling and a very low Custom look.

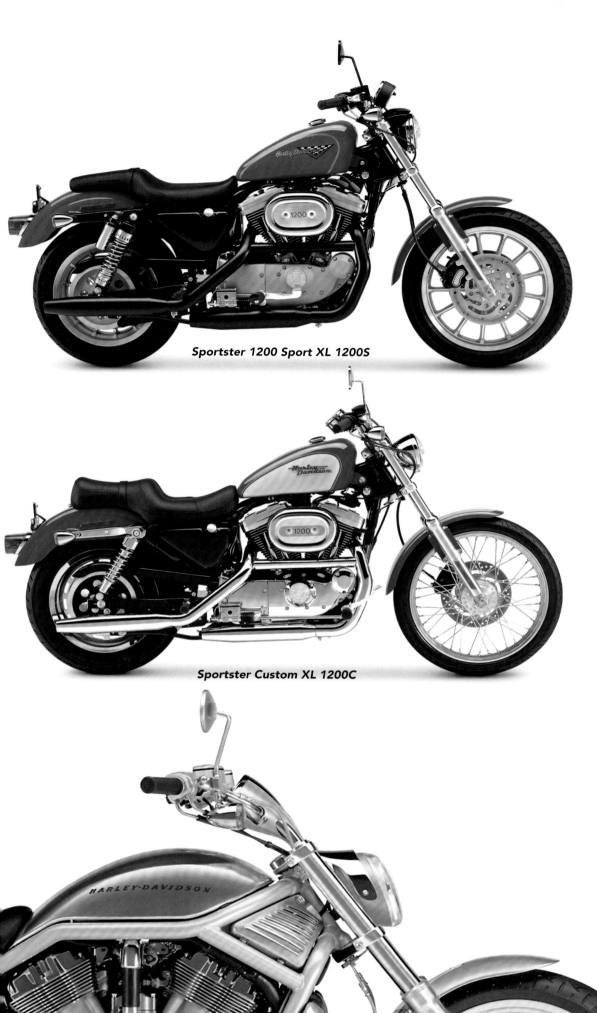

Sportster 1200 Sport XL 1200S

Sportster Custom XL 1200C

E-Harley-Davidson V-Rod 2002

BIG TWIN MOTORS

Flathead before and after 1936: 45 ci (750 cc), 74 ci (1200 cc), 80 ci (1340 cc), side valves, made from cast iron.

Knucklehead 1936-1947: 61 ci, 74 ci, made from cast iron.

Panhead 1948-1965: 61 ci, 74 ci, made from cast iron.

Shovelhead 1966-1983: 74 ci, 80 ci, made from cast iron.

Blockhead 1984-1999: 80 ci, cylinders and heads made from aluminum (Evolution).

Fathead 1999: 88 ci (1450 cc), cylinders and heads made from aluminum, 2 camshafts, chain-driven transmission with chain tightener. Named Twin Cam 88, and fitted to the Dyna and Electra Glides in 1999. The Twin Cam 88B version, with internal rocker arms, was fitted on the Softail range from 2000.

SPORTSTER MOTORS

From 1957 to 1985, the Sportster motors were similar to the Big Twins (cast-iron cylinders, aluminum heads). Since 1986, the Sportsters have been fitted with Evolution-type motors.

V-ROD MOTORS

Revolution 2002: 1130 cc, 60° V-Twin, 4 stroke, dual overhead camshafts, 4 valves per cylinder, push-button operated, liquid cooled. This motor was a development of the Twin-Cam 88.
Harley-Davidson has sold the new V-Rod bike, presented in July 2001, as part of the 2002 range since November 2001.

318-319 Harley-Davidson personalizations that focus on women can get pretty daring, sometimes mixed with cartoon heroes.

PART TWO

HARLEY DAVIDSON
EVOLUTION OF THE MITH

HARLEY-DAVIDSON

321 The Harley-Davidson tank is one of the essential elements to have contributed to the image of this American motorcycle.

322-323 Arlen Ness decided during the late 1990's to create a V-Twin motor.

324-325 With this Harley-Davidson dedicated to the actor James Dean, Cyril Huze succeeded once more.

326-327 In 1990 the designer decided to place major importance on the pictorial decoration of this original Softail.

328-329 This Softail Heritage is a good example of a customization.

THE HARLEY-DAVIDSON AND CUSTOMIZATION

THE HISTORY OF THE CULT

Since the very first Harley-Davidson model, designed by William Harley and Arthur Davidson, made its début in 1903, the V-Twin engined motorcycle has attracted a crowd of fans, some of whom have woven their lives and personalities around the machine.

Modernized and updated without changing its contours or hiding its Vee-shaped engine, it has ridden down the years for a whole century, with a series of V-Twin engines incorporating increasingly advanced technology: the Flathead, Knucklehead,

Panhead, Early Shovel, Shovelhead, Evolution, and the most recent Twin Cam 88. This bike has remained faithful to the spirit of its designers without disappointing the passion of those who over the years have become its apostles. It has survived sometimes dramatic situations, intensified by the passion it arouses, in one of the most fascinating adventures of the 20th century.

The Harley-Davidson is an American bike, conceived in the United States and designed for the vast American continent, featuring comfort and style that have remained

unchanged over the years. It has, however, incited other passions all over the world, even in countries that rejected the American capitalistic model. It inspired a new language with its own peculiar technical and universally understood vocabulary, as well as its own uniform: the legendary Perfecto jeans, leather boots, and sometimes a pair of chaps – leather leggings held up at the waist by a wide belt. The ensemble is completed with the compulsory leather jacket, preferably in black and festooned with the colors of various bike clubs,

Harley Davidson

330-331 You can expect to see just about anything at American custom bike shows because anything goes, but on occasion you have to wonder how on Earth it's possible for such a lack of taste to exist! The judges, however, have seen it all before. In general there are few real innovators – they can be counted on the fingers of one hand – and they are not worried at all by the level of the competition, which generally is no more than copies of customizations by famous artists or, more simply, bikes bought from famous artists. These are often exhibited by their new owners in the hope of winning a prize with a motorcycle that has already been exhibited by its true creator.

331 The quality of the bike, its age, nationality, or even the degree of transformation it undergoes are all of little importance if its owner wants to try his luck. In line with the principles of the Harley-Davidson's home country, the owner may freely and democratically display his mount, freshly polished so that no marks might spoil his chances of glory.

including perhaps the Harley Owners Group, which was set up by Harley-Davidson in '83 and now has over 200,000 members.

The years have left their mark not only on engine design but also on the wide range of available customizations, which dazzle the eye in a glistening frenzy: incredibly accentuated curves, highly chromed engines, and billet-alloy fittings. Now more than ever, the Harley-Davidson allows living legends and enthusiasts of the open road to live alongside everyday bikers.

Customization has become a new form of expression, honoring the artistic and creative impulses of every owner of the legendary V-Twin motorcycle.

Of course, customization of motorbikes has been around for a long time and appeared long before the first Harley-Davidson. The term refers to changes made to suit the customer's taste and covers both mechanical and aesthetic modifications.

In the early 1900s it was not uncommon for people to construct their own bikes by assembling elements, such as the frame, the engine, the wheels, the fork and other pieces, manufactured by a variety of craftsmen. It is therefore easy to imagine how incompatibility between pieces often led to badly assembled engines and gearboxes. One had to be an accomplished mechanic to take a ride on one of these machines – or at least be prepared for a lot of walking.

The reliability of Harley-Davidson's "Silent Grey Fellow" reduced customization to a bare minimum and focused it especially on technical, rather than aesthetic, changes.

It was only towards the 1920s that

332-333 This is a teardrop tank that has been shortened in the style of a very restrained chopper and splendidly decorated with portraits, landscapes, and flames in a tightly packed whole. The tasteful combination of colors emphasizes the relief of certain items and accentuates the chosen theme of the paintwork.

accessory catalogues appeared featuring practical and useful items such as windshields, saddlebags, leg shields, and chrome-plated headlights. The availability of these parts soon led to competitions with prizes for the Bike of the Month or the Most Original Bike, encouraging bike owners to personalize their machines and render them more suitable for long-distance rides or more sporty or aggressive, according to their individual tastes and personalities. Customization was also an excellent way of boosting business.

At the end of the 1950s a number of bikers began modifying their machines in very specific ways – greatly lowering their center of gravity and further simplifying the body's overall contours. These modified versions were often quite difficult to ride, with their large rear wheel generally

contrasted by a very slim front one perched far ahead of a small, frequently decorated tank. Baptized "choppers," they were a new and original way to affirm the rider's freedom and distinguish him from all those who didn't share the same outlook on life.

Custom, a typically American word, soon earned connotations of rebellion, of consciously being different, and of breaking away from the mainstream. Bikers' dreams of wide-open spaces and the endless roads across the vast American continent soon fired a subculture's passion for these bikes.

An archetype of this subculture is the legendary Keith Ball, who went out into the two-wheeled world at the tender age of 16 and has never looked back since.

As a boy, Ball used to constantly dream of riding down the highway astride his own customized chopper. He mentally redesigned all the two-wheelers that he went crazy about in magazines, and soon, although he's quick to point out "too late," discovered the charms of the large V-Twin for himself. Its sensual curves, its rhythmic and guttural engine sound, the smell of hot oil...all of these inspired wild dreams of thrilling rides and literally made him shiver with anticipation. Later, while riding one of his dream machines, he came to the realization that he couldn't help but start designing bikes himself. It seemed the only way to satisfy his urge to be ever faster on California's highways and the envy of all bikers. Keith Ball seems to have always lived the biker's lifestyle. Yet now he's a designer and manufacturer of commercial custom accessories, an accomplished novelist, a metal sculptor, poet, journalist, and even the vice-president of the $35 million Paisano Publications group. Paisano's best known title is *Easyriders* magazine, the bible of the biker's world, now published in English, Japanese, French, Spanish, German, and Italian. The magazine is devoted exclusively to the biking culture and designed for an ever-changing readership. Even at the threshold of the third millennium, the Paisano group still undertakes surveys and quality studies to better understand the needs of Harley-Davidson users and provide them with sector-specific news stories, advice, entertainment, and information.

336-337 A Softail Springer customized in the Native-American style and produced by Paragon Locomotion, which has not hesitated to create a splendidly detailed job right down to the seat. As far as the engine is concerned, despite its artwork and S&S carburetor, it's still an original Evolution.

338-339 A simple custom bike by Paragon Locomotion. It's still an almost original Softail Springer but has the single addition of a Harley Performance Screamin' Eagle carburetor. The Harley front fender has been brought as close to the wheel as possible to make the bike as slender as it can get.

334 top This is an Arlen Ness bike from the 1990s based on a Softail Custom. The swingarm has been replaced with one by the Arlen Ness Co.

334 bottom This simple design reflects the taste of the owner of this Softail Springer. Its customization was limited to the replacement of the original rear fender with a wraparound model, the installation of ape-hanger handlebars, and a paint job designed to glorify a star.

335 Here's a multicolored row of tanks painted to reflect the themes of a famous name in the world of Harley-Davidson customization. The skulls and flames reflect the imagination of another American artist who lives and works in California, Ron Simms. Ron is the builder of classically designed bikes with impeccable finishes, but unfortunately his work is copied by many others whose limited means impinge on the quality of the designs and their realization.

EASYRIDERS AN EASY READ

Paisano Publications launched the magazine *Easyriders*, mainly targeted at Harley-Davidson fans, in 1971. Over time the magazine gradually bought up or created various other titles to enable the publishing group to reach the largest possible number of biking fans in the greatest number of segments and focusing on all different centers of interest. The company Easyriders Inc. was eventually taken public, and its first purchase offering on the New York Stock Exchange saw an initial capitalization of $76 million. Four years later the company began licensing its name for use on a large number of products, and it now owns a retail franchise chain of 30 outlets and growing. The group's policy with its outlets is to boost visibility, and therefore readership and advertising income, along with selling motorcycles and accessories. Easyriders' business is of course very dependent on the popularity of Harley-Davidsons as well as that of the handful of other US motorcycle brands.

At the close of the 20th century, there are some 900,000 Harley-Davidsons registered in the US. The customer profile is of course critical. The typical Harley-Davidson (or other US-brand bike) owner is male, between 35 and 65, has an average income of $70,000 per year, and enjoys a new image in the eyes of the public – not least because politicians and businessmen don't hesitate to pose for the press with their bikes nowadays, which are naturally all – American brands.

One last figure worth mentioning: in December of 1997, the publishing group's total circulation topped 4,100,000 copies.

WITNESS

Keith Randall Ball is known worldwide under the pen-name "Bandit," and from the start his work has fascinated *Easyriders'* readers. In the 1970s his first two stories, *Prize Possession* and *Outlaw Justice,* were instant hits with bikers.

During his long career Ball has restored virtually all of Harley-Davidson's classic models and customized all types of two-wheelers, including choppers. He is unquestionably one of the greatest international authorities on American bikes and, in his role with Paisano Publications, often the first to inspect new customs. In his writings, his expert analysis pays tribute to the talented designers and craftsmen he has come to know who have made customization a fine art form.

TIMES PAST AND FUTURE

Since it's impossible to elaborate on anything Keith Ball can say on this subject, I have asked him tell us the story of the classic chopper (and its impact) in his own words. As a firsthand witness and participant in this unique and crucial stage of American biking, Keith is able to bring back to life a piece of aesthetic history that left its mark on an entire generation, creating a lifestyle legend and inspiring the dreams of thousands of fans.

Keith Ball lived through this period and felt all of its effects firsthand. He knows all the key players of the era and was himself intimately shaped by their influence. Without question, he is uniquely suited to explain the role of the chopper in the history of custom bikes.

340 and 341 This is Keith R. Ball on the Street Stalker Harley-Davidson. The bike has been fitted with bodywork manufactured and sold by the Harley-Davidson Motor Company in an attempt by the Milwaukee firm to enter the custom market. These products allow anyone to transform their Softail without great expenditure, thus giving the bike a personal touch without spoiling its standard qualities. The model being ridden by Ball was assembled by the California dealer Bartel's with the addition of a Screamin' Eagle ignition and a carburetor transformed with the help of Departure Bike Works. The Harley kit used to customize a Softail is called the Street Stalker. Nor should it be forgotten – as Keith reminds us – that it is due to Wyatt Fuller and Little John Buttera that the Milwaukee company finally entered what is known in the States as the aftermarket parts business. Now any fan of the V-Twin can easily transform the appearance of his Softail.

THE HISTORY OF THE CUSTOM CHOPPER

WHERE DID IT ALL START? BY KEITH RANDALL BALL

Was it Von Dutch who invented the first chopper in the midst of an avocado plantation in Santa Paula, California? Or was it Ed Roth in his hotrod stronghold in Los Angeles' South Bay area?

Did it all start in the 1950s with the film *The Wild One*, or just before that when Harley fans started stripping their machines to make them lighter and faster on the flat-track circuit? Did it start like skateboarding, with kids nailing 2x4 planks to their roller-skates, or did the craze catch on during the 1940s when Harley-Davidson launched its classic black-leather jacket?

No matter what, it truly took hold with the hotrod mindset of the 1950s, when a few teenagers decided to simplify and lighten their bikes to boost speed for drag, flat-track, and hillclimb racing. This was just after the War, when bikes went for ridiculously low prices. A Harley Knucklehead would fetch next to nothing at the time, and the new owner's aim was to strip it immediately of its fenders, add a raised single

342 left Brother Ben Hardy is an unknown name to most American bike fans, yet he has played a significant role in the development of the customization business. From his workshop in the Florence area of Los Angeles, Brother Ben supplied the parts used to build the bikes ridden by Peter Fonda and Dennis Hopper in the film Easy Rider. These were quite possibly the most influential custom motorcycles of the last 50 years.

seat, mount quick-throttle handlebars by Flanders, and head straight for the track and their first breakneck ride.

The chopper started off the same way most other trends do: with the same yearning to be different, to be noticed, to shock, and to provoke one's friends and acquaintances. All this was easily possible, thanks in large part to the untapped talents of the machinists, welders, mechanics, and bodywork experts who had recently discovered the full scope of their creative potential working on customized cars.

Ed Roth and Von Dutch are shining examples of talented men who worked on both cars and bikes. The hotrodders were just a bunch of bad guys who stuck to four-wheelers until they discovered what they could do with a Harley stripped of its superfluous elements. After that they decided to take up the challenge of bikes and re-invent them from scratch.

After a short flat-tracking period, this group of rebels decided to abandon the conformist milieu of the American Motorcycle Association. They also distanced themselves from the more conservative of the hotrodders, refusing to follow in the footsteps of tradition and deciding instead to simply enjoy themselves as much as possible. They created a whole new social fabric in the process: They became Outlaws, the so-called "One Percents."

Apart from Motorcycle Goodies (a division of Harley-Davidson Los Angeles), there were no suppliers of custom pieces for bikes at this time. Hap Jones, Gary Bang, and Flanders were not yet involved in customized bikes; their sole aim instead was to supply flat-trackers and the fans of British bikes with spares such as Bates headlights, solo seats, and aluminum footrests. If you wanted an extended front fork you had to go to the junkyard, fish out a pair of Ford pipes, and mount them on a Harley Springer frame. Well into the 1960s bikers used to make their own sissybars, and the only rear fenders available that weren't Harley-made were the ones sold as spares for Triumphs. In short, what couldn't be found at the local dump was simply stripped off another bike.

As Barry Cooney puts it, "Most custom bikes were built using a combination of parts mainly stripped off Triumphs and Harleys. The first custom V-Twin with a Narrow Glide front fork was built using Sportster parts. The guys cut their rear fenders at their fixtures, simply removed the front fender, and replaced the Fat Bob gas tank with a peanut tank from a Sportster. Then they mounted 19- or 21-inch front wheels." This was during the era when Barry worked on BSAs, Nortons, and Triumphs; when Easy Rider aroused renewed public interest in biking, Barry decided to open his own workshop specializing in Harley-Davidsons.

342 bottom right This is the front of Ben's shop, Hardy's, which built choppers and sold second-hand bike parts during the 60s.

342-343 and 343 Peter Fonda on his "Captain America" chopper will always be part of the Harley-Davidson legend. Easy Rider was released at the end of the turbulent '60s and attained worldwide acclaim, perhaps for the concept of freedom that it preached. The theme of the film was how the lifestyle of the two heroes was not accepted in the South and how they were treated with hostility by the locals. The film was a call to freedom and a tribute to wide-open spaces. As soon as it came out it became a rallying cry for bikers.

FONDA'S EASY RIDER

"Before the film *Easy Rider*, only bike-club members chopped their bikes. But after the film, a new generation of hippie bikers emerged. They were not violent; by and large they were strictly interested in free love, sex, experimenting with new drugs, and rock 'n' roll."

In the early 1970s' bike workshops proliferated like mushrooms. AEE Choppers and D&D Distributors started manufacturing and distributing accessories, while Santec began producing frames. Dick Allen got into the production of Springer forks.

The custom-bike boom was under way, and it was then, in 1971, that Arlen Ness opened his first workshop: "Up to the time I opened my shop, the general rule was that you built your own bike," Arlen recalls. "You started with rigid frames, ribbed Triumph fenders, Bates headlights, and nothing was more cool than a 21-inch wheel. You could then throw in a few accessories, such as an English peanut gas tank, Hap Jones' ape-hanger handlebars mounted on dogbone risers produced by Flanders, and Dixie mufflers. The accessories had to be transformed one by one. It was only at the end of the 1960s that we started changing the frame significantly and increasing the angle of the steering column."

D&D was founded by Jo Teresi and Mill Blair. The distribution company started off with five accessories for Harleys. Then the two partners discovered a local bike workshop and asked the engine technicians to manufacture other accessories, especially attachment fixtures for Springer forks. Boyd de France, D&D Choppers' machinist, could come up with all the two partners needed. The business took off immediately with a series of frames, extended forks, and spares for Panhead Harleys.

Paughco was also one of the first companies to manufacture chrome-plated

"the bike builders encyclopedia"
Choppers magazine
NOVEMBER 1969 75¢ a Roth publication

A grand tour thru the Harley factory with "PIG" from Milwaukee.
Closeups of Pe... nda's "Easy Rider" bike! Plus Boris Murray from drag strip to Bonneville. ...ey mechanic ...ck Blythe builds a ... ...d chopper!

Easyrider

primary chain guards for Knuckleheads and Panheads, plus a range of mufflers and frames. Ron Paugh started his bike business when the aerospace industry crashed in 1969. "In fact the guys at Laidlaws approached me in 1967 and asked me to think about a design for chain guards for bikes. It took me two years to really get started in this. When the aerospace industry crashed in 1969, my team immediately produced 500 chain guards. The very first day, Laidlaws picked up 100 and my new business was launched. We got into manufacturing one chain guard, one universal carburetor box, and a muffler set. The aerospace industry rose from its ashes

but it was too late for me – I was simply far too happy making accessories for choppers. I just went straight ahead with my new business, never looking back."

The East Coast was not immune to the chopper craze either. In Brockton, Mass., Dave Perewitz set up Cycles Fabrications, which at the time focused exclusively on Sportsters. As Dave explains, "I was transforming Sportster frames into rigid frames. I used to extend them to the limit, build sissybars, and install Springer forks." In 1976 he became the king of engraved accessories and for two decades has supplied the custom-motorcycle industry with his rocker-arm covers and engraved fork tubes.

344 and 345 left The cover of the July issue of a monthly trade mag, published by Roth Publications in 1969, shows a truly unusual chopper. The front fork is intriguing and, while quite original, could not have been very satisfactory dynamically. Although its unusual style was worthy of appearing on the cover of this magazine, a periodical dedicated solely to choppers could probably not survive today. Choppers were part of a particular period, long gone, and now are rarely seen in shows. They have been superseded by bikes boasting modifications made possible by the advances of technology seen in the last 30 years.

345 top and center Arlen Ness brought out his first catalogue in 1976, six years after he opened his workshop. It was a simple document that showed his customers the first accessories he designed and sold himself. Since then the Ness catalogue has come out bigger and better every season.

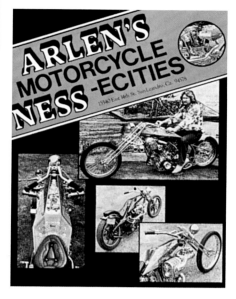

CHOPPERS MAGAZINE
NOVEMBER 1969

this month features...

Easy Rider 16

Harley Factory 22

Nichols' Jewel 34

Heavy Harley 46

also...

BIG DADDY SPEAKS

I just got the latest show program from the big show car promotor in the east. More chrome fantasy! Useless junk to clutter the big auditoriums! All types of bodies mounted on the T frame. From telephone booths and beds to Popcorn vending machines. One hundred and thirteen pages of this trash. One page was devoted to three bikes of national fame. (Finch's Kaleidascope, Lonscar's "Dr. Jeckyl" and Heitman's Invader) We (the public) will again be subjected to more of these dream cars that never hit the streets. They are nice, sure! But why do these shows stress cars? Because the image of the bike is a necessary evil to these shows. They are afraid of the troubles that plagued the N.Y. Show . . . the troubles caused by so called bike riders. They arrived in buses. Picture that if you will . . . So instead of all the promotors getting more and bigger trophies for bikes, they get cars like George Barris' Ice Cream Wagon and cover 'em with tinsel and forget the truly soul bikes around. The laws say America is free! On a cycle you can dress like an astronaugt or wear levi's, but if you're gonna wear the grubbies, there are a lot of kids that are gonna be watchin' and a lot of promotors that are gonna say yes or no on better bikes for next years show circuit. It's up to you riders!!

CHOPPERS MAGAZINE is published monthly by Roth Studios . . . a private business located at 4616 E. Slauson Avenue in Maywood Calif. 90270. Managing editor is Jim Jacobs and publisher and sole owner is Ed Roth. One year subscriptions are $7.27. BACK ISSUES available to Feb. '68 for 75¢ ea. Advertising rates and circulation figures available from Robert Williams. SECOND CLASS mailing is paid at MAYWOOD Post Office. 90270

PHOTO TECH...Howard Roth
LAYOUT...Jake Jacobs
MAGAZINE FRIENDSHIP...Robert Williams

Dave says that Kelsey's Customs, set up in Beverly, Mass., customized Triumphs and Harleys for years before finally focusing on hotrods. The East Coast also became a large accessory-distribution center after Larry and Mike Coppola set up the Nempco organization in 1969. Nempco's accessories, such as oil tanks, fork tubes, battery boxes, and forks, were produced by Danny Puccio, whose father had a large factory. Danny used to secretly slip into the machining room at night to fabricate accessories for choppers. It was only when Danny became the Great Imperial Genius of custom Harley-Davidson accessories on the East Coast that his father got wind of what he was up to!

Then publishing veteran Lou Kimsey and his partner in the magazine *Big Bikes* joined up with Joe Teresi and Mill Blair to found *Easyriders*. As we said earlier, the fledgling chopper industry came to fruition between 1961 and 1971 with companies like AEE Choppers, Motorcycle Goodies, D&D Distributors, Paughco, Mother's Choppers, and a handful of others.

Then, from early 1972 onwards, motorcycle workshops started sprouting all over the country, making way for the continuous creation of new types of accessories. The rules of

345 bottom In 1990 I photographed a copy of Peter Fonda's Captain America chopper, a model of extraordinary importance to the world of Harley-Davidson. Today the California Motorcycle Co. builds new copies of Captain America using the Evolution motor with Panhead-style covers, creating impressively reliable facsimiles of the original. The company also builds copies of the "Billy Bike" ridden by Dennis Hopper in Easy Rider.

the game haven't changed much since then: a chopper's outer appearance is the visual reflection of the creative talents (and shortcomings) of the men who designed and fabricated it. In other words, a custom bears immediate witness to the talent of its fabricator: his intimate knowledge of the machine as well as his skill at aesthetic and technological innovation.

The more a biker personally customizes his own bike the more respect he earns in custom-bike circles, and vice versa. It would, however, be a mistake to think that accessory manufacturers suffer because of this. In fact, the market grows in step with public interest in custom bikes. It was in the early 1970s that D&D started manufacturing extended forks that were much safer than home-made custom forks. Paughco

kept constantly busy. (Of course, each workshop still featured at least one person dressed in the obligatory black T-shirt, his hair a lot longer than the others' and his long beard swaying dangerously close to the machinery.) During the 1980s many workshops began producing billet-aluminum accessories, a costly, new, high-tech category for the costly, new, high-tech Harley-Davidson. A whole new concept of Harley customizing had been born.

Harley-Davidson was making the most of its return from near-death, manufacturing increasingly advanced pieces throughout the 1980s. The V-Twin Shovelhead engine was totally redesigned to produce the Evolution mill of 1984. At a stroke it erased the company's reputation for unreliability and dealt a positive twin impact to the

sale and manufacture of V-Twin accessories. However, this did not stop many Harley customers from abandoning the brand in the 1980s after being sourly disappointed by the marque's lack of reliability.

In short, the industry hit a lull just as its quality and technology began to rise. Much of this was also caused by simple social trends. Many drug aficionados were either sitting in prison at this point or had settled down to start families and take up stable jobs. Other bikers had grown up, slowed down, passed on, settled in.

Harley seemed to be in its death throes yet again, but finally managed to struggle back to profitability at the end of the 1980s with the emergence of a new group of customers, the RUBs (Rich Urban Bikers): People who had raised their families and

produced frames featuring new angles in the steering column, eliminating the risks involved in making one's own changes in the garage. Custom seats were introduced to the growing list of available accessories, gradually replacing the ubiquitous Bates pillion seat. Whole ranges of sissybars designed to adapt to special bikes were also launched on the market. Besides providing greater comfort they eliminated the risks linked to improvised sissybars, which often tended to rub against the rear tire. And so a leisure activity was transformed into a multimillion-dollar industry.

By the late 1970s the custom industry was in full bloom, with a few large distributors and a network of 3000 specialized retailers. The industry had taken off after the cult film *Easy Rider* debuted, and was soon identified with the rock 'n' roll scene as well. It started leaning heavily towards the drug culture at the same time, creating a lifestyle featuring ongoing parties and easy women.

This was dangerous living: high-speed bikes, all-night blowouts, the use and sale of illegal drugs, music that made you lose both your hearing and your memory. At this pace no one really wanted to live a night longer – except perhaps to see the following weekend. Despite all the offenses, however – the prison time, the women, and the deaths – the industry somehow managed to produce increasingly innovative machines right up to the beginning of the 1980s, a decade which happily opened a new era for Harley-Davidson.

Even as motorcycle workshops replaced single-function machine tools with CNC mills capable of operating in four axes sim-ultaneously, their engineers and staff were

industry. On the one hand the Evolution engine was sturdier, more sophisticated, and set in new rubber mounts, making it possible to travel long distances without the slightest trouble. On the other hand, the new engine was placed inside a Softail frame, affording greater rider comfort.

The new generation of bikers could also now customize their bikes using a range of billet-aluminum accessories. The seemingly endless and constantly updated list of available parts included new brakes, wheels, controls, fenders, etc. Former aerospace workshops were converted to the

proven themselves in their jobs and now wanted to return to the thrill of biking.

The 1990s would be marked by a boom in manufacturers of billet-aluminum accessories and costly customizations. High-end shops and manufacturers started popping up all over the United States, their aim to reach the market with the modified bikes that Harley could not produce fast enough themselves. It started with the notorious Illusion Motorcycle Company, and today we have Titan, California Motorcycle Company, Big Dog, American Iron Horse, Ultra, and a list that grows by the month. Custom-bike producers

346-347 This chopper perfectly shows how technical progress now allows a frame to have bodywork fitted to it which reflects the tastes of the owner. For example, note the wraparound rear fender, the addition of saddlebags, and the shape of the fenders. Today the chopper has become a middle-class nostalgia item and, though still a means of expression, it is now simply a matter of design.

347 top Choppers have changed with the passing of the years but they still retain nostalgia and an air of rebellion. Today they are a means of artistic expression, mostly as a result of technological developments of the past 30 years. This V-Twin motor is an Evolution mill originally built for a Softail frame.

who struggled to make ends meet in the 1970s have now become household names at the head of multimillion-dollar manufacturing, retail, service, and mail-order businesses.

Arlen Ness and his son Cory now run a company with an annual turnover of $10 million. Dave Perewitz distributes his own range of accessories. Rick Doss, Donnie Smith, Ron Simms, Randy Simpson, Cyril Huze, Eddie Trotta, and a handful of others have been around for nearly three decades, and their companies continue to generate profits year after year.

Now another generation of motorcycle fans are in the making: The X-Generation. What will become of the chopper, customized bikes, and the biking industry in general under their influence?

No one can tell. Is the Harley bad-boy image going to survive? Are Japanese cruisers going to continue attacking the market? Are bikes in general going to continue to remain popular? Will new laws finally put an end to the lifestyle of those who live for biking and its industry? I doubt it, but I'll be there to watch and report.
—Keith Randall Ball

348-349 This custom bike is a creation of the famous brake manufacturer Jay Brainard (better known as Jay Brake) and his son. The bike benefits from all the advantages offered by their company regarding binders and the design of wheels and transmissions. As far as aesthetics are concerned, the lengthening of the frame allows this model to hide its battery and oil tank. What is not surprising about this bike is the quality of its braking components. The system has been built so that friction is applied to the edge, not the middle, of the brake discs. The manufacturer claims this process allows better rotor cooling and more-progressive braking action.

THE LIVES AND PHILOSOPHIES OF TWO GREAT ARTISTS

TO UNDERSTAND AND ACCEPT

It is not easy for just anyone to understand why and how a person expresses his art and passion on a motorcycle. Bikes are often considered noisy contraptions of metal, plastic, and rubber intended to provide a simple end result—transportation.

A Harley-Davidson cannot, however, be considered as just an engine-driven machine on two wheels. It must also be perceived as the cornerstone of a complete lifestyle, something part and parcel of its owner.

Harley-Davidson bikes have aroused passions for nearly 100 years and drained the creative talents of various movements, each hoping to express itself through a subculture based on a vibrating machine with contours that always seem in fashion.

Harleys are also a very important economic phenomenon – first of course for the Harley-Davidson Motor Company, which has taken full advantage of the fashion and following related to its marque, but also to a vast and varied aftermarket based on travel, meetings, and a wide array of useful, less-than-useful, or purely decorative parts.

The range of accessories stretches from

simple tin models manufactured in limited series (a very successful commercial technique in the USA) to a collection of watches, Zippo lighters (another American legend), glasses and goggles to suit all types of bikers, helmets, boots, jackets, and all kinds of matching, signed clothing *ad nauseum*. All of these things are presented in a collection of products that are for the most part renewed every year and are often used by those who are not even motorcycle owners or riders.

There are lines of specially customized furnishings and musical instruments available which honor – or cash in on – the legend of the Milwaukee V-Twin motorcycle. Harley and its style have even inspired the world of traditional artists, many of whom now paint canvasses focusing on these motorcycles in a variety of natural, contemporary, or futuristic

situations. Even the toy industry has been able to benefit, actively nurturing future bikers with small-scale reproductions of Dad's motorcycle. Some toys even incorporate such realistic effects as a digitally produced V-Twin engine note.

Beyond all this, serious technicians work constantly to develop new mufflers, wheels, carburetors, leather saddlebags, seats, etc. All these things are made available so that each owner can transform his bike into a unique model, thus giving customization its true meaning as a creative technique without limits (especially prized in a country that encourages private initiative).

To illustrate this world I have chosen two master builders who, although from different origins and cultures, are equally talented in the creation of two-wheeled art.

350-351 Here are two master builders: Arlen Ness (left) and Cyril Huze (right). Their creations are both gracious and elegant, but they use widely different themes which reflect their differing personalities. Neither builder accepts compromises and both demand perfection. Work for both is a joy and creating an obsession. Both are considered great artists, and both have become legends in the biking world.

LIVE AND CREATE
OUT OF PASSION

Arlen Ness

" *Customizing and redesigning parts for*
motorcycles has always been a passion
and natural ability for me.
I have never been formally
trained in design.
I have always been partial to smooth-flowing,
well proportioned lines.
Art Deco styling has always been a
favorite of mine. "

ARLEN NESS

352-353 Arlen Ness poses with pride on one of his later creations, the SmoothNess, a work of art whose body is made entirely from hand-smoothed aluminum. Once again the master builder surprised the public (after all, he had to), this time by creating a near-envelope body for his motorcycle. SmoothNess is powered by a V-Twin quite similar to a Harley 1340, but which is in fact an assembly of non-OE parts supplied by different companies. It dates from 1992 and the motor was built by Jeff Border. The pistons are from Harley stock, the cylinders from S&S, and the cylinder heads come from the hotrod specialists at Edelbrock. The carburetor is once again an S&S model, but the air filter and exhaust are unique, both being made entirely by hand. The frame of this aluminum monster is a 1992 Arlen Ness version of the Smooth Tail Rubbermount design; the engine had to be mounted on deformable block supports so that its vibrations would be damped and absorbed rather than transmitted through the frame to the fragile light-alloy bodywork. The tank was built by Craig Naff, the rear lighting came from Arlen Ness himself, and the seat was done by Ness's faithful collaborator Danny Gray. The fork – an important element of this bike – is a Japanese-sourced 39mm with two inches of travel and the wheels are both 18-inchers. The result is an elegant machine with great lines. SmoothNess further increased Ness's reputation, raised the standard of the industry again, and provided endless inspiration to others.

DIFFERENT PALETTES FOR THE SAME PASSION

Arlen Ness was brought up in the midst of hotrods and chopped Harley-Davidsons in San Francisco, California. He launched his career by painting his first bike while continuing to work as a trucker and a carpenter to fund his passion. His wise choice would soon bear rich fruit, as is the case with many persistent amateurs of talent. Not until the age of 28 could Ness manage to support himself by working as a full-time motorcycle designer and constructor.

Since that time Arlen has consolidated his reputation across the United States and the world in a field where the exceptional talent of those known as "creators" is readily recognized. Arlen Ness's career developed very quickly, in fact, lock-step in tune with the cadence of a V-Twin Harley-Davidson. Though recognized early on, his commercial fortunes only truly began soaring at the end of the 1980s. He was among the first to use computerized CNC machine tools to mass-produce and commercialize superb aluminum accessories for V-Twin motorcycles.

This success spurred him to try and conquer the European market, where he encountered French decorative art and the majestic lines of antique automobiles and sensually curvaceous Italian sports cars. His creative capacity was enlarged in Europe, and on his return he produced range after range of custom bikes with bodywork that was at once daring for its technical difficulty and harmonious for its soft, non-aggressive lines. His bodywork has become a milestone

354 and 355 A few strokes of a pencil: Arlen Ness is seen while he is creating. Ness feels a sketchpad is the best way to express creativity; this is far from the image many have of a sophisticated design loft with computers and CADD programs. Once he has embarked on a project and found a theme, Arlen transforms the initial idea into a realizable concept by studying the laws of air penetration, fuel use, and constructability. Creating what may seem unimaginable is his goal, and also a business necessity. Today, his name is not only added to bikes but an entire line of clothing.

in the world of custom bikes and assured his eternal fame as a designer.

Arlen Ness has gradually built a family-controlled empire specializing in custom motorcycles. Today his catalogue includes everything required to build a custom motorcycle from scratch, plus special sections dedicated to a biking-wear line for men and women. Ness has influenced a large number of other designers, his philosophy being ceaseless innovation without imitation.

Fully aware of his skill as a designer, innovator, constructor, and pioneer, Arlen Ness has clearly expressed his intention to devote most of his time and energy now to creation. His heir-apparent, Cory Ness, has comfortably assumed many of the business aspects at the company.

but about almost anything under the sun. He makes unforgettable dinner company because of his knowledge, simplicity, and kindness. When Ness is at ease, he opens up and talks freely about his passion and how it all started.

"When I was about 14 years old my father gave me a scooter, a Cushman. I improved it a bit and used it to ride around the neighborhood. At 16 I sold that and got my first car. My father was dead against buying me a real motorcycle, although he didn't mind the scooter. In fact, I didn't actually own my own bike until my 20s. I had been already married for a few years and my wife didn't want me to buy a bike, but I would often visit one particular neighborhood where bikers hung around.

A CLOSER VIEW OF A LEGEND

Up close Arlen Ness has nothing in common with the classic image of a biker. He seems more of an informal executive, dressed in a light-colored cotton sports shirt with a buttoned-down collar, flapped pockets, and his company logo embroidered on the breast. Black jeans over lizard-skin boots and a matching lizard belt complete his ensemble.

Ness is a true artist who has become, to some extent despite himself, another legend in the dreamy universe of biking. Naturally friendly, he is always ready to give an autograph on almost anything, but he is most at ease when quietly dining with two or three close friends in a San Francisco restaurant, chatting not only about bikes

At the time I knew nothing about it, much less about brands and the various models available. I simply fell in love with the low shapes and the looks of what I learned later on were Harley-Davidsons.

From that time on I started saving - without letting my wife know about it. I bought a secondhand Harley without even knowing how to ride it. A friend had to help me bring it home. Imagine how Bev (his wife) reacted to that!

Since I was already used to repainting and making changes on cars and hotrods, I started doing the same thing on this bike. Later some friends started asking me to repaint their bikes. In this period I didn't have much spare time; I was working six days a week driving trucks. But for the sheer passion of it all, I changed jobs and became a carpenter, which left me 4-1/2 days a week. That left me more free time to repaint friends' bikes."

356 and 357 Arlen works in his company office with various engineers who are familiar with his ways, his requirements, and his customers. After years spent working with these men, some of whom have shared his rise to success, Arlen assigns them work with complete faith in their abilities. Nothing is done on the customers' bikes without the opinion of the boss; he spends a lot of time talking to his collaborators. Ideal solutions are easier to find when working together with people who have plenty of experience with the V-Twin and customization. Arlen works only in his personal workshop when it is necessary to make transformations to his creations or simply to get construction of a new custom under way. Still, he does like working in an environment where he has all his points of reference handy. The workshop is a tranquil, uncommercial setting that is eminently suitable for producing work far removed from the mundane.

At first Ness was fascinated by the bikes themselves: their beauty and their dangerous, exciting appeal. It was only much later, when he met real bikers for the first time, that he realized that motorcycling could represent something else. At that time a huge portion of bikers were outlaws, the so-called "One Percents" who exclusively rode Harleys.

As a teenager Arlen had never been particularly rebellious. Now his only real interest was working on bikes, something that put him into contact with a totally different world. He eventually dropped his job as a carpenter and devoted himself entirely to working on two-wheelers. Ness was a father, and for a short time his two children were raised with gearboxes, V-Twin engines, wheels, and machine tools right inside their mortgaged house.

It was then that he decided to rent a tiny, simple, rundown place in San Leandro, California. His workshop was only open to customers between six and 10 in the evening; that left him the entire day to devote solely to his work without interruptions.

It was a time of growth and expansion in the world of customization, and Arlen Ness started designing his first accessories, such as raised handlebars. Quite naturally, as his customer base grew the workshop was forced to open earlier. Arlen took on employees and recruited the help of his brother. He was almost 30 years old.

At this point Ness was fascinated by the chopper look. With each successive customer his dream was to build the simplest bike possible. What had attracted him to Harley-Davidsons in the first place was the sound of the engine, the narrowness of the bike, its symmetry, and above all its infinite room for being tidied up. When he started out, Arlen Ness had no examples or points of reference, which left him free to innovate and invent all alone. His only conscious influences were the Art Deco lines he admired on certain cars. These continue to influence his designs today.

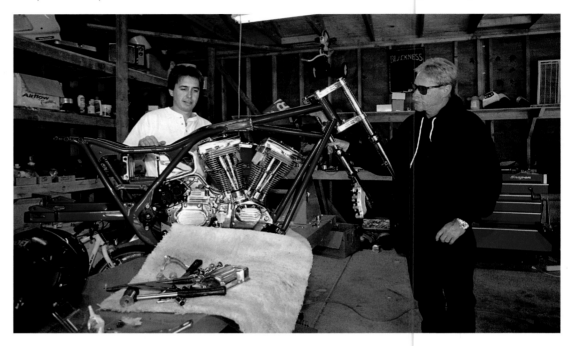

His main concern was linear harmony and the balance of proportions from front to rear. Arlen eschews unbalanced forms such as forks that are too long and sissybars that are too high; his style is totally rooted in a designer's Golden Mean.

The company started becoming noticeably profitable in the mid-1980s, and this allowed Ness to hire talented professionals to assist him - especially people to put his designs on paper, since he feels he doesn't draw well (!). It was at this time that he was able to fully pursue and develop his more adventurous ideas.

Ness's inspiration comes from everyday life: the colors he sees, the shapes he observes, the cars he likes. (SmoothNess was inspired by the superb lines of a Bugatti.)

358 top Arlen Ness is not alone in having a workshop in the garage of his house. His son Cory has one, too, and though it is less well-equipped than his father's this doesn't prevent Cory from expressing his own creativity. The two men's results are different, but equally interesting in their forms, choice of colors, and quality of finish. Cory's work is difficult to criticize; he is now making more and more of an impact in the field in which he grew up, forever surrounded by positive examples.

358 center and 359 Arlen Ness and one of his engineers are discussing a detail about the top pieces of a fork. This custom bike has an 88-inch engine and only the bodywork and the fork, the tank, the seat, and the handlebars are made from parts readily available on the market.

His dream is to further extend his catalogue, which already includes nearly all of the pieces needed to build a Ness bike from scratch. His most cherished wish is to produce his own range of motorcycles priced at under $30,000. He's been playing with this idea together with his son Cory and a few choice friends for several years.

Today Arlen seems to have distanced himself from managing his business, deputizing his wife Beverly and their children to handle the routine management. Arlen can therefore divide his time between shows, promotions, and exhibitions. When he gets back home he often fiddles with one of his new concepts in his own garage workshop.

Ness swears that never in his wildest dreams did he think he would be as successful as he is. Working on bikes and still being able to make ends meet had been his original goal. Decades later his business is worth millions and 30% of its accessories are exported overseas, mainly to Japan and Europe. (While his Japanese and European market shares seem about equal, the actual proportion fluctuates with the economic situation in each region. A curious problem for a guy who set out three decades ago to build a few custom choppers.)

Arlen Ness is aware that his bikes are not the only things that have made him a personality or a legend. His success is also due in large part to the fact that the biking public has made him their reference point, a sort of icon of the industry. He's aware that bikers have placed him on a pedestal, but happily he has gotten there by really being able to do what he's famous for.

Ness is fond of telling the following anecdote: "When I was very young - I had only been painting bikes for about two years - I was riding my bike one day when a car stopped beside me at a red light. The driver lowered his window and said 'The paintwork on your bike is really good. You know, I just heard of another guy in town who does fabulous paint. His name is Arlen Ness.'"

It was the first time in his life that he realized that people really appreciated his work.

360 and 361 This Arlen Ness bike created an absolute frenzy. Baptized "Two Bad," it was built back in 1979 - a time when you really had to take risks to tie together two Sportster motors, a single transmission, two carburetors, four oil and fuel tanks, and a central lubrication system. Ness managed to fit this bike with two 900cc engines fit with 1100cc pistons and cylinders. The technical work was performed with the help of a friend, Jim Davis, to whom he had illustrated his idea of having one motor placed behind the other with a very low center of gravity. The technical problems seemed insurmountable, but Jim came up with a frame that included a very low torsion-bar suspension. Arlen's design for Two Bad ran the power of the front engine into the rear unit, which then fed the single transmission. Two batteries were hidden below the bodywork. The result was one of great elegance; Arlen keeps Two Bad on show at his shop, and it never ceases to amaze.

362 and 363 How could he do something old using something new? Arlen Ness picked up on the interest of customers who were able to afford such luxuries and installed a Sportster engine in a completely rigid (but heavily modified) frame. In particular the oil tank was worked on, as it was to be given the added function of acting as a support to lend the frame more vertical rigidity. The old drum technology of the braking system was replaced with modern discs and the casing of the gearbox behind the engine was transformed by a small plate which protected the vulnerable pinion while simultaneously supporting the kick-start mechanism. The project surprised everyone with its jewel-like appearance but, despite the modern hardware, a lack of amenities meant it was hardly a long-distance tourer.

364 and 365 Similar frames once again, though the inclination of the steering column has been slightly transformed on some. Arlen Ness's logo appears on each tank as a sign of the exclusivity of these slim, graceful, explosively powerful machines. Their extra urge comes partly from work carried out on the engines and partly from an array of compatible high-performance parts mounted by expert mechanics, their aim being not only to please the customers but also to provide reliability. All the bikes shown are fitted with a single seat, as the pleasure of the rider is supposed to be complete even when travelling alone. This pleasure is supposed to be created by the characteristics of the engine and its supporting structure; items which only the rider is able to appreciate. Without entering into a philosophical quagmire, it's safe to say that a custom bike is first and foremost a vehicle for giving selfish pleasures. If the original Harley-Davidson had become just another piece of transportation, its legend would never have continued for 100 years. Today anyone can transform this splendid motorcycle according to his own tastes, resulting in a unique model that will give plenty of satisfaction and which others will envy. Just be sure to consider your options carefully before choosing the basic bike which will someday become your passion.

ARLEN NESS

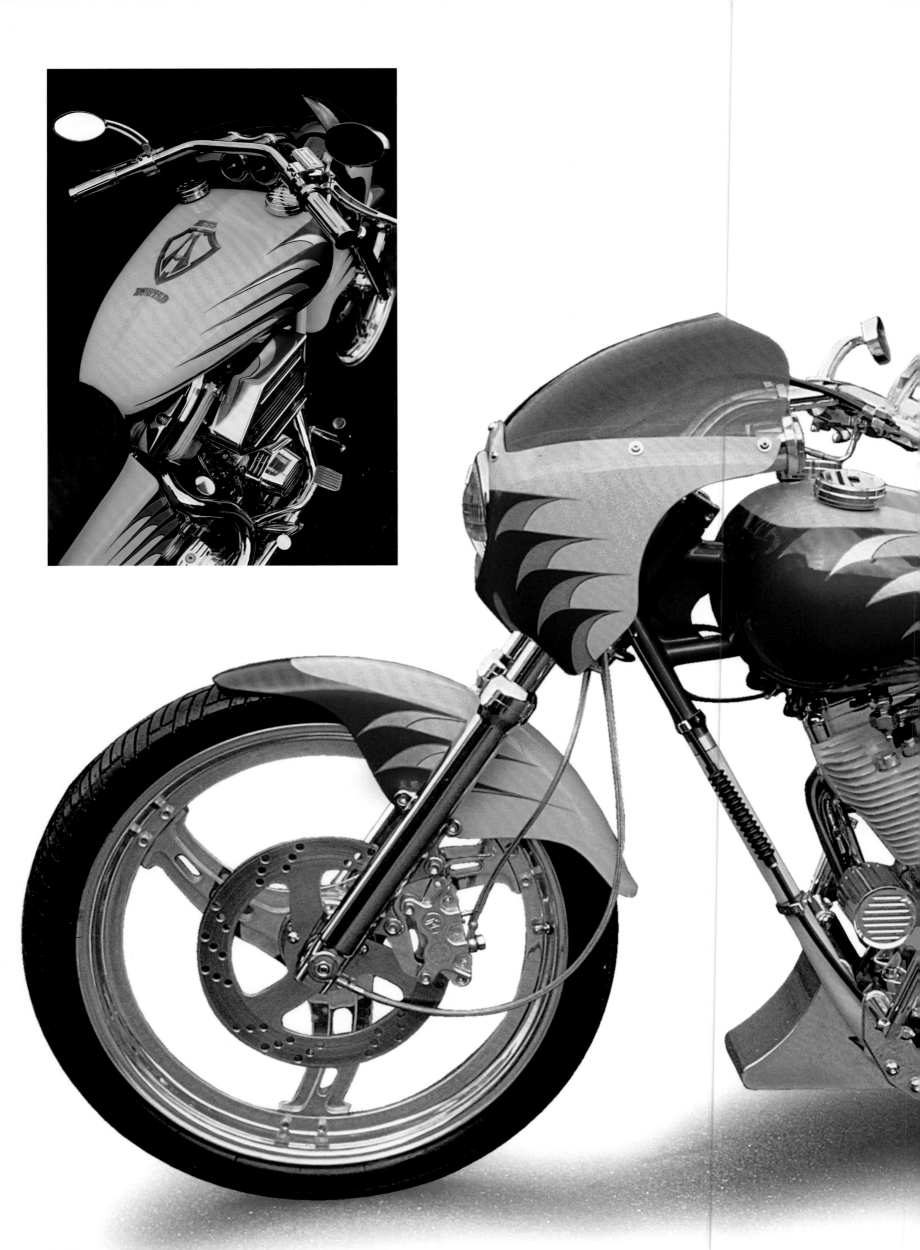

366-367 Here's another model that anyone can purchase for fast riding and which didn't cost a bundle to build. Fit with a Barnett clutch and an 88-cubic-inch engine it took just four months to construct in Arlen Ness's workshop. The pistons, rings, manifold, connecting rods, and air filter are all by S&S – a fact that just goes to show how the parts made by this company are among the most versatile and reliable on the market, assuming the mechanic who mounts them knows what he is doing. The frame has been lowered, the swingarm is by Arlen Ness, and the fork has been shortened by two inches. The front wheel measures 19 inches while the rear one is an inch smaller. This bike has maintained its pure lines, being just a little restrained in character. Its carefully designed artwork in the scallop style gives it a touch of individuality and nostalgia which distinguishes it from the many similar models. It is fit with a single seat – an excellent way of stating that it is just as fun to ride a Harley alone as it is with a passenger.

368 and 369 This is the Convertible, an exercise in adaptation – or, even more accurately, in how to have two bikes in one. That was the challenge faced by Arlen Ness in 1993. The resulting motorcycle featured the powerful lines and Indian-style fenders so typical of its creator, but could be turned into a much more sober road machine in barely half an hour. Screws, clips, roller bearings, and other means were used to support a body worthy of an Arlen Ness showstopper, while hiding below this was a much more restrained and roadworthy set of panels. This custom once again shows Arlen Ness's genius and originality. He has created two separate designs around the frame and the lovely V-Twin, the more restrained of which nestles neatly inside the wilder. All the proper technical details are there as well: a 1340cc motor with polished cases, cylinder heads modified to accept a high-voltage double ignition, a prototype Arlen Ness air filter, Accel ignition parts, a clutch by Barnett, and a rakish steering-column angle of 40°. The paintwork is based on candy colors and violet.

370-371 Flames are another classic way to decorate Harley-Davidsons. As a symbol of rebellion, freedom, and speed, flames are one of the most popular motifs in both motorcycle and auto customization. They were especially popular on early choppers. Also synonymous with hell and suffering, many early flame jobs were appropriately galling to the eye; crude, unrefined versions have long been used to decorate the bikes of rebel motorcyclists. But today flames are often very different, especially when produced by a master builder as a means of creating balance in the lines of a bike. The flames are less violent on this model and represent a style often used by Ness in which he attempts to hide them in geometric patterns. In this example Arlen shows how flames can decorate a custom without adding any untoward aggressiveness.

372 and 373 This bike was built at the start of the 1990s, but it still receives as much attention today as it did then. Its adventurous, if rather busy, design led it to appear in magazines all around the world and become an instant two-wheeled classic. This is the NessRossa, a motorcycle honoring the Ferrari Testarossa sports car so widely appreciated by Americans. Arlen built the bike as a tribute to Ferrari (he himself owns one). The motor is a two-liter V-Twin fed by four Dell'Orto twin-choke carburetors, two 80° Jerry Magnusson blowers, and two containers of nitrous oxide. This model is frequently ridden by Arlen himself and often exhibited to the public.

374-375 top At first glance these two bikes by Arlen Ness may seem identical, at least in concept. But they are in fact totally different; the one above was built from a Dyna chassis and fitted with a Sportster Evolution engine. It has highly accentuated lines – dear to the heart of the designer – and all the work centers on the bike's aesthetics. The frame is one of Ness's own manufacture and allows the engine to be mounted on rubber blocks. Being long and low, this makes the Sportster almost unrecognizable.

The work is once again exceptional, and it has allowed the appearance of the original Sportster engine, smaller and more compact than Harley's bigger V-Twins, to be modified. This customization was a real success, as it's rare to find a small-Harley design that is so well balanced and pleasing to look at. All the components of this bike come from the Arlen Ness catalogue, so any enthusiast is in a position to try this one themselves. Sportsters have everything to gain from such a transformation.

374-375 bottom This other bike is a perfect example for custom enthusiasts who enjoy doing work themselves. One such fan used components available from the Arlen Ness catalogue to create this custom (named "Pro-Street") based on an Atlas frame. It just goes to show that with a budget of $30,000 you can build a real jewel of a racing bike with unique style. In this case it took its builder a

year to see the final result. Apart from the camshafts, points, pushrods, valves, and springs (which are all by Crane) and the carburetor, downpipe, and exhaust pipes (by S&S) there was almost no mechanical transformation. Now the proud owner (who is also a neighbor of Arlen Ness), Carl Brouhard, has a custom bike with Arlen Ness style and components at a very affordable price.

COMMERCIAL RESTRAINT

Between 1992 and 1994 it was simply impossible to purchase a new Harley-Davidson engine, even at an authorized dealer. But while Harley-Davidson could perhaps block the efforts of many fans, large-scale designers such as Arlen Ness were prepared. Ness had long before purchased a large number of ex-police motorcycles at auction, broken them down, and reconditioned their engines and FXR frames. After all this painstaking work, he was well equipped with raw materials for his customs.

It was at roughly this point that Sputhe Engineering grabbed considerable marketshare by developing an engine block very similar to the original V-Twin produced in Milwaukee. Sputhe manufactured its own aprons, cases, cylinders, and heads, all of which worked in perfect harmony with S&S reciprocating parts. These engines would also prove very reliable, a highly appreciated plus point. Their output was also higher than that of genuine Harley blocks.

As an increasing number of professional designers started using these engines in their custom bikes, Sputhe Engineering continued developing its range of powertrains, especially five-speeds.

Even though it was well equipped with Harley mills itself, it didn't take long for the Arlen Ness Company to see the wisdom of Sputhe's move. Soon Arlen was quite eager to give his public a kit of his own that would be competitive with the various engines on the market at the time or in the near future.

Harley-Davidson eventually returned to its senses and made reasonably priced OE engines once again available. However, the damage to its marketshare (and even reputation) had already been done.

376-377 Similar frames once again; though the inclination of the steering angles differs from bike to bike, Arlen Ness's logo appears on each tank. These bikes boast typically (for Ness customs) powerful engines, and all have been fitted with sporty single seats. The red custom is a Ness creation based on a Day Tec/Rubbermount frame. Avoiding solid mounts means the rider suffers less vibration, as on the Electra Glide and Dyna. It also allows the owner of a Harley-Davidson to give his bike the appearance of a Softail without having to suffer through that design's less pleasant aspects. It can, for example, be given a large rear wheel, as shown in the photograph. The width of this one's tread is 180mm, which means that the chain drive need not be lost in the conversion. The fork is a 41mm Wide Glide model with a single disc, and the braking is provided by a high-performance four-piston Performance Machine caliper. The mirrors are Big Eyes Grooved models from the Arlen Ness range of aftermarket supplies. The lines are a modern interpretation of the true Arlen Ness style; fully balanced and unified.

377 top This bike, too, has a lovely appearance. It represents the Arlen Ness's goal across the range of custom bikes, which is that the design should not be allowed to compromise performance and vice versa. The starting point was familiar — a second-hand FXRP that was stripped down and given a second youth with the addition of new bodywork. Despite its smooth lines, tasteful decoration, and refined style, Ness's cruisers are made for riding. The look is largely original but with a typically sophisticated color scheme; the paintwork is different for every bike, giving each customer a unique machine.

378 and 379 Would da Vinci have customized an American motorcycle this way? This odd question may in fact be valid, since Arlen Ness named this bike "Mona Lisa." Even so, the important aspects of the machine are technical, in particular its Monoshock rear suspension. The Mona Lisa name actually comes from this fact: It is a play on words based on the American pronunciation of "mono," which usually comes out "monna." The bike's main design feature is the view of part of the rear tire seen through an opening in the fender. The idea aroused wonder, but it harmonizes easily with the elegant lines of the black motorcycle. The Mona Lisa's rear light and license plate are positioned low down and the exhausts are parallel to the road. Particularly elegant are the chrome seals on the sides of the rear fender, which perfectly match the style of the front. This is a refined, agile, and dashing motorcycle. As with all of his creations, Arlen Ness spends most of his time on the design of the model and the mounting of special parts. The frame of the Mona Lisa was made to measure specifically for this bike and exceeds the normal models by some five inches in length. The fork is a Harley-Davidson stock model, while the engine is equipped with Crane ignition, camshaft, and manifold. For the record, Arlen Ness built a second bike just like this one for an Italian enthusiast who loved the custom's lines and appreciated its homage to the great Italian artist.

380 and 381 Low and gentle, nothing disturbs this bike's overall appearance; this pure Arlen Ness shares key elements with both the Convertible and the SmoothNess. It's an elegant bike without any affectation in its decoration, and its success rests entirely on its sophisticated shape and the cut of the body. Note the symmetry of the lower lines and the exhausts, which follow the shape of the amazing bodywork: this is clearly a design worthy of the Arlen Ness trademark. Many of his creations bear something more than his signature, in fact: the logo that he places on either side of the tank can be seen here as well. The basis of the logo is the Bar-and-Shield trademark characteristic of Harley-Davidson and recognized around the world. However, Ness's own variety carries a stylized "A" in the center (for Arlen, of course). To Ness this is not an imitation but an honorable reference to a company that is in large part responsible for the world in which Ness flourishes. Even without Ness's touches, the Harley-Davidson name alone is enough to light up the faces of enthusiasts.

382-383 bottom At first view, this model dedicated to Pepsi-Cola (the fizzy drink that provides Coke with its main competition) might appear uncomfortable. While the bike represents above all a new style, to its corporate owners it is just another toy to be added to the collection. Nonetheless, Arlen didn't want to build a rigid frame for the "Pepsi," and so installed a Monoshock rear end directly behind the engine. This bike was ordered by the promotional department of Pepsi-Cola and, as you no doubt already recognized, uses the company's logo as the basis for its front and rear fender lines.

382–383 top The Ness Patrol is certainly not a substitute for the fuel-injected Road King used by many US motorcycle policemen.
It is simply a new decoration scheme, and one which is as close as Arlen Ness comes to building "standards." Ness produces this design regularly for customers who want to cross the country on one of his machines. Fitted with a reliable motor and an S&S carb, the Ness Patrol is a very usable long-distance motorcycle that, despite its limited transformations and relatively uniform design, still attracts the attention of the public.

384-385 Similar to the powerful V-Twins described in detail elsewhere, the Team Ness is another success for the designer. Sporting in spirit without actually having an outrageous level of horsepower, this custom bike uses fairly standard Ness accessories to give its performance an extra kick in the pants. Among its features are twin-piston brake calipers acting on dual front discs, freestanding exhausts, and a rear section made more substantial by incorporating the fender into the monocoque that supports the battery and oil sump. (This leaves just enough space on top to mount a small single seat.) The sporty style of this model is emphasized by a checkered strip; while unusual for Arlen Ness, this design fillip helps make the creation a visual success. The same basic design was later taken up by Arlen's son Cory for The Wave; customization is a family affair for the Nesses.

386 and 387 Here are three models from the Arlen Ness collection which seem visually identical but are again in fact quite different. The fieriest of the trio is the yellow and green custom done up in scallops. Its engine is one which Ness recently developed for use not in bikes but in custom cars and hotrods. Arlen wants to develop a complete kit for this engine and put it on the market. You can find out more about this powerplant in the section covering the LightNess, a model made entirely of polished aluminum. The overall package was meant to be a prototype of an all-Ness GT motorcycle. Arlen lengthened the frame (replicas of which are now available) and fit a standard Wide Glide fork. Equally important for any Gran Turismo offering are the fairing, fenders, and saddlebags, all of which are fundamental to comfort on long rides. The bike is aesthetically pleasing while remaining faithful to Ness's policy of only offering personalized designs. All the other accessories, including the handlebars, airbox, engine cases, and so on, are straight from the Arlen Ness catalogue. An important detail is the seat, for which either a single- or a double-rider setup can be specified. Although all three bikes shown are similar, each has its own characteristics and each is considered an individual product. Customers can order them turnkey from the factory or piecemeal from the catalogue. Even so, these bikes are immediately recognizable as Ness designs to those in the know. Their components and, above all, their balanced, well proportioned style makes their parentage clear.

388 and 389 With Carl Brouhard, Arlen Ness produced the Ness-Stalgia, a motorcycle that honors one of the most famous cars of the past. The dashing design is clearly based on the visual cues of the 1957 Chevy Bel-Air, a legendary automobile straight out of American Graffiti and Daytona beach racing. With this bike Arlen wanted to reproduce the car's famous fins at the rear and, on the top of the fork, the upper part of its front fender and headlight cowl. It was another model that greatly excited the public; some were perplexed by Ness-Stalgia, but most loved the idea and understood its symbolism.

CORY AND THE INFLUENCE OF HIS FATHER

Cory Ness has been influenced by his father's style his entire life. He grew up to the pace of the V-Twin with customization under his skin. But it was only much later, when he started working within the family-run company, that he started transforming motorcycles of his own. Since then Cory has brought his personal touch to the company, especially in custom theme paint jobs, sensitive colors, and personalized handlebars and mufflers. Today Cory, who

has followed the rise of the family concern and its successful sales strategy, now sits at the head of a company that he knows in and out, dating back to experiences earned sitting on his father's knee and watching his projects come to fruition. A full-fledged designer in his own right, he has gained a following of his own as an innovator and sensitive stylist, bringing a "newNess" into the business of custom motorcycle design. The future of this highly prestigious brand now seems even more consolidated. It is, therefore, with confidence that one can invoke the old cliché, "like father, like son."

390 and 391 In 1988, Cory Ness presented a surprising new custom at Spearfish in South Dakota that was quite outside the stylistic canons of the Ness family. Cory's design had a radical, streamlined shape but was also rather restrained in execution. It was thoroughly dressed in components from the company catalogue, such as the fork head from the Extraterrestrial family. The bike took Cory a year to design and produce; the final cost was some $75,000. It was fitted with progressive suspension, Patrick Racing pistons, special exhausts by Bob Munroe, dual halogen lighting on the fork head, and a specially shaped seat by Danny Gray. The tank was made entirely of aluminum and the carb was an S&S.

Rear lighting was given by made-to-measure LEDs. The fork was a 39mm combination of Arlen Ness and Harley-Davidson parts. The front wheel was a 21-inch Ness Tech Smooth 7, the rear an 18-incher, both made completely from aluminum. As for tires Cory stays faithful to Metzeler, like his dad. A last important detail was the color, a special hue called True Blue Pearl and provided by House of Kolor; this complementary shade was a surprising and attractive final touch.

392-393 top While the tank of the Low Rider bears the logo of the Arlen Ness Company, it was not Arlen that designed it but rather his son Cory. Surrounded by the world of customization since childhood, Cory has worked with his father for years and taken Arlen's work as his own example. By sharing the same passion and working in the family business, Cory will soon be able to assume responsibility for the company. This Low Rider is from 1993; its various transformations have put a price of $35,000 on it. It is fitted with a low Sputhe Engineering engine with pistons, piston rings, cases, cylinders, and cylinder heads all by the same company, the aim being that problems of non-compatibility are therefore avoided. The gearbox has five speeds and the FXR frame was made by the Ness Company. The steering column has been lengthened five inches and the front fork shortened by two.

392-393 bottom The Wedge is another design by Cory Ness. The bike's bodywork is worthy of Arlen but has Cory's distinctive personal touch. Despite its thick and heavy rear, the bike is still well-balanced. Its ambiguous styling sits halfway between a sportbike and an elegant Harley custom. Note the fork head integrated with the front of the frame, which blends into the whole to form a single unit: It took 200 hours for Don at D+D Metal Works in Grass Valley, California to shape the metal to fit Cory's drawings! The steering head is fixed to the forks by Harrison self-locking bolts and the braking system is by Performance Machine. The enlarged, 104-cubic-inch engine contains high-performance parts from Sputhe Engineering and S&S. Cory specified that he wanted a Stock-class engine (as designated for drag racing) mounted under this wild bodywork. The motorcycle cost around $60,000 all told.

THE FRENCH CONNECTION

394 Cyril Huze used a 1977 FLH Electra Glide when he created Miami Nice, a custom that partly evokes the Art Deco style as originated in France. It's a very recherché design, dashing as many of Cyril's creations are; he has introduced innovations to this bike, such as exhaust pipes which appear closed at their ends. (The fumes actually come out of holes cut into the bottom of the silencers.)

395 Cyril has always been attracted by the art of Native Americans, and that was the theme he chose for his first serious customization, a design based on a Harley-Davidson Softail Custom – a model from the Softail range that resembles the choppers of years gone by. That particular Softail only had a few transformations made to it, but the most important was a paint job executed by talented craftsmen who made

liberal use of gold leaf, a trick which had not yet become common. The combination of gold and turquoise corresponded fully to the spirit of the bike, which was extremely successful in competitions.

Cyril Huze

● *Good design is a balanced combination of boldness, deliberation, and deep awareness.*
● *Simplicity is the top of elegance.*
● *Just because an accessory fits a bike and looks good on it doesn't mean it is the right one to install.*
● *A good bike appeals to reason, but magnificent bikes arouse emotions. There are no limits to the emotions that can be marshalled around them.*
● *Designing and manufacturing a motorcycle is like writing the words and music of a song. All songs use the same notes, but only a few can become internationally successful.*
● *A good designer is not simply the person that takes you from 'what you've got' to 'what you want,' but the one who takes you from 'what you want' to 'what you wouldn't have been able to come up with even if you'd tried.'*
● *Having mechanical talent will only take you so far in producing a bike, while creativity is indispensable. Experimentation is the only route to innovation.*
● *When I customize a bike, I don't do what the others do; I follow my own dreams. A customization workshop must first of all be a dream workshop.*

THE BIRTH OF A MARVEL

We set out to follow, step by step, the birth of a work of art; not just a statue, a painting, or a modern or contemporary sculpture, but all of those put together using various media: metals, leather, rubber, and small amounts of plastic. These are the materials it takes to build a custom, that term which is all-too-often used loosely to mean the mounting of a few accessories on an otherwise stock bike. The word only takes on its full meaning when a creator starts from a bare frame and transforms and adapts it to the point that it has little or nothing in common with any mass-produced model – *without,* however, eliminating the values of the original.

It is perhaps thanks to the design of the V-shaped engine (whether it's an original Harley-Davidson or one by S&S, RevTech, Sputhe, or soon Arlen Ness) that serious customization

has taken hold within the sect of the Disciples of Milwaukee. Far from being stocky, the lines of most customs are stretched to the utmost, something which can only be done around the narrow, lithe footprint of a longitudinal powerplant such as a Harley or Ducati twin. The transverse cases of a Japanese Four, a German Boxer, or an Italian Triple or Six would simply not allow it.

And let's not forget the emotional pull of the American V-Twin, an engine type synonymous with Brando and the Blues Brothers, with diners and the desert, and with racing and rebellion. Whether one knows the United States intimately or merely dreams of it from afar, one can't help but fantasize for hours on end when faced with this most American symbol of freedom. The images which cinema and advertising have chiseled into our very being cannot be denied.

The reality of things may not be the same as our fantasies, as cyril Huze is quick to admit. But following him during and after the creation of a custom gives us great insight into how he walks the line between the two.

THE CONCEPT: BIRTH OF THE DREAMLINER

Here we will follow the creation of the Dreamliner, one of Cyril's most recent designs. His vision was to create a very low, long, streamlined motorcycle built around a a wide rear tire and a simple rigid frame. The challenge was to marry chopper nostalgia with what Huze calls "state-of-the-art technology." Dreamliner was intended to convey feelings of elegance, speed, and modernity even while standing still; to put it in a nutshell, a chopper for the 21st Century.

As is usual for Huze, a name had to be found before he could even draw the first sketches. Knowing that he was leaning toward a streamlined dream bike, Cyril immediately went for "Dreamliner." It must be pointed out that most designers know what their next projects will be even before finishing their latest work. According to Huze's philosophy, the name is the synthesis of this concept; it spurs creativity and obliges the designer to imagine lines, parts, accessories, and paint in harmony with the title. The bike's name becomes a sort of guide, keeping the designer focused. Throughout the process of styling and building this motorcycle, Cyril continually asked a single question: "Am I correctly expressing the 'Dreamliner' idea?"

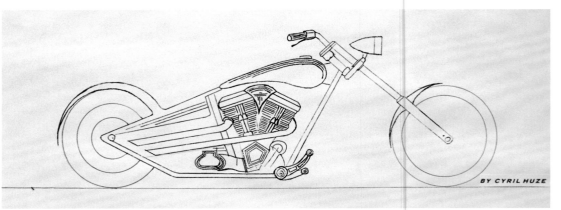

THE FIRST SKETCHES

Choosing the overall shape of the motorcycle is the most crucial task. For Dreamliner Cyril tried to imagine a body offering the least possible resistance to the wind. Visions of streamlined automobiles, airplanes, and trains danced in his mind. Each time he tried to put his thoughts into practice, Cyril envisioned straight lines sculpted into the body flowing organically from front to rear.

This process eventually became so all-consuming that Huze resolved to make these horizontal bodylines the visual center of the bike. Before making the first sketches, he jotted down the constraints set forth for this bike.

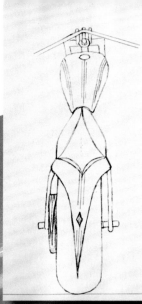

DEFINITION OF THE CUSTOM

● The bodywork itself would constitute the main graphic element of the art.

● The pipes would flow smoothly from the cylinders to the rear with only one turnout and absolutely no angle relative to the road.

● One-off chrome emblems featuring a racy imaginary animal would adorn the flanks of the gas tank.

● The bike would have a simple blue-steel look; a monochromatic paint job would avoid visual conflict with the bike's bodywork.

With these ideas in mind, the first sketches were drawn of the right and left sides, a rear view, and a few custom parts designed to emphasize the streamlined look. The airbox, coil cover, fender brackets, and some other parts designed and fabricated by Cyril for this specific motorcycle were intended to be marketed later as aftermarket parts, but this was not to influence any component's design. To some extent Dreamliner would be a showcase for Huze's other products, but its

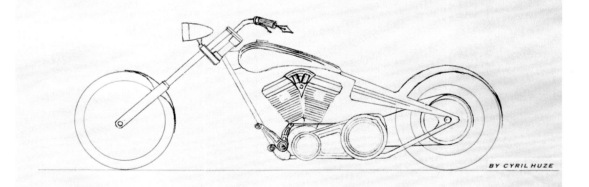

BY CYRIL HUZE

main purpose was pure aesthetic expression.

The frame was pegged at four inches above the ground and Huze's visualized body lines would be made of aluminum rods attached with epoxy. The taillight and turn signals would be frenched (i.e., built into the rear fender), while the handlebars' center riser would hide the electric wiring.

Brigitte Huze, Cyril's companion in life as well as in design, scaled and blueprinted every part. When all seemed right, templates were made to guide the fabrication.

396 and 397 The marvelous creations of Cyril Huze Custom begin on this simple office desk. After careful reflection, the ideas begin to flow between Cyril and Brigitte Huze and the first sketches soon appear. These will be the basis for what is to become, just a few months down the road, the Dreamliner. The bike will be very long, just as Cyril wants, and worthy of designer Brigitte's talent. Its tank is to follow the line of the bike while accentuating its curves and making it seductive. The rear will have a slightly molded form so as not to hide the classic elements of the front and rear cylinders.

Before starting fabrication, a basic full-scale mockup had to be made. Both wheels were perfectly centered in the frame, a fake engine was bolted in (so as not to scratch the final engine, whose cylinders were polished aluminum). All the various drives and belts were set to the correct tension and the bike was adjusted to ensure its perfect horizontality above the ground. (This was done using adjustable triple trees.) An extra 10° rake was added to the original 38° angle of the steering head, giving a final setting of a racy 48°.

Since the shape of the rear fender is one of the most important elements of any custom, Cyril decided that this would be fabricated first. A cardboard mockup of the part was placed over a large, generic steel fender and the styling began.

The frame used as a base for this bike was Ness Tuff-Tail. Designed to accept an eight-inch rear tire and therefore carrying an offset on the left side, many adjustments would be required to make it appear symmetric in the end. Each side of the fender had to be rolled down to fit the tire's radius perfectly. This was facilitated by the

398 and 399 These photographs show how much care must be taken so that when this custom hits the roads a few weeks from now it will be reliable and perfectly safe. The oil tank will be welded onto the frame and then rubbed down and painted; after filling and painting, the joint between the two parts will become totally invisible. This is a job that has caused Cyril and Brigitte a great deal of worry; since Cyril's search for originality is constantly pushing him to the limits of technology and fabrication, his construction methods are often untried and risky. It's the price that he and Brigitte pay for customs that are stylistically original and technologically unique.

fact that the Tuff-Tail is rigid; no rear-suspension travel would therefore interfere with Huze's calculations. The Dreamliner's tire would run very close to the fender, with only about a 3/4-inch gap between the two: just enough to accommodate the taillight box, its wiring, and some running clearance. The taillight was also a unique, custom-built part, with LED optics in place of bulbs. After all this had been checked, the rear fender was welded to the frame.

Starting from another cardboard template designed by Huze, the front fender was then made out of fiberglass. Perfect left/right symmetry was checked first, then the fender's fore/aft position was determined by running a tape from rear of the back fender to rear of the front fender. The distance between these points was set as a factor of the distance between axle centers. Spacing to the front forks was then double-checked and the fabrication of custom fender brackets commenced.

DELICATE PHASE: THE SIDE PANELS

For this project Cyril wanted the side panels and oil tank to look like one piece. Starting with a stock oil tank he fashioned a new part that was both longer and narrower. This slimming required that something be done about the battery, however, which in the Tuff-Tail usually lies at the center of the oil tank. A small dry-cell battery was chosen in place of the larger conventional wet-cell type. Placed horizontally, it afforded extra room at the rear to accommodate electrical modules and fuses. The new oil tank was then pressure-tested with water to ensure against welding leaks.

A piece of steel was then wrapped around the tank to temporarily attach it to the frame. The critical side panels could then be cut out and welded to both the oil tank and the frame's rear tubes, a task performed by Michael Durocher.

The gas tank would of course not be neglected, as it is one of any bike's key parts. For Dreamliner, a very narrow aluminum fuel tank was extended in front to cover the ugly frame neck and further elongate the design. This aluminum extension was then scaled back 1/8-inch from the front tube to avoid scratching the paint as the bike rolled and vibrated.

To avoid conventional tank brackets Cyril resorted to an aesthetic trick. Two brackets were welded onto the top tube and two others affixed to the inside of the tank tunnel that housed the upper part of the frame. These brackets slid into each other with just enough play to be compensated for by the Dreamliner's final paint layer. Two other small brackets were then welded

to the lower part of the gas tank to ensure the stability of this key piece. Two bolts ran through the main brackets to firmly fix the gas tank to the frame and preventing all movement, even in the case of severe vibrations. During final assembly, a rubber sheet was placed between the gas tank and the top tube.

With the tank in place at last, the patterns of the aluminum side rods which would be fabricated later could finally be drawn on cardboard tank-side templates.

BRIGHT AND EFFICIENT LIGHTS

The bike's taillight and rear turn lights were fabricated from scratch solely for this model. Since bulbs are less bright and intense than LEDs the latter were used all around. LEDs also boast a longer life span than bulbs and are more resistant to severe vibrations.

The taillight for this bike naturally had to be very streamlined, and its installation proved troublesome. The rear fender was set to run just a tiny bit over 3/4 inch from the tire, following the rubber's contours from end to end. This meant that the taillight box could not be thicker than half an inch at any point. (While there is no rear-suspension travel on a rigid frame, tire expansion at speed demands an allowance of extra space.) Several broken LEDs and seven hours of trial and error later the box was finally perfectly sized and fabricated. Vibration tests were then carried out to check the system's reliability. The same general fabrication process was then used for the turn-signal lights.

All lights were frenched into the rear fender by Michael Durocher so that they perfectly followed the lines of the body. Finally, a narrow steel channel was welded up under the fender to convey the necessary wiring from the rear lights to the battery system.

THE SEAT: DESIGN BEFORE COMFORT

With the gas tank in place, a very precise template of the seat base was cut out of thick cardboard. The rear of the seat was to end in a point reminiscent of the rear fender and taillight. The seat pan was then made of fiberglass and, after drying, trimmed to fit flush against the frame. Three screws (two in front and one at the rear) had been 'glassed into the pan earlier.

"streamlined." All the steel and aluminum parts of the bike would be carefully ground and polished to a smooth, glassy finish. This grinding took an entire day in itself.

Cyril absolutely wanted this model to give an impression of speed even while standing still. To create this illusion he decided to use thin aluminum rods permanently fixed to the metal bodywork with epoxy. This proved easier said than done, however.

A large number of tests were carried out on small pieces of metal, and everything seemed to be going smoothly until it came time to try bending the aluminum rods. Rather than smoothly following the metal's contours, they tended to snap off or detach from their supports instead. After a long period of trial and error, a workable method was developed using thinner, more flexible rods than Cyril originally imagined. These were stuck to the bodywork one inch at a time and the bonding epoxy was allowed to dry each time before continuing. It was a painstaking process, but patience carried the day: the final fit of the rods was eventually tested by hammering, and they didn't move a micron!

A new problem did turn up, however. How would the ends of the rods be blended into the body without a sharp, ugly transition point? Epoxy was eventually used to taper the end of the rod into the bodywork smoothly. This painstaking sculpture work was carried out to cause a smooth transition until the rods seemed to melt into the body.

After insuring that the motorcycle was free of all imperfections in its metal, the entire structure received a first coat of primer. Start to finish, the bodywork and sculpturing took three weeks to finish, with two technicians working full time.

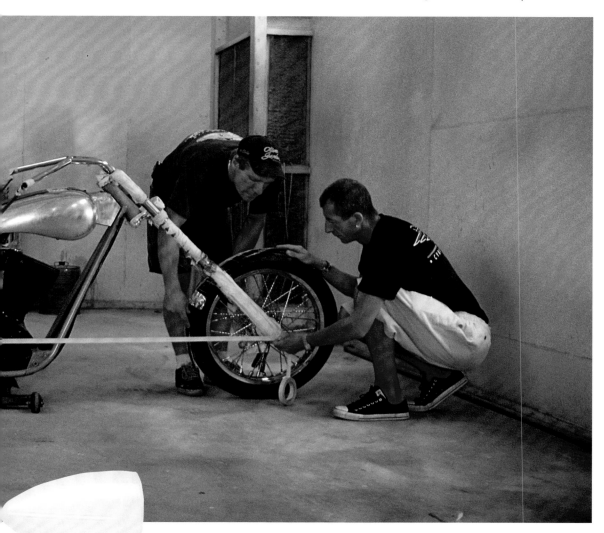

THE HANDLEBARS

On a bike of this quality it is out of the question to use handlebars already available on the market. The handlebars were therefore custom-built, bearing in mind not only their technical considerations but also the lines and spirit of the bike.

Since the electric wiring to the controls must run inside the handlebars, three handlebar risers were used in place of the usual two. The central riser served double duty, conveying all the control wiring down in a single band into the front of the frame, where it could be easily routed out of sight. A hole was cut into the upper part of the left top tube near the base of the gas tank. The electric wiring was then slipped through this hole and threaded through the top tube all the way back to the battery. The clearance of the handlebars in relation to the gas tank was then tested with the owner seated on the bike.

The two front screws would go into the frame while the rear screw seated in the fender. With the seat pan and gas tank both in place, the distance between the top of the fiberglass pan and the top of the metal gas tank at the point where both meet was carefully measured. This value would represent the overall height of the seat, which when viewed from the side should sit along a fluid, unbroken line from the tip of the tank to the tail of the rear fender. Cyril's choice for the seat covering was black stingray (a most suitable skin if ever there was one!) mixed with matching black leather. The stitching pattern was designed to evoke the shape of the taillight. The upholsterer, Jeffrey Philips, had worked with Cyril on a regular basis for several years and fully understood his desires. This helped him to once again come up with a masterpiece.

Once the main body elements were complete, the motorcycle had to be

MOCK UP

All parts to be mounted onto the bike at final assembly were installed after the initial priming. To do this Cyril was seconded by a skilled mechanic. This mock-up stage included fabricating a large number of exclusive accessories such as the pipes, airbox, license-plate bracket, fender brackets, and the dozens of other pieces that turn a custom-built motorcycle into a sophisticated piece of jewelry. This phase also involved routing the control lines to clutch and brakes, always ensuring the most fluid runs and curves. This process entailed drilling new holes into the frame and filling up some of the ones made earlier. To avoid confusion,

EMBLEMS

Cyril commissions his emblems to be made by Marc Fabre, a talented European artist. Fabre creates the emblems overseas without ever seeing the tank itself.

To make his jewelry, Huze's drawings for the right and left emblems are rendered, inverted, and scaled directly onto the gas tank by Brigitte.

A fiberglass casting of each side of the gas tank is then made, and inside each resin print Brigitte re-draws the emblem so that Marc can faithfully size them while thousands of miles from the US. Made of thin steel (to look like they are integral parts of the tank), the emblems are polished to

perfection after casting and manually adjusted to fit the tank sides without any gap. After final forming, the emblems are finally chrome plated. Tension runs high when it comes to fixing these custom emblems onto an already-painted tank!

PAINTING

Cyril Huze works with a certain logic, but above all it is artistic honesty that forces him to paint his custom bikes as he does. For this project, Cyril wanted to invent an exclusive steel blue. After goofing around with various color mixtures literally for days, he came to feel that a slight reddish tinge in the blue would provide the perfect steel effect.

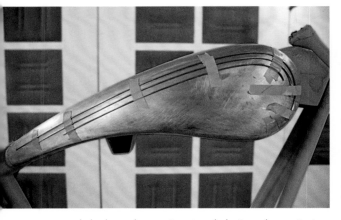

each hole to be maintained during the painting process was circled in green; all those to be filled were circled in red. A simplistic approach perhaps, but essential to avoid errors.

Once the mock-up assembly was thoroughly checked and adjusted, the motorcycle was again stripped down to its frame. Parts to be painted were separated from those to be plated or polished, all the small nicks and imperfections created during the mockup phase were corrected, and the entire bike received its final coat of primer, which Huze's crew sanded glass-smooth.

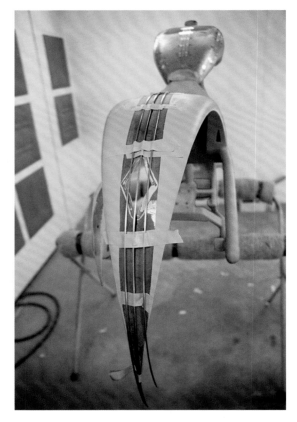

400 and 401 bottom These photographs show the attachment of thin aluminum bars to the rear fender and upper fuel tank. This job was another worry for Cyril, the bike's creator and technical engineer, as at first he used dowels that were too thick and rigid. Once the heavier rods were in place they became impossible to shape and fix; a thinner gauge was the answer.

402 and 402-403 Once the frame is finished and the fenders are ready to be mounted, the designer has to turn his attention to the mechanical aspects of the bike. These have to be assembled with the maximum of care, as even the engine is a custom part. The V-Twin, whether or not it is made by Harley-Davidson, is the heart and soul of the bike; it will receive the same attention as a beautiful gem in the setting of its ring.

403 top The designer has taken the trouble to attach adhesive tape to the sections where the bike's identifying logo will be placed. It only takes one clumsy slip while applying the Dreamliner logo to ruin the painstakingly prepared tank surface.

403 bottom The double ignition system has been installed in a housing that Cyril has personally prepared. This is typical of the care he takes to make his creations suitable for the marketplace. This housing is just one of the accessories Cyril has developed for the aftermarket.

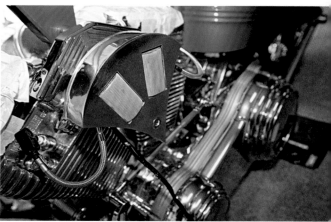

404 and 405 *The result at last sees the light. The project's difficulties were resolved one at a time as they cropped up, and now the Dreamliner is ready to meet the public. Every year, however, these same fans become more critical and severe in their judgement of master builders and private enthusiasts alike. True professionals such as Huze wouldn't have it any other way; it is exactly those expectations that keep the artist moving forward.*

Cyril Huze shares Arlen Ness's passion for American motorcycles but, having come from a different culture, he views them through a totally different lens. While still in his native France Huze could only dream of America: its open spaces, rock 'n' roll, Harleys, and film stars. Although his work is not as plentiful as Arlen's, it equals it in quality. Looking at his creations one understands that Cyril Huze is a man out of the ordinary. Each of his bikes provides a new thrilling surprise, but common to them all are elegance, power, and a deep sensitivity to the chosen theme.

Cyril Huze was brought up in Paris. At 18 he left the family home to become more independent and went on to fund his higher education on his own. By the age of 28 he had opened his own successful advertising agency and made a name for himself.

Following his personal taste and intuition, he did everything possible to attract a clientele of US companies with European ambitions. For nearly 20 years Huze would be steeped in marketing concepts, creative strategies, radio jingles, and television spots with the goal of helping large American corporations to become household names in Europe. He assimilated the two commercial cultures and took what was best from both.

But despite Cyril's professional success in France, during his very first visit to the US he immediately felt at home and knew that he'd reached a turning point in his life. In his own words, "Although I was born in Paris, my entire youth was spent in an Americanized environment. The 1950s marked the height of American opulence and I belonged to what was, perhaps, the first generation of Europeans to really be exposed to American culture: rock 'n' roll, Cadillacs, James Dean films, American TV serials, and so forth were my passions. To really feel like American teenagers we wore the same blue jeans and the same leather jackets. Of course, we had to make our hamburgers at home; they weren't available in restaurants back then!

"Growing up we used to compete with each other to be the first to buy authentically American products: a new record, a T-shirt, a car license plate, things like that. Even our language was Americanized, we used a lot of American words. It was all very cool, not least because our parents were horrified."

"America fired our dreams, and imitating American culture was, for us, a way of moving beyond our parents' generation; a way of rebelling. Like teenagers everywhere we were trying to forge our own identities. America appeared to offer a new and different lifestyle virtually off-the-shelf; we didn't even need to invent much."

"As a teenager I was both rebellious and sentimental. I often felt like a lone wolf. I identified with James Dean, both in real life and in the roles he played under Elia Kazan. He was my idol, provided the escape route that I needed so much."

BLUES

408 and 409 Few Hollywood figures are as closely associated with custom motorcycles as the Blues Brothers. Huze, who is also a passionate fan of the blues, built Harley Blues on a modified rigid Pro Magnum frame into which he fit a 1997 Harley engine bored oversize and sparked by Crane Fireball ignition. The gearbox is a modified unit from Andrews Shafts & Gears which has been buffed, painted, and engraved. The brakes feature four-piston calipers and both tires are Avons on 18-inch wheels front and rear. Cyril was also of course responsible for the bike's color scheme, which uses shades of silver and blue that are very close to his favorites. Nor does the rear of Harley Blues lack originality or care: Cyril used a Pro One Marker fender that was specially modified and trimmed for the project.

410 and 411 *The decoration of this motorcycle was carried out by painter Chris Cruz on a modified Fat Katz tank which Huze lengthened by three inches. The rocker covers come from the Arlen Ness workshops and the carburetor is an S&S Type E. The electric wiring passes through the rod connecting the handlebars to the ICS Roadforks tines. The oil tank is a chrome Ness model with Blues Brothers engravings while the seat, as far as can be seen, has been designed for looks rather than comfort. The bulk of the upholstery was made by Jeffrey Phipps while the covering and faces of the Blues Brothers were done by Ralph Bailey. The headlight comes from the Headwinds range, and both wheels are Stealth models from RC Components. The high-performance brakes are RC Teardrops.*

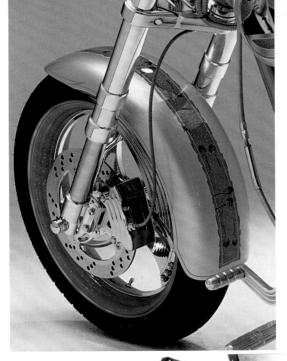

America; an America that never speaks about differences and which lives up to its stated ideals. It is the America of his teenage dreams, an America where lovely rhythms transport the free on fabulous voyages of discovery. It is during these voyages that Huze sees and appreciates the landscapes and people which have fired the artistic chroniclers of America.

The image of America that Cyril Huze envisioned before ever laying eyes on the country was a multifaceted prism, one of whose aspects bore the image of Harley-Davidsons. To a dreamy young Frenchman, these motorcycles seemed to symbolize all the most basic American values: freedom, adventure, and new friendships with whomever one might meet at the end of the highway. As a child he listened to *Heartbreak Hotel* while admiring the jacket photo of Elvis on a red-and-white Harley KH. He discovered that Roy Rogers rode a Harley Sportster. He saw the film *Spirit of St. Louis*, in which Jimmy Stewart (as Charles Lindbergh) rode a Harley. Later, like many of us, he was forever changed by Peter Fonda,

Dennis Hopper, and Jack Nicholson in *Easy Rider*. To Huze, the Harley-Davidson to some extent encapsulated America.

On the other hand, Huze goes on, the factory itself now makes bikes which increasingly look alike. He feels that motorcycle owners are more desirous than ever to show off their individuality and express their personalities through customs. He continuously points out that the only mission of a motorcycle designer is the "building of personalities," and the only way to do that is by giving the bikes an added element of aesthetic, technical, or financial finesse. When Cyril Huze dreams, he dreams of building bikes that will be stars on two wheels, just as James Dean and Peter Fonda have been stars on the screen.

MIDNIGHT RUNNER

412 and 413 *The Midnight Runner is the result of an intelligent and inexpensive customization which has preserved the bike's capacity for long-distance travel without resembling the standard Road King. For this bike Cyril used a large number of accessories available on the open market, though many were adapted and personalized to ensure harmony. Cyril's handiwork can be seen by looking at the bike*

from all angles and noting that while he started with a much less refined machine than customs are generally built from, he nevertheless succeeded in eliminating the heavy looks of the Road King.

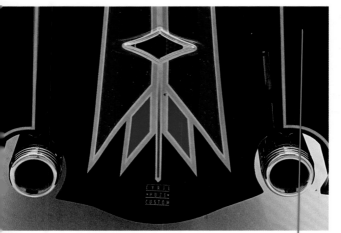

In fact, Cyril treats each bike on which he works as a real person. It's what he calls his "star strategy." To better understand and appreciate this technique, one must understand that Huze's logic quickly deviates from that of a pure designer into that of trained communications professional. In fact, his entire approach to the business of creating motorcycles is close to that of a commercial analyst creating new trends. This is why Cyril always asks and answers a few key questions to provide a quick outline of the motorcycle's personality: Will it be nostalgic or futuristic? What's the bike's name (this must be easy to remember)? What is its style, both for its own sake and in keeping with that of the owner? Will it go beyond the owner in elegance, tradition, or aggressiveness, greatly magnifying a trait that was only hinted at before? And what will be its language, expressed through the shape of the accessories, colors, and paint? These elements must always be in perfect harmony with the chosen theme. After asking these questions (and looking back on 28 years of experience), Cyril Huze is more than qualified

to write the storyboard of his new bike.

All of his projects, whether simple or highly sophisticated, are first drawn on paper without the help of computers. The adventure begins by looking for a theme and a name. After that come sketches from different angles, blueprints for custom accessories, and graphic experimentation toward the colors and the paintwork. Even the drawing of the seat must remain in perfect tune with the rest of the design.

This initial conceptualization is affected by at least two economic factors, and these may either be complementary or in conflict. If the bike is done on commission Huze must obviously consider the customer's wishes. If, however, the bike is to be only for his showroom, Huze enjoys much greater freedom in his reactions, choices, and expenditures. Whatever the case, it is under Cyril's close supervision that his team of talented craftsmen build, paint, and finally assemble the new bike.

For Cyril, building a custom motorcycle is a complex art form that demands creativity, careful engineering, discipline, and above all a great deal of patience. And, as is the case with all art forms, only those artists who are not fully satisfied with their work can evolve and grow. That is the constant challenge; the possibilities are infinite, so likewise are the chances for stagnation.

Great designers surprise the public with each of their creations. Their responsibilities and commercial obligations seem to be constantly questioned and revised. *Always surprise*: That is the sure formula to become a great designer who can impose himself on the market. The job involves passion, but for

413

414-415 This photograph shows the elegance of the rear light, the Arlen Ness license frame with indicators incorporated, the shape of the rear fender (which has had its lines emphasized by Brigitte's paintwork), the painted profile of the saddlebags, and the protruding section of the exhausts. The bags have been lowered using a kit by Arlen Ness which has been modified to hide its attachment points. The dashing lines of this motorcycle are actually accentuated by the shape of its saddlebags, enabling the viewer to appreciate the thoughtful work Huze must have put in during the design stage regarding forms and colors.

a particular style to be recognized the designer must also be keenly aware of customer expectations. Being too far ahead of one's time is as meaningless as not moving far enough to the front.

If a designer manages to get his style recognized, his customs gain prestige. They are highlighted in the media, often being placed on the covers of trade magazines. Cyril Huze can spend hours talking about his passion for the bikes he has created, but he can also wax forth on the passion instilled by the work of others and by those motorcycles which are still to be built.

He seems unstoppable once he starts talking about V-Twin engines, custom accessories, the search for themes, the emotional value of shapes and forms, or the symbolism of colors. In the heat of a topic he can become, from moment to moment, a poet, a philosopher, or a seller of dreams and ideas. Yet while his passion is seductively attractive, his convictions can be so firmly set as to prove exasperating.

Huze has helped many with their first steps into custom biking, and he feels he has brought true joy to those who have shared his ideas and trusted him with their dreams. Nevertheless, he feels a heavy responsibility for having directly or indirectly incited so many to spend uncommon fortunes in the name of God Custom. So far, nobody seems to have any regrets. Huze likes to comment that his customers have become his close friends; they are now "religiously" linked, as he puts it, by the same passion.

All of us have felt, at least once, a click for something or someone. Cyril felt the click that changed his life while riding a Harley-Davidson through the American Southwest, fulfilling another childhood dream and making new friends of bikers, Indians, farmers, and cowboys.

The emotional shock was such that while he had spent nearly 20 years of his life in advertising, he felt he needed to find a way to make a living for the next 20 years in the biking universe, only going back to advertising if necessary to make ends meet. During this long trip a meeting with the Hopi Indians of Arizona left a permanent mark on his heart. He decided to dedicate his first custom to them.

Before making the slightest change to the mass-produced Softail he drew his concept completely out on paper, then set off again to show his design to the Hopi. They admired its authenticity, and one of them prayed before his sketches. The motorcycle went on to beat the pros at Sturgis and Daytona.

416 and 417 Cyril Huze borrowed the style of the famous art deco hotels on Miami Beach for Miami Nice. He takes pleasure in describing this bike as having "long bags and a low profile, a miniskirt and a high profile." The bike was made for cruising along Ocean Boulevard and for giving the impression that life is good. The decoration of Miami Nice harmonizes well with the scenery of Miami, especially its incessant sunshine. Huze actually lived in Florida for many years.

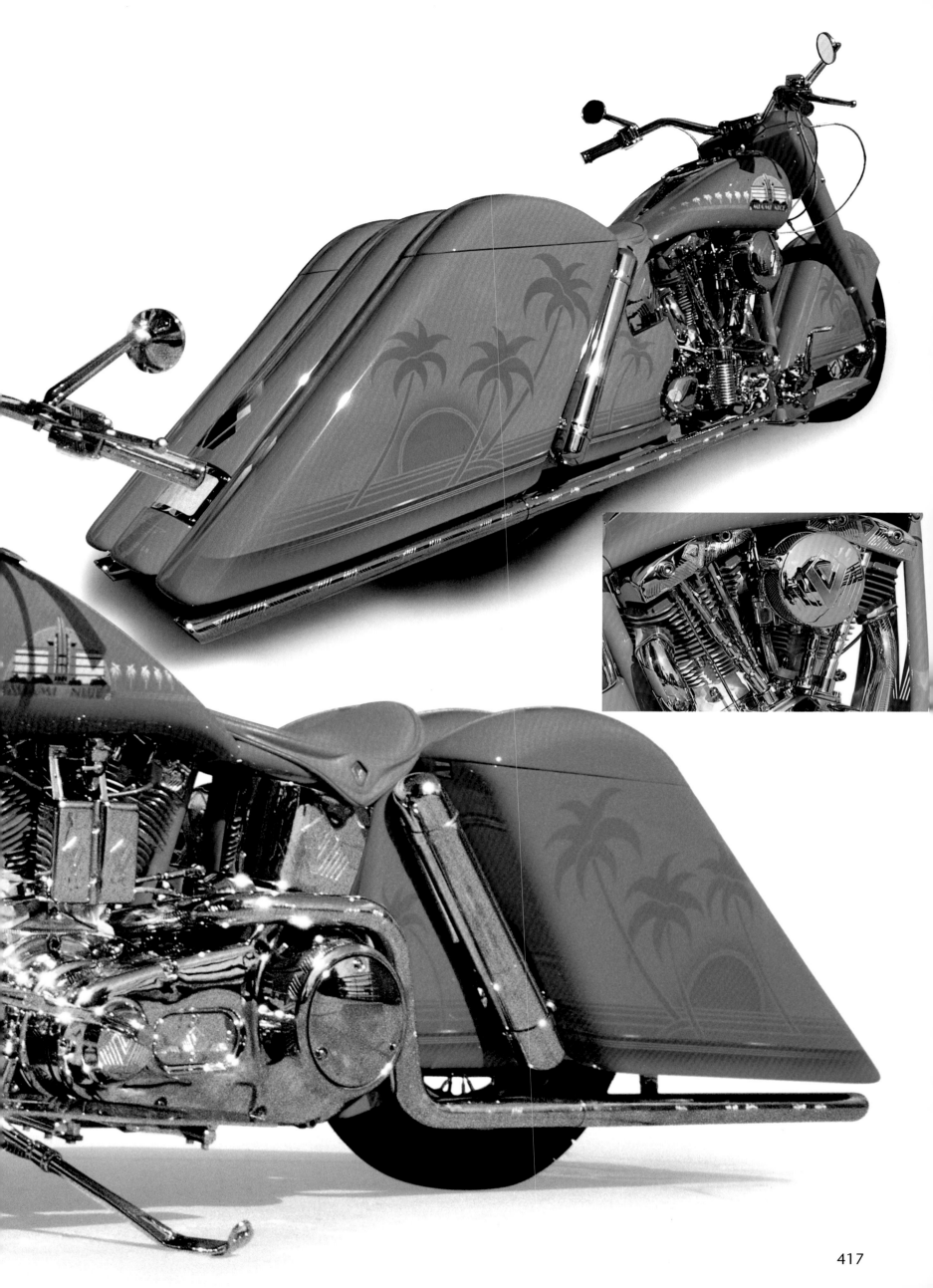

417

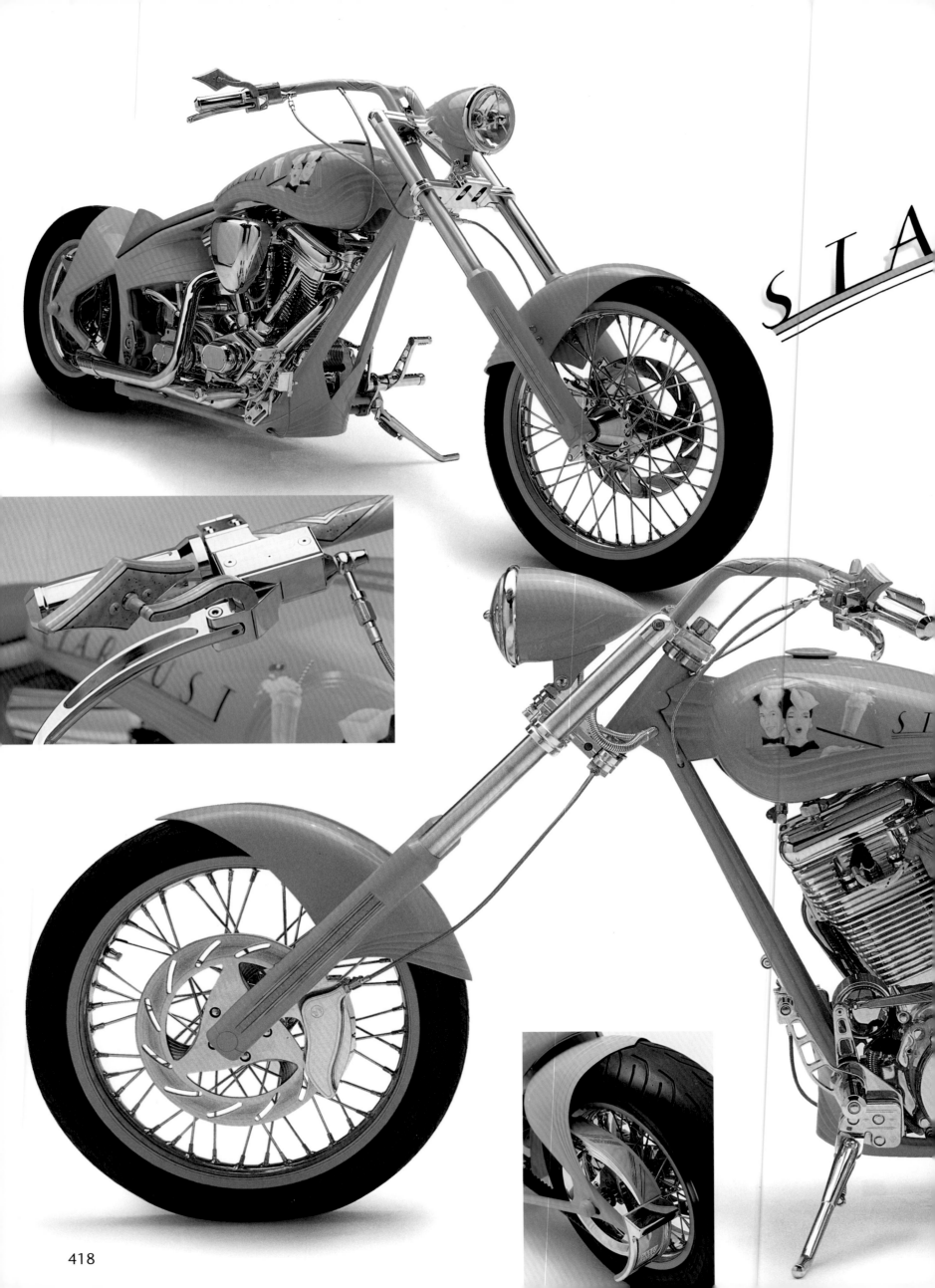

S L A

THE GREAT RIDDLE
BY CYRIL HUZE

In this job, where you express your passions and ideas through chrome, steel, and paint, it is easy to settle into the illusion that you know everything about customization...until the day when a journalist, perhaps a little smarter than the rest, stretches his mike and asks you the one question that no one else had thought of asking a designer: "Tell me what the Harley-Davidson and the V-Twin engine means to you." What he is asking me to do is not to talk just about my passion, but to explain its very basis!

I instinctively tend to hide behind the famous Harley-Davidson slogan at such times: 'If you have to ask, you wouldn't understand'. The guy who came up with that was very, very cunning. I'd like to meet him and congratulate him. But is this slogan really true? Are one and the other impossible? In any case, the saying has been printed on hundreds of thousands of T-shirts and has allowed the people who know it to avoid this question for generations.

To tell the truth, I have never worn this T-shirt. Unfortunately, perhaps, I wasn't wearing it on the day in question, either!

So now I will try to answer that journalist: If not to explain the inexplicable, at least to attempt to make it clearer. My thoughts drift to Martin Jack Rosenblum, the Holy Ranger, the extreme poet of the V-Twin, the official historian of the Harley-Davidson Motor Company. One day after a reading of his poems he said to me: "Cyril, what's really wonderful is that we'll never be able to explain what makes us so attached to Harley-Davidsons." And after listening

418 and 419 "Wide-Drive Softail Custom" is the rather more pretentious name of Stardust, which takes its theme from the 1950s era of drive-in movies and drive-in restaurants. The decoration of the tank is entirely the work of a Frenchman no less in love with the United States than Cyril Huze. It was Cyril's idea to place the discreet and ingenious rear indicators just at the ends of the exhaust pipes at the base of the sides. Notice again the attention to detail and innovation shown by the rear fender, which is connected to the swingarm and incorporates the license-plate mount at its tip. The rear wheel is a 40-spoke Ness model, Huze naturally choosing wire wheels over anything that smacked of trendy technology. The front part of Stardust's frame is painted to harmonize with the general design of the bike. A section of the handlebars includes the controls, various Ness Petite switches, and an American Legend mirror (the latter obviously added more for looks than any practical purpose). The mirrors are of course decorated with a fineness of detail worthy of the rest of the bike.

to his poem I had thought I understood it perfectly! Rosenblum shook my certainties, but in the end he is right. Harley-Davidson is like a beautiful flame that never stops burning. Just when one thinks it has gone out it flares up again from its ashes. It's also a very beautiful flame, ever-changing. One can see it and feel it, but words can never describe it perfectly.

So I'm finally ready to send my answer to the journalist who asked that question. These words will be written in my most beautiful hand: *"It's a mystery."*

Deanager

But a seemingly banal occurrence gave Cyril new courage. After visiting his company's website, a couple sent him an e-mail that tackled this very question. "The art of the Harley," it said, "is at once the art of travel, the art of adventure, the art of freedom, the art of living in harmony, and the art of sharing."

Cyril was touched by the simplicity and strength of these words, and struck by the repetition of the word "art." With these notions he thought he had found the basis of the Harley-Davidson phenomenon. To him the brand is a great equalizer that transcends generations, professions, countries, races, and religions. It is the American way of clearing psychic baggage and returning to true values.

A little abstract, perhaps, but at least it's a start. Why Harley? Well, what are legends made of? How are they born? How do they become universal? How do they survive?

420 and 421 James Dean certainly brought good fortune to Huze; the success of this glorified Softail boosted Cyril into the ranks of the world's best designers. Called "Deanager," this bike has won many of the industry's most coveted prizes. The reason becomes clear when one looks closely at the unusual, intelligent, and tastefully understated details of the finish, which easily seduces any admirer. Starting from a Fat Boy Huze massaged all the details without completely altering the original lines of the bike. Artist Chris Cruz provided a fantastic and precise paint job. The color scheme (blue, gold, and burgundy) is both luminous and soft at the same time, and it really allows James Dean's black-and-white portrait to stand out. This bike began life as a 1992 Harley; its rear lights were imported from France, the risers are from the Pro One range, and the footrests are by Arlen Ness and Razorback. The deerskin seat was specially ordered from Mike Corbin and made from a single hide. The mirrors are by Drag Specialties. The swingarm was carefully mounted to emphasize the bike's lines and the design of the rear fender. The oil tank was engraved using a style and motifs reminiscent of American Indian art. The rocker covers have been engraved for added visual interest (though they're still discreet compared to the decoration elsewhere).

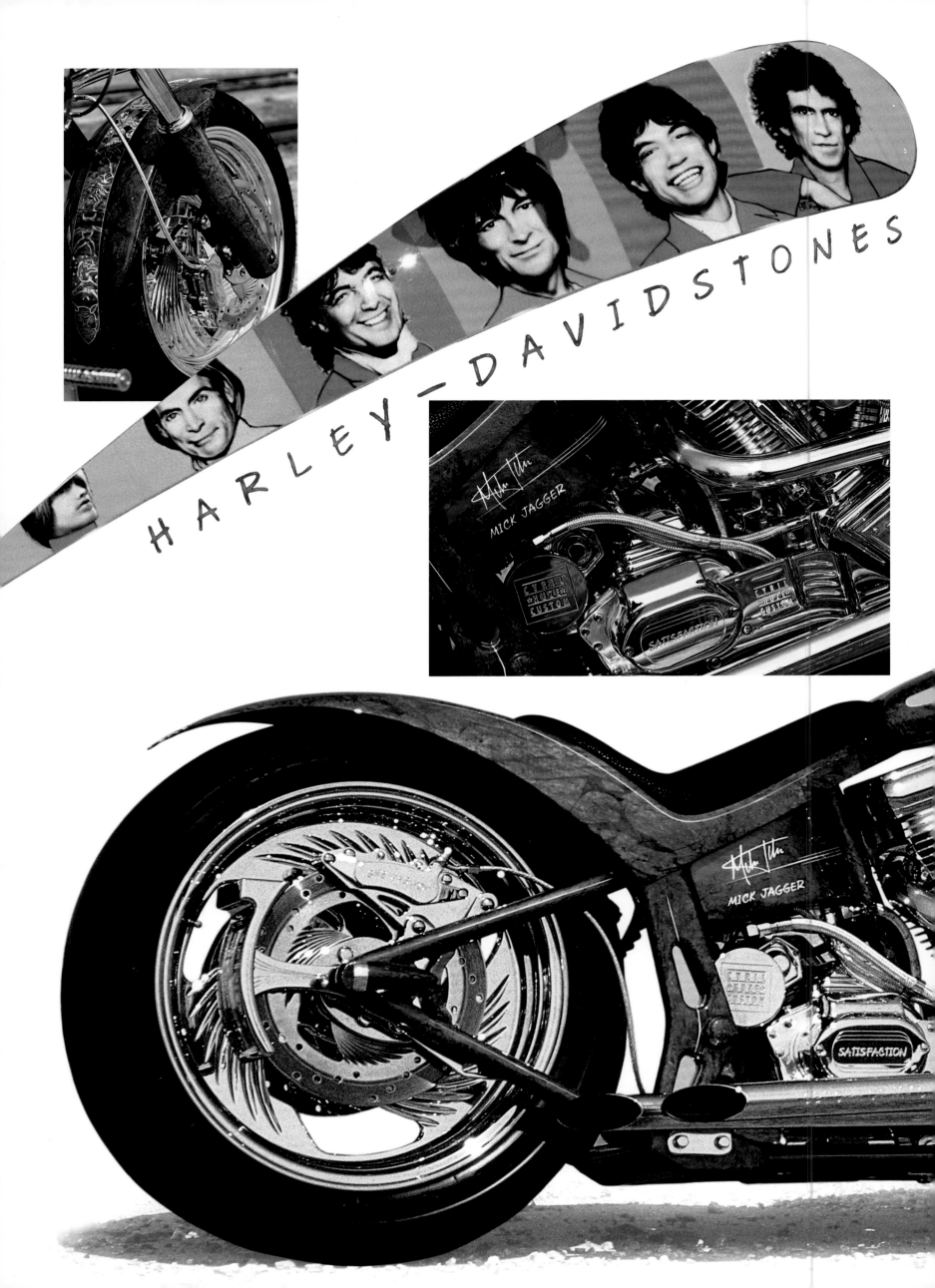

HARLEY-DAVIDSTONES

MICK JAGGER

MICK JAGGER

Cyril picks up the commentary. I'm trying to remember what made me fall in love with the Harley brand initially; what made me buy my first Milwaukee V-Twin and drove me to make their customization my profession.

The first thing that comes to mind is the beauty of the symmetrical engine: the curve of its profile, the power of its lines, the sound of its engine, the 'Made in America' label. But those things alone are hardly enough to explain the things that go beyond buying my first bike.

A first possible answer is this: Man is naturally a conquering animal, close to nature, in love with freedom, and always seeking new adventures, new territories, new meetings. What's more, for historical reasons America, more than any other country, is the cultural incarnation of these values. Notice the similarity between the clothing and accessories of cowboys, Indians, and bikers: same leather, same fringes, same boots, same headwear, same saloons, same attitude, and so on. The Harley-Davidson is, I believe, the horse of the modern highway. In an increasingly aseptic society where most human relations are conditioned by financial interests and where 'adventure' is used to mean package vacations, the Harley is a haven for those who want real adventure, want to find their real identity, and are interested in the sincerity of human relations without any particular agenda. To my mind, this explains the psychological closeness between the

422 and 423 Harley Davidstones is a tribute to the world's most famous rockers by a music-obsessed designer. The bike is typical of Cyril Huze's preferred lines, while the color scheme is based on shocking purple with wild marble effects. The spectator can't help but be amazed at the detail Huze has included in honor of the Stones: The musicians are all portrayed on the body, while the titles of their greatest hits grace even on the most discreet mechanical components such as the oil sump and brake calipers. The photographs of this custom's details show that nothing has been neglected and that every element has been embellished with great care.

HARLEY-DAVIDSTONES

brand and its fans, generation after generation, in the US and abroad."

Indeed, Harley-Davidson and its engines are today much more than a legend. They have become a veritable myth: a folk tale whose resilience is tougher than the steel used to make its motorcycles. The first feature of a myth is the possession of ancient roots. In Harley-Davidson's case that would be 1903, which is ancient enough for Americans.

The second feature is to glorify a hero. So how has a profit-based corporation morphed into a modern-day hero? Huze offers some answers. "The brand went through all the dramatic times of this century. It has seen the same wars as America and fought alongside its country. It has been knocked down in times of depression or recession, but it always fought back to win the most important commercial battles – even when its

424-425 Despite its already wild marble paint scheme, Huze hasn't left a single space unoccupied on this bike. Titles of Rolling Stones hits have been engraved just about everywhere, especially on the chrome parts, and the name of each band member is inscribed in the center of the tank. It is a no-holds-barred homage to the rock 'n' roll artists who continue to excite both the young and the not-so-young, destroying generational barriers and demonstrating yet again that quality is everlasting.

HARLEY DAVIDSTONES

competitors refused to fight fairly. So many battles fought and so narrow escapes from death have certainly contributed to making the brand a likeable hero. Returning from the very brink of death is another key feature of every mythical hero.

The Milwaukee V-Twin is a hero by nature, too. Because it's simple and easy to maintain, it has often been very affordable. Its unchanged lines make it familiar at a glance. Its exhaust noise, almost like a sound bite, is a universal signature that immediately arouses the demons inside us all. Its weaknesses compared to the Japanese speed monsters only serve to make it human. The Harley-Davidson is what I call an 'object with a face,' and what could be more attractive than a hero with a face? Yes, to me this bike has a human personality, a human style, a human way of dressing. All these just make it seem to be waiting for us to decorate it, to make it more agile, faster, more attractive, and so on. So now the Harley is a hero that you yourself can make even more heroic.

Art is the tool of this transformation. All of a sudden, individuals and independents

Glamour Girl

look at this machine and are convinced that they can make it more seductive or better performing. They hope to transform the hero into a god.

Thus the art of personalization becomes the art of customization, and the art of customization approaches purely spiritual levels. New techniques and ideas are assimilated by the manufacturer and integrated into the mass-produced model; in turn, the ever-more-beautiful customs nurture the V-Twin legend all the more and the Harley-Davidson myth is amplified.

What makes it all continue is that the myth is also quite contagious. For many the V-Twin becomes the object of all passion.

True legends are made of mysteries that will never be really explained. The Harley-Davidson remains a riddle, just as it should be. While one can always talk of one's passions, is it really necessary to find the foundation on which they're based?"

426 and 427 *There's no doubt that this elegant custom bike belongs to a woman (Kaylin Rionesse), while the skill in the use of color and the choice of an overall theme confirms it as another Cyril Huze creation. The starting point was a Harley Fat Boy and the result a work of art, thanks in large measure to the talents of the legendary Vargas – the American specialist whose surname is now synonymous with Esquire magazine and its series "The Vargas Girl." As a fan of Vargas's work the owner of this custom wished to pay tribute by offering his Harley as a canvas. Built in 1995 by Teddy Brach and Cyril Huze, it now has a value of $75,000. The underlying Fat Boy was rebuilt by Red Racing. The engine is standard with the exception of an S&S E-Type Shorty carburetor and modified White Brothers exhausts.*

428-429 The most important element of this bike is its paintwork, which is attributable to Shelby Good for the molding, Cyril Huze and Brigitte Le Jeloux for the design, and Chris Cruz for the actual work. The background color was prepared by House of Kolor using a special mixture of silver-white pearl, purple, and magenta. Chris Cruz's brilliant paintwork was applied using an airbrush and 24-carat gold leaf. The front fender is a modified Arlen Ness piece and the rear a Storz/Huze. The rear light was made by Cyril Huze and the footrests are a combination of Ness, Doss, and Huze components. The fuel tank is a modified five-gallon CCI and the oil tank comes from Doss. The mirrors are by Aeromach and the levers from Arlen Ness's catalogue. The fork is a Wide Glide built by Pro One that was shortened by two inches and fit with double discs. The rims are 80-spoke, 16-inch Pat Kennedy units while the four-piston brakes came specially prepared from Performance Machine. This is an exceptional and totally original machine, as the care in its accessorizing attests.

A WORLD APART
FOR A MEANS OF EXPRESSION

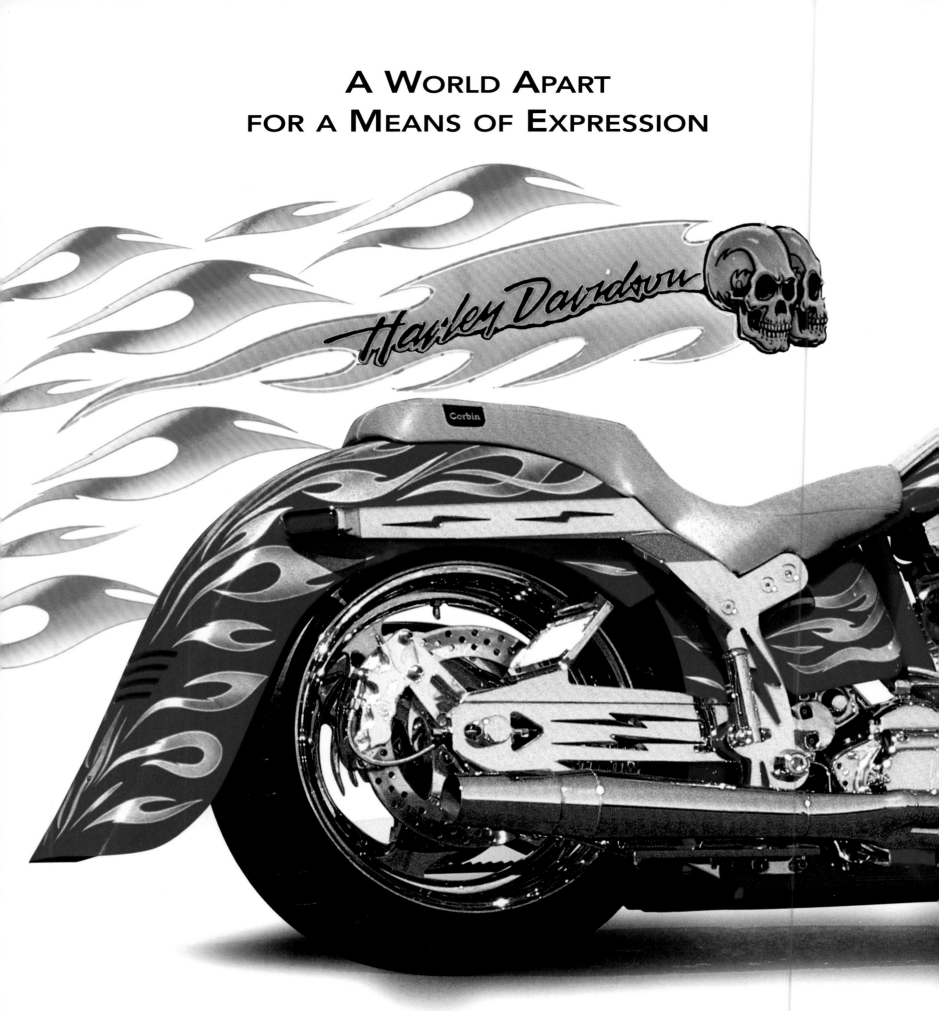

The Harley-Davidson world is really quite different from the biking universe in general. For one thing, it is different in that this bike, created nearly 100 years ago, has run the entire gamut of adventures in every social field.

At the outset Harley-Davidson seemed to be just another motorcycle brand on the US market, where competition was already fierce. Manufacturers would battle each even over a tiny share of a military order.

But the Harley Davidson Motor

Company eventually won all these battles, and seems to have overcome all the vagaries of history as well. At various times in this century the company has expanded its market share for reasons of technology, symbolism, status...even because it was once the cheapest way to travel across America. The Harley has also, in its day, been emblematic of a certain social terror, with impressive gangs of bikers roaring into towns and frightening the locals. Oddly, at the very same time it was gaining

headway as a symbol of freedom, as reflected in *Easy Rider* with Peter Fonda and Dennis Hopper.

The customization virus, which has revitalized the Harley brand in the '90s and moved it into the highest social strata, first appeared in California in the early 1960s. During the 1970s the bug gradually ran all throughout the States and Northern Europe, continuing on to eventually conquer Asia.

The later 1990s saw men and women of

all ages and classes infected by this madness; suddenly doctors, realtors, and lawyers became chap-wearing bikers on the weekend. But while many now ride Harley's as a quasi-active hobby, others still make the bike their total lifestyle. This everlasting core may explain the continuing Harley magic.

The public at large felt quite protected from the customization rage until it, too, fell victim to the charms of delirious patterns of paint, chrome, aluminum, and

steel that turn these machines into rolling works of art. At once childhood dream and adult plaything, iron horse and silver bullet, a means of escape and a means of seduction, the customized V-Twin has become a recognized pop-art form even amongst non-riders.

A growing number of companies are now using this craze to bankroll their own customs with the sale of innovative accessories and highly professional services. While these products won't turn

their consumers into a Ness or a Huze overnight, it's quite common to be pleasantly surprised by a new talent who comes up with an astonishing creation seemingly from out of the blue.

Still, it is the works of art which seem to continually flow from the shops of the master builders that attract the most attention from the media, the public, and of course collectors. Even museums (New York's Guggenheim) and galleries (London's Barbican) have come to celebrate this art form in the '90s, with travelling exhibitions drawing both the the dedicated aficionado and the merely curious onlooker. The general and specialized media frequently interview creators, publish photographs of their works, and treat custom bike builders as modern industrial powers.

Large Harley-Davidson events attract ever-growing crowds who are eager to break away from the daily grind and personally exchange a few words (or even just a handshake) with one of the elite master builders. While the masters' new customs are quite capable of being ridden, they are first and foremost for exhibition. Perfectly suited to the showrooms and salons which ultimately support the entire customization business, these two-wheeled sculptures are part artistic statement and part commercial advertisement. Besides furnishing their private garages and corporate showrooms with concours-worthy automobiles or historically significant race cars, today's private collectors also go in for custom bikes – particularly those that have been built and signed by the foremost

432-433 This bike was designed by a private French customizer whose starting point was a Softail Heritage. It is useless to ask how much the machine cost, as even the builder does not know. (Perhaps this is the reason it's such an excellent piece of art!) It is impressive that one individual could modify all the components (including the frame) and do the paint job himself, and still engine up with such a balanced, professional result. With pure lines and a great profile, it almost looks like a dragster for the street. The primary drive is external, and the power of the engine is directly related to how much air the massive twin carbs can ingest in a gulp. One detail not to be overlooked is the placement of the indicators, which are incorporated into the rear fender. A truly intelligent idea!

designer names of V-Twin *haute couture*. Some collectors may think nothing of paying the cost of an average home for a truly spectacular showpiece.

Nevertheless, it's easy to see how the custom craze has caught on. Explaining its origins and evolution, however, requires analyzing a whole series of phenomena, many of which occurred at the same time.

As Cyril Huze points out, "...the Harley-Davidson has always been the object of envy because of its emotional value." It is a symbol of power, escape, and freedom, yet it is also a beloved underdog. The fact that the brand has frequently flirted with bankruptcy (during the Great Depression, then again in World War II, and during the 1970s and '80s as the result of lousy

management and fierce competition from the Japanese), yet always managed to survive, can only reinforce the public's affection for it. The bike's unique, seductive lines and characteristic engine note have become universally recognized signatures and made this brand's following the envy of its Japanese, German, and Italian competitors. Virtually every cycle maker in the world has, at one time or another, tried to foist their own custom bikes on the public which are largely lukewarm copies of the unbeatable Harley-Davidson design.

The Harley-Davidson is far and away the most widely chosen raw material for motorcycle personalization. Its soft lines contrast with its hard and robust accessories, lending it a presence that

434 Yellow is one of the best colors for custom Harley-Davidsons, and the paintwork shown here allows you to make out some of the interesting features of these bikes, such as their steering heads' rakish angle and the attractive rocker covers of their V-Twin motors. The first bike has OE covers from Harley-Davidson, the second a set of pieces from the Arlen Ness range.

435 top and center Virtually everything about this Harley-Davidson Road King, which has been customized to look like a New York taxi, is original. The most important accessories are those which the creator salvaged from a real NYC cab, such as the tank decorations, the front fender ornaments, and even the speedometer. This customized Harley is one of the best on the show circuit in terms of its originality of design and the skilful incorporation of genuine theme parts.

435 bottom The owner of this bike is a member of the exclusive Hamster Club, which is limited to approximately 200 members. The Hamsters love to party at their meetings, which are ostensibly organized to exhibit members' bikes. Needless to say, a Hamster custom must be of very high quality, like the one shown. It was done in the Ness style with a Dyna frame and a high-performance S&S carburetor.

436 and 437 This bike looks a lot like SmoothNess, from which it probably received its inspiration. As with the original by Arlen Ness, its creation could not have been easy. The builders were Brian Olson and Mark Kennison, both of whom live in Indiana. The value of their creation is some $140,000 – about the cost of the average home in their state. The skeleton which supports this amazing bodywork is a five-speed FXR with a 122-cubic-inch engine. Pistons, cylinders, and heads are by Patrick Billet, the ignition system by Fire Ball, the carburetor and air filter by Edelbrock, and the exhausts by Kennison and Olson themselves. The transmission is a high-performance Harley unit and the fork a standard Narrow Glide. Performance Machine made the brakes and the tires are Metzelers. Note that the bike's headlight was not originally designed for a motorcycle but rather a Ford Taurus automobile! This attractive bike includes an ingenious method for accessing the rear wheel: a sort of "hood" which opens up like a shell. Unless the passenger is willing to sit in that hollow like a rumbleseat, this bike is strictly for one-up riding.

is simultaneously graceful and distinguished and wild and aggressive. Its narrow-angle engine architecture adapts easily to modifications, so each customization has a fighting chance at aesthetic success.

Californian motorcycle clubs formed by World War II veterans were the first serious customizers, and in the earliest days their efforts were not confined to Harleys. Indians and British motorcycles often received the same treatment. The same was true for the first hotrod-constructor crossovers. But by the time that Hollywood lionized biker culture in *Easy Rider* and a raft of successive, far less worthy motion pictures, Harleys were the only bikes to have.

As the Harley-Davidson brand gained ground as a symbol of new social attitudes, other motorcycling clubs were set up specifically around the marque. More people joined the bandwagon of those who would spend their nights in garages cutting, welding, and devising new accessories for their own personalized Harleys, each bike reflecting their personalities, expressing their tastes, and in many cases venting their feelings of rage and rebellion.

The Harley-Davidson factory has been mass-producing motorcycles since the beginning of the 20th Century, but only fate, chance, history, and destiny have connived to make its motorcycle a mythical object. Still, the owners of these bikes have actively perpetuated the legend by modifying their machines. After customization their bikes become unique, creating a strong psychological link between the brand, its customers, and simple observers. Each one nourishes the rest.

Like a virulent affliction, the Harley virus becomes more contagious with every passing day. At the threshold of the 21st Century this US bike is called to play a prime role in the lives of hundreds of thousands; part engaging hobby, part escape valve, and part a definition of personality.

The irreverent choppers of the 1960s were the first blatant symptoms of this passion for customization, and in those years Harley-Davidson ownership was not an expensive pastime. Used bikes were cheap to come by, and necessity was truly the mother of invention when it came to customization. Though these motorcycles were already clearly a passion among many, it was a passion that was well within the reach of

the working classes. Only later, when these bikes attracted fans from other strata and their ability to represent the personality of their owner was appreciated by a wider audience, did the Harley hobby become a costly and competitive activity.

Clubs and events had begun popping up all over the place even before the customization bug infected the greater American population. It remained little more than a hobby with social attitude until that fateful day when many of the more talented customizers began realizing they could make a decent living by offering their creativity to others. In the beginning one didn't need to be a recognized figure in the art of building bikes; one simply started off helping to make custom bikes for friends, and then for friends of friends, until word of mouth grew to the point that a professional business had been born. It was through this very process, however, that soon the best craftsmen, painters, and bodywork specialists became the heroes of a new lifestyle. That lifestyle grew up against a backdrop of rock 'n' roll, hallucinogenic drugs,

438-439 Boy, this color is unusual for a member of the Hamsters! Its owner, Tank, took two years to build this massive bike. His friend Tom Pokorny was responsible for the engine, in particular cutting the cylinder fins and mounting and adjusting the Andrews camshaft and Dyna Single-Fire ignition. The remaining mechanicals are essentially factory standard: a Harley-Davidson Evolution 1340 engine fit with several Arlen Ness parts and a Dell'Orto carburetor, which was chosen to suit the throaty character of the engine. Tank started with an FXR frame and made several alterations, first inclining and lengthening the steering head and then stretching the swingarm two inches. A shortened Electra Glide fork was used to slightly lower the bike. Some 300 hours were spent building this bike, largely because many parts had to be made as one-offs. The headlight is a good example, being a combination of a 1940 Ford and original Harley-Davidson parts. The front fender is from a '46 Indian, the rear was made in-house, and the taillights began life on a '59 Cadillac.

FLIGHT DEVILLE

440 top Customizing this bike was a big decision, as it started out being a stock 1938 Knucklehead. Knowing the costs of customization and the high value of the bike if kept original, it would certainly have been fiscally wiser to leave well enough alone. But when moved by passion, prudence is not a consideration. The engine, frame, and transmission were largely left original, but the rear fender, lights, and brakes are all modern. The fuel tank was been lengthened at the rear and fit with new side panels to hide an oil tank. The fork fittings, supplied by Milwaukee Iron, hold a a modern telescopic fork with internal locking caps. The front braking system uses a four-piston GMA caliper and a thoroughly up-to-date rotor. The motor is almost completely stock, save for an uprated modern oil pump.

student revolts, and questioning authority, but soon it spread out into the American culture at large. Indeed, very few of the early customizers actually made a living from their passion. Those craftsmen who unknowingly pioneered and defined an entirely new art form were, for the most part, purely amateur.

Customization was still perceived by the public at large as a marginalized hobby even after it had become a legitimate profession for dozens of US designers, and the industry went on to follow the ups and downs of America's economy throughout the 1970s, 1980s, and early 1990s. A few small and medium-sized businesses managed to make a healthy profit supplying custom accessories thanks to the cult-like

dedication of those in the Harley lifestyle, but biking was hardly a major economic force in this period.

Even Harley's rabid (but limited) following seemed doomed during the Reagan years, abetted by the company's technological and managerial difficulties under AMF ownership and the incredibly good value of its faster, lighter, more reliable Japanese rivals. Additionally, a consumer society demands that its member have a real job, not just a hobby. Harley owners abandoned their passion by the thousands at this time, many selling off their American bikes in favor of Japanese alternatives or, even more frequently, a family and career. The reign of the V-Twin seemed to be at an end.

But two important developments then

440-441 and 441 top The particular combination of chrome and paintwork is what gives this bike its interest. It was made by Raymond Demers from Quebec, but he does not wish to reveal his technique. After the brightwork was prepared, a special treatment was clearly applied which allowed paint to adhere in certain spots. The areas which seem to be tears in the metal were protected while the remaining surfaces were roughed up and then re-smoothed prior to receiving their yellow coat. Raymond says it took 90 hours to finish the job. The engine is a 96-incher with a Crane cam, S&S carburetor, and SuperTrapp muffler. The ignition came from Dyna, while the rod, bearings, and pistons are by S&S. The frame is a Softail type and the steering-head angle rests at a conservative 38°. The fork is a shortened Wide Glide.

came to pass which reversed this course. First was the release of Harley-Davidson from AMF control, which eventually allowed technological and managerial advances to make up much of the brand's lost ground. The second was that among the Harley fans who had given up their machines for a more settled, established lifestyle, after a minimum of creature comforts had been attained, the children had grown up, and the mortgage was paid

442 *This custom, like so many others, has an almost standard engine but a seriously modified finish. The bike was built by Paul Yaffe and Mac Daddy for customer Bob Lowe, and it gives the impression that it was designed and built as a single piece. The continuity of the frame and fenders make this machine look large, light, and unbreakable. The final tab for customization came to some $68,000, not including the 1998 Softail frame on which it's built. In addition to its 36° steering angle this bike features pistons*

and rocker covers are by Edelbrock, stylish new handlebars by American Legend, and a revised, centrally positioned speedometer that gives the front of the bike a fine sense of equilibrium (besides offering greater visibility). The fenders were made by the customizers from scratch, while the tank was sourced from Metal Works and the fork is a standard Wide Glide. The flashy front and rear wheels were built by Carriage Works, and the twin-piston brake calipers are from Rev Tech.

442-443 *Most of the components on this Softail Springer have been gold plated, including the pushrods, instrument bezels, fork springs, various screws and levers, cylinder cases, air filter, and so on. Even the wheel spokes have been given the 24-carat treatment! This customization is probably unique; in ten years of attending motorcycle shows I've never seen anything else like it. This machine showed up in a recent Bike Weeks competition at Daytona Beach, Florida.*

444 Frankly, this modified Softail looks more like a Hollywood monster than a Harley-Davidson custom. Its lack of elegance and questionable taste in details leave me puzzled. A close look reveals a forced-induction engine with visible compressor, and discreet flames have been superimposed on the piping (presumably to indicate the temperatures a poorly engineered blower can reach?). Then come the dual containers of nitrous oxide on the rear fender, which must certainly give more power to this Milwaukee V-Twin than any tire can handle. Besides the interest in sheer oomph, this Harley does show some sculptural work at the rear.

off, the members of this new middle-class very often decided to strip off their masks of conservativism and return to the Harley fold. Today a whole generation of baby-boomers is once again returning to the ideals of its youth: ideals that are often rooted in the Harley creed of independence, freedom, and camaraderie. In its own way, the return to Harley-Davidson is a return to basic values.

The timing for this change was just right: Harley-Davidson had just launched new, more reliable, more comfortable models. The baby-boomers defined a new socio-cultural tendency in which one's quality of life was deemed more important the quantity of

objects one acquired. The new V-Twins are left to become the object of all their passions. At this point, thanks to its precursors of the 1960s and the arrival of fresh new talent such as Ness and later Huze, customization is at last about to come of age.

The masks finally fell in the 1980s and '90s. Out on the road the CEO, the plumber, the lawyer, carpenter, surgeon, and gardener all became men sharing the same passions, the same risks, the same joys, the same disappointments, and the same bonds of friendship. Astride a Harley-Davidson, men and women who had grown up worried about America's divided interests found that

445 top This is another Springer Softail by California designer Ron Simms, and it has been transformed in ways that you, too, could effect on your own Harley-Davidson. The bike boasts a personalized paint job, double discs with twin-piston Performance Machine calipers, S&S carburetion, a wide rear fender, chrome wheels, and a 180mm back tire. These are all simple, and in many ways intelligent, elements if you want to change your Harley. To replicate this work, just arm yourself with a reasonable budget and loads of patience! This particular customization required a single seat; a double would have interrupted the lines and made the tail of the bike look too heavy. It would also have spoiled the looks of the wide rear fender, which gives the machine a certain air of mystery.

445 bottom This Softail has been customized in a rather sober manner. While fit with a one-off swingarm which alters the rear aspect nicely, as a whole it is somewhat lacking in originality. Only the cut of the oil tank seems innovative, connected as it is via simple alignment to the base of the swingarm support. The spoiler clearly has no other function than decoration, yet it tends to make the bike look heavier than it should. (One must always ask if less decoration would make a greater improvement than more!) In a major competition, this machine could only win a prize for its paint.

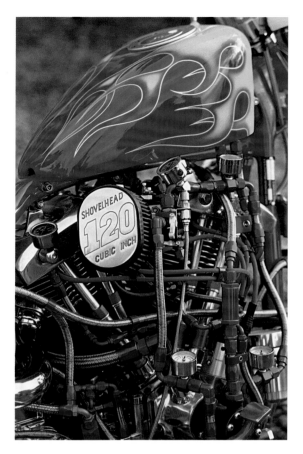

profession, status, race, religion, and all the rest began fading into the background. What was left was purely passion. The bike had the peculiar power to eliminate social barriers, all the while providing a fresh sense of adventure in an otherwise sterilized society. No surprise, really, that the Harley would soon become the object of all longing for such a huge group of people, both in America and later across the world.

One must also not forget how the brand has maintained its nostalgic image while quietly introducing new technology. Those who had gone through the chopper period naturally remained faithful to the brand out of nostalgia, while those who at the time wanted to be part of the lifestyle but didn't dare (or were simply too young) now clamored to buy a V-Twin out of romanticism. Lastly, those who had never abandoned the lifestyle found themselves surrounded by old friends and a whole new generation of enthusiasts.

Finally comes the matter of self-definition.

A universally accepted rule, common to all men and women, is that a person is measured by his or her personality. Thus everyone wants to affirm their personality, and everyone does so on a daily basis: through the way they manage their private and professional lives, make their day-to-day choices, choose their friends, surround themselves with their favorite objects, etc. A Harley-Davidson is, at least partly, an affirmation of its owner's personality. The brand becomes a sort of rallying call, bringing together all those who want to express their attachment to certain values: adventure, freedom, independence, friendship, nostalgia, and so forth.

Within this framework, however, each individual also seeks a specific identity. Since by its very nature the V-Twin adapts more easily to customization than other bike models, it is hardly surprising that this tool of inclusion often also becomes a tool of personal distinction.

The desire for personalization is a way

446 and 447 I find it difficult to understand why so many people are prepared to pump thousands and thousands of dollars into an engine when the only return will be increasingly useless amounts of power. A super-output V-Twin is really only suited to a dragster, the aim of which is to beat back all comers on the quarter-mile. In most cases, however, the designer falls into the false belief that increased power automatically equates to increased speed and increased interest. In fact, after some fairly simple mods have been made, the acceleration of a Harley-Davidson becomes limited not by its output but rather by the traction of its rear tire and the skill of its rider. This is why revamped carbs, hotter ignitions, and tanks of nitrous oxide are such popular additions; these fast and inexpensive customizations can generally supply all the extra bite that a V-Twin bike can handle. Monstrous blowers, multiple carburetors, grossly enlarged cylinders, and so forth may be impressive to see and lots of fun to imagine, but they're rarely the most sensible route to greater performance. What shown on these pages is the work of a Canadian who has only altered his bike's looks – steering head, spoiler, fenders, seat, and paint. It's a nice bike, but it wouldn't get anywhere near the top in a show.

in which owners communicate with each other and the public at large. People sharing the same ideals can recognize each other through the outward manifestations of their motorcycles. Once customized, the Harley brings together kindred spirits who would otherwise have never met. New relationships are thus born, and the art of customization is itself nourished by the resulting exchange. New exchanges give rise to new designs, new aesthetics, and new technologies.

Nevertheless, V-Twin customization only really became an art form, albeit a pop-art one, when a new class of practitioner joined its ranks. These new talents came from backgrounds in painting, engineering, advertising, and manufacturing as well as classic styling and design. What's common to them all is a love of the Harley-Davidson and a history of customizing their own bikes before selling their skills to others.

By introducing new shapes, materials, techniques, colors, and accessories to the field, these geniuses have risen to the top of the most hotly contested commercial art form of our time. Their talents inspire all V-Twin lovers, and one must only observe the public's passion for their work to understand that this particular movement is bound to last. The custom designer is the conductor of the orchestras of our dreams; a magician of shape, sculptor of sheetmetal, and poet of color all rolled into one. His work, already fought over by collectors, represents one of the great artistic statements of the age.

448 Promotion Motorcycles has attempted to make this Electra Glide Sport look more youthful without depriving it of its solid appearance. First it was lowered as much as possible, then the steering angle was raked back. The tank and the fenders were lengthened for a more sultry appearance, and a full set of accessories from Pro One was tastefully installed to finish the job. (Pro One is a new company in the Harley world, but it already has a great deal of experience in the custom-car and hotrod fields.) This Harley did not receive any structural changes beyond lengthening the front fork by two inches. The powertrain is still standard right down to the intake, exhaust, and gearbox. This customization, undertaken for a private client, cost around $30,000.

448-449 Look carefully at this Fat Boy. Its customization could easily be done (or even commissioned) on a tight budget. First disassemble the bike and paint the frame. Then consider each element of the bodywork, taking care to first work out the desired style, accessories, and colors on paper. The seat is easily altered by any reputable upholstery shop, and voila: a perfectly admirable custom.

449 top In this overview of custom jobs for which price was clearly an object, this simple Softail Custom with an excellent paint job stands out as a fine example. Made strictly according to the owner's wishes, double front discs and dual-piston calipers round out the main mods.

450-451 Ron Simms' preferred formula is to alter the line of the steering column by chopping the front fork, a time-honored method which he's used throughout his career. Over the years Simms's shop has turned into a serious business whose employees, like Ron, are dedicated to the task of designing custom components. Today Simms' company, Bay Area Custom Cycles, builds its bikes using Paughco frames specially made to Ron's own specs. Bay Area Custom Cycles likes to receive its frames already adapted with extra-wide swingarms. This allows them to use impressive rear tires without having to forgo chain drive. The company has eight employees and produces about 50 bikes a year. This example took about two months and cost nearly $50,000: It has a 98-cubic-inch engine, an S&S carb, and of course a special Paughco frame. Original parts elsewhere guarantee the bike's reliability and quality.

452 and 453 Transformation of this tourer was a delicate job because of the original bike's strong personality. Donnie Smith, a customization professional, knows the Harley-Davidson scene well. He wanted to strip this Electra Glide Classic of as many accessories as possible while still keeping the operational parts, such as its S&S carburetor and cylinders. He simply removed every part which, according to his own sense of balance, reduced the bike's elegance. To finish the job off, he lengthened the standard fuel tank to make it more visually united with the frame that supports the seat.

The overtaking lights were replaced by two small, equally effective headlights while the windshield was cut and shortened – an idea that has since been taken up by Harley itself and is available in its catalogues. The Electra Glide Classic is still a real cruiser despite Donnie's modifications. He in no way wanted to change the bike's vocation. Shown in three different views, the bike is still very original and consistent with Harley's design. It maintains its original spirit and quality, and is still very comfortable for one or two riders. Donnie did not replace the double seat with a single, since touring is most fun in pairs.

454 and 455 Sporting dynamics and a relaxing, pleasant ride…. One bike can indeed possess both qualities, even though they are usually exact opposites. The latter is desired for long journeys, while the former – which requires a certain nervousness at the helm – generally demands constant attention from the rider. The bike shown here has managed to strike an impressive compromise between both extremes. Its looks have also been made more interesting by the indenting work done to its tank. This involves cutting out the steel sides, swapping them left to right, and then welding them back in. A superior custom paint job and a gutsy automotive-type ram scoop finished off the job. The same bike's owner might appreciate the dragster shown underneath, which is slightly reminiscent of the streamlined speed-record bike Jo Petralli rode to reach 180 mph on Daytona Beach in 1937. If you use a little imagination, the bike in the picture looks a little like that old racer, with its oil tank, exhaust pipe, and streamlined rear end wrapped around the transmission. Note the pair of nitrous containers on the front uprights of the frame. Because this bike calls the dragstrip home, only a single front rotor and dual-piston caliper are required, despite its considerable power.

454-457 top and 457 top In 1992, Bob Dron took a Softail Heritage and made a splendid Bugatti-inspired custom which he called the "Royale." Since then he has created the Royale 2 and Royale 3, both of which maintain some of the spirit of the original. Although the model shown has a fair degree of bodywork, it is designed to allow easy access to the mechanical parts. This particular job took only three months in the workshop, but over a year was necessary at the design table. When the bike was first presented its visual solidity, an illusion caused by Dron's decision not to lengthen the frame, didn't please everyone. It did, however, give the machine the appearance of utter indestructibility. The mechanical parts are all original; Bob Dron was not looking for performance so much as aesthetics. This bike was made in 1994 at a cost of $100,000.

456-457 bottom This Harley was ordered by a millionaire who collects outstanding bikes. Baptized "Dragula," it is was made entirely of hand-worked metal around a Softail frame. The exhaust has a single rear outlet and is mounted on the rear fender. Production took six months and the total value is some $70,000. Dragula features a Dyna ignition, an engine good for 75 hp at the wheel, S&S pistons, rods, and cylinders, Delckron guards, and camshaft, points, tappets, springs, and valve seats all by Crane. S&S was again tapped for the carburetor, while the clutch work went to Barnett. The custom's telescopic fork is a Wide Glide built by Storz that has been shortened two inches, while the wheels are Performance Machine models. The color is a urethane pearl black that was individually chosen and mixed.

458-459 top This custom bike was built not to be an extension of a single customer's personality, but rather as a dressmaker's dummy for an entire corporate lineup. It was designed to display a wide range of components made by its owner, the Samson Company, which manufacturers a line of popular exhaust pipes suitable for Harley-Davidsons. In order to present its products to the world of customizers and fans, Samson produced this unique model strictly as an attention-getter. Samson then entrusted a lucky representative with shuttling the bike from show to show. The Softail Heritage has been lowered by changes to the frame and fork.

458-459 bottom This yellow-orange bike is partially decorated with flames. The bodywork is relatively simple while the Shovelhead engine is mounted in an Arlen Ness frame. The bike stands out mostly for its bright colors and its curious lack of balance, being particularly weak in the area of the rear fender. Almost 100 years after the creation of the Harley brand, the transformation of its shapes and external appearances still easily separates talented stylists from backyard tinkerers.

459 top Drag Specialties is a company producing numerous aftermarket components for Harley-Davidsons. It uses this bike (and several others) as rolling ads for its products. When companies employ this method of marketing they usually entrust the design and construction of the bike to the industry's best known customizers; it is hardly a corporate benefit to be associated with an ugly custom. The same professional designers will often also perfect other accessories which will bear their client's logo in the marketplace. This bike was built by Dave Perewitz over eight months of hard work. The transmission case has been smoothed, and the steering column and frame (both built in-house) are considerably sleeker and lower than stock.

460-461 top This bike has a Softail frame, a pronounced steering-head angle, and a large front wheel in the Heritage style. It seems slightly unbalanced, however, due to the line of the tank. This doesn't meet the line of the single seat, resulting in a visual hiccup. An S&S carburetor, twin front calipers for safety, and a satisfactory (though not marvelous) paint job round out the customization. This project would have benefitted from more planning, especially in the area of the the front fender. The paint job would also have benefitted from more uniformity – though admittedly, the background color is a hard one to work with.

460-461 bottom The highly visible signature and the low, beefy style hint that this bike came from Bay Area Custom Cycles. Ron Simms's shop produces highly functional yet suitably customized machines, and all of his trademarks are here: the huge swingarm, chromed Wide Glide fork (thick, but nevertheless slimmer than that of the Softail Heritage), and low yet traditional lines. Simms offers the advantage of traditional Harley-Davidson style (a low center of gravity and a solid, heavy, very proud look) with world-class paintwork and top-quality parts. His customizations are frequently mysterious, deep, and technologically surprising. This particular bike was made entirely in the firm's Bay Area workshops in Hayward, California.

462 top American Indians have always been a source of inspiration to designers at all levels, but many amateur stylists ride into an ambush in their attempt to exploit the easy elements of such a vast theme. The owner of this Springer, however, must be satisfied with his bike's splendid finish. This motorcycle was probably created more for aesthetic appreciation than absolute performance. Aside from the Dell'Orto carb, the entire design evokes tranquility more than power. A single, perfect line runs from the head of the fuel tank to the tip of the rear fender, below which hides a fashionably wide tire, freestanding exhausts, and a 120-spoke wheel. A lovely bike.

462-463 bottom This is another Ron Simms custom. It bears a lot of the characteristics typical of his other bikes, especially in terms of its frame, swingarm, and accessories. What makes this example more unusual, however, is that while every Bay Area Custom Cycle product features an outstanding paint job, these all seem to center around Ron's favorite icon, the skull. This time there isn't a skull to be seen – just metal-flakes so big that they're practically poking out of the bodywork.

463 top This custom was based on an almost standard Harley-Davidson Softail Heritage but it has had some modifications made, mostly to the bodywork. You can see that the front and rear fenders have been changed, allowing the builder to give it an air of agility. This is helped in part by the aftermarket carburetor cover, but mainly by its paint scheme: descending blue flames. The Heritage is already very low, and this characteristic is further emphasized by the extra-long exhausts and oversized handlebars. All of the elements are impressively well matched.

464 and 465 The bulky Electra Glide Sport appeared in the Harley-Davidson range in 1990. It's a difficult bike to customize, but Florida's Paragon Locomotion had a whack at it. The changes were largely aesthetic, mostly concentrating on embellishing the brightwork and adding a deep, transparent paint job. Together, these add a surprising amount of beauty to this beast. Paragon's entirely manual engraving task took 150 hours, 50 of which were spent on the cases alone. The points and tappets came from Crane, springs and valves by Manley, carb and air filter are Screamin' Eagle parts, and the silencer is by Bartell. The frame was lowered two inches and the Wide Glide fork shortened the same amount. The price of this surprisingly attractive bike came to $50,000; not an awful lot, considering that the engraving was done by hand.

466 and 467 The Softail Custom and Softail Heritage are universally popular, perhaps because their various elements are easy to customize and transform. Professional designers and amateur enthusiasts can easily copy the examples already produced by this builder or use them for inspiration. Note the lengthened tank on the model at the top, which is accentuated by the shortening of the rear fender and forward-placed controls. The modifications made here center on the two fenders and the paintwork, which is good but hardly original. The bike at the bottom seems to have received more attention in its details, and even the logo on its

tank has been touched up. The aluminum swingarm is a model sold by Arlen Ness for the Softail. The rear fender is in unit with the seat support and with much of the oil sump. The bike is attractive for its finish, and it's interesting to note how the paintwork is simple, effective, and harmonious. This is a lovely machine; its character is more sporting than most, and the cutlines of the bodywork show that it has received a great deal of attention. Though created by an amateur, this job is worthy of a professional. This unique and modern bike can hold its head high amongst all those false sports machines coveted by tyro riders.

the front fork has been shortened by two inches, the double-disc brakes are GMAS, and the equal-diameter wheels are both by Performance Machine. The bike was ordered by Drag Specialties to be used as a traffic builder and advertising tool. Lowered as far as possible, it's a veritable jewel of creativity.

468-469 bottom The bike at the bottom was envisioned and built by professional designer Donnie Smith from an FXSTC base. The mechanical preparation was done by Donnie and Pat Obringer and the ignition parts come from Crane. The frame started life as a 1992 Softail,

468-469 top The interesting points of this rather sober FLH don't immediately leap to view. The decoration has been well carried out, particularly on the central part of the tank. The fleeting fenders and the taillight are also quite interesting. This model was made by an amateur customizer, but one with great tact. He has also added an OE speedo on a modest support which harmonizes perfectly with the fuel cap.

470 top and 470-471 bottom This custom was built from an Electra Glide. Substantial and boasting a great profile, it cost about $45,000. S&S parts are everywhere: the bottom end of the engine, the pistons and rings, the cases, cylinders, and heads...even the camshaft, valves, valve springs, and seats. The carb, ironically enough, is from Carl's Speed Shop! To achieve this bike's visual effect, the frame had to be lengthened by three inches and the steering angle inclined an extra 6°. The engine is a 1574cc monster and the the bodywork is made entirely from hand-beaten aluminum. The rear fender has been cut at the base to leave space for the chrome ring nut of the single exhaust pipe. About the only thing that hasn't been subtly (or not so subtly) tinkered with is the gearbox, a bone-stock Harley-Davidson piece.

471 Here we see a rigid and amply modified frame holding a Shovelhead motor. The bike also boasts open exhausts and impeccable mechanics. While its unsprung frame and tiny, flat seat would make it unsuitable for fast riding, it is certainly welcome at shows. This type of bike offers an interesting combination of parts from different eras – especially those eras in which Harley-Davidson's mechanical prowess left a lot to be desired. This is a fine animal with geometric patterns on the tank, a Harley-Davidson motor with genuine historical interest, and an ignition casing that's been tastefully customized to match the rest of the bike. The air-filter cover is an over-the-counter Arlen Ness part which has carefully been decorated in harmony with the fuel tank.

472-473 top This bike, like many others shown in these pages, was built by professionals who simply wanted to give it a slightly more personal touch. For the most part it remains a standard bike, meaning that its reliability, durability, and value are pretty much unchanged. This is an FXR, a model which is often used as a basis for custom Harleys. Here the designer has attempted to achieve his aim by slightly altering the frame and engine cases, changing the carb and exhaust pipes, and modifying the headlight and fork angle; in other words, changing all of the major elements which alter the bike's appearance without substantially changing its essence. Unfortunately, the final color detracts a bit from the effort.

472-473 bottom Gran Turismo bikes only hold limited interest to designers, who generally prefer to work with models that are closer to the performance realm. This bike features a raked steering head and a White Brothers kit which allows the forks to be lowered. At the rear the swingarm has been inverted and shorter shock absorbers are now used. This particular customization took Donnie Smith two months, and that's without even touching the original engine aside from repainting its cylinders. The front fork was shortened 1.5 inches while the wheels remained 16-inchers front and back. The covers of the saddlebags were modified and the front indicators were moved to the sides of the steering head. Removing the stock passing lamps visually lightened the front end.

473 top This fine custom bike is one of the latest from South Florida's Paragon Locomotion, which is based in Deerfield Beach. Once more a Softail was used as the basis for this top-notch custom job – as one would expect to see in Florida, the state second only to California in the production of excellent Harley customs. The rake of the Wide Glide fork was increased by 3° and the entire rear end was carefully redesigned to integrate the fender and seat into a single unit, giving this model a real touch of originality. Paragon's innovative bodywork and tasteful accessorizing have given this Softail admirable balance and beauty. All in all, this bike should be a breath of fresh air for any fan of Harley-derived customs.

474-475 top Ron Simms gets the honors on this page with two different V-Twin models. The first bike is the result of a customization of an FXE; it was fit with a Dyna ignition system for better performance and, as with so many Harley-Davidson engines, numerous internal parts were altered. These include the rings and pistons, carburetor, and bottom end, all of which came from S&S, plus standard balancing and blueprinting. The fork is a Harley-Davidson original, and Ron Simms created the following items himself: the handlebars, risers, grips, rearview mirrors, rear fender, instruments, footrests, and main engine cover. The whole shebang ran to about $30,000 in parts and labor. Don't forget that this is a Shovelhead motor, a very different animal from today's technologically advanced powerplants. This is a bike that will give a lot of pleasure, but by its engine's very nature it will always be miles behind the performance and reliability of the newer Evolution and Twin Cam series.

Harley Davidson

474-475 bottom This is a much more recent model which Ron Simms has designed. It is fit with an Evolution engine that's been bored out to 98 cubic inches and heavily modified internally. Numerous S&S components (including the bottom end, pistons, rings, and carburetor) were added and all the reciprocating parts have been balanced and blueprinted. The oil sump was made by Paughco in Arizona (the same company that supplies Ron's frames), and the motorcycle's custom lubrication and electrical systems were both done by Bay Area Custom Cycles, though the exhausts and mufflers were brought in from Thunder Products. Looking at these two bikes together, it's clear that their designer was the same, despite their technical and aesthetic differences.

476 and 477 Surprise: The Softail Heritage has been customized yet again! For some reason this bike lends itself to all kinds of crazy paint jobs and accessories. The model above boasts custom handlebars, grips, and mirrors. The latter meet US regulations (just barely), but they're really less for looking back than looking good. The original Heritage had a solid fork, so the designer must compensate for this if he does not want his custom to look heavy up front. This model has been decorated with cartoon characters, a theme which might seem a little out of context (the bike will surely be viewed by more adults than children) and is probably a trademark lawyer's worst nightmare—quite possibly, the nitrous system is intended to carry the owner beyond the reach of court-ordered "cease and desist" letters.

Dick Ross began customizing his own Softail Heritage in the early 1990, first adding its conspicuous paint job. This was in an era when scallops were very popular, but the durability of this treatment shows that this particular painting motif never goes out of style. The Harley's rather small original brakes were replaced by beefy Performance Machine components and the factory leather seat was reworked and re-colored. Dick's customized engine was surprising for its day and became widely displayed in professional magazines. Dick Ross's work has evolved over the years, to the point that he is now on the verge of becoming a widely known figure in the field. Ross now works as a stylist for Custom Chrome Inc., an American company that makes V-Twin accessories for the United States and export markets.

478 top and 479 top This custom Harley was designed and built by Ron Simms in an almost classical style. Views of both sides of the bike enable you to get a better idea of his work: It is an extensive custom job but also faithful to the bike's traditional lines, which seems to be a combination of Softail Heritage and Softail Custom. This type of styling symbolizes determination, solidity, stoicism, and quiet power. A wide rear tire, an elaborate fender that ends high up over the wheel, the addition of a license-plate support, and a bevy of custom decorations – once more Simms's ideas cover the whole of the bike, including his trademark skull on the fuel tank. This Harley-Davidson owes its impressive appearance to the care expended on it by Simms and his team. It respects the long tradition of stolid customization.

478-479 bottom This Harley-Davidson is more closely related to a record-breaking prototype than a customized production motorcycle. Its 1.6-liter engine is right at the limit of what can be achieved with Harley-based castings. The engine is also turbocharged, as if size alone weren't enough. Anyone wishing to create such a monster must always bear in mind the tremendous pressures and forces that act on any engine that operates so close to its absolute tolerances. Only through careful planning and uniformly excellent materials can reliability be had in addition to performance. Nor can the quality of the transmission, brakes, rear wheel, swingarm, drive pieces, or frame tubes be neglected. This bike was prepared by Sputhe Engineering, a company that specializes in performance engines. Then supporting structure was lengthened and lowered to allow the turbo system to be installed. While its rear-wheel output of 115 bhp might not seem huge, remember that this is a (relatively) small-displacement engine with air cooling and only two cylinders. Many large automotive V8s with all the advantages of liquid cooling, four valves per cylinder, and multi-port fuel injection would be happy with similar specific outputs.

480 and 481 This is a modern chopper with an extra-wide rear tire and a thin, long fuel tank. This chopper has remained faithful to its 1960s roots, painted as it is with intense designs of purple, canary yellow, and red. Even this wild treatment has left enough room for some classic design fillips on the teardrop-shaped tank, however. This custom chopper features hand-painted images of monsters and skulls on the bodywork, all of them posing in the attempt (not always successful) to transmit a message of power and fearlessness.

480

482 and 483 These two completely different Harley-Davidsons are good examples of how it's possible to transform a bike by carefully adapting accessories to the principle visual components (fork, wheels, bodywork, and lights). Of the two models shown, the Flame model has undergone more transformations. The Wide Glide front fork now has a functional strengthener to which the indicators have been mounted – an interesting solution that avoids having to install these parts on the handlebars, particularly on the Softail range. The lower half of the bulb is chromed and fit with an orange cover. Not even the fenders are like that of an original Softail, and the tank has been flattened to give the impression of greater sportiness. This is a fairly complex and expensive customization, given the number of transformations and the quality of the paintwork. The second bike is more an amalgam of over-the-counter accessories from different manufacturers who specialize in Harley components. The front fork is from a Softail Heritage and the headlight cover originally came on a 1970s Electra Glide. The fenders and handlebars have been replaced by aftermarket parts and a single seat was inserted to bridge the gap between the fuel tank and the rear fender. An effective, and surprisingly economical, transformation. These two examples show just some of the possibilities available to the average Harley enthusiast.

484 and 485 All choppers have extraordinary forks (of extraordinarily varying quality) and wheels of different sizes. Look carefully at these photos and you'll notice how similar modern choppers are to their predecessors despite the passing of the years and the differences in technology. The bike on the left is an "old," machine with long forks of questionable safety and a Shovelhead V-Twin around which the owner has veritably wrapped a frame and sculpted steering column. The machine at the top right is visually quite similar, but its Evolution motor, modern, professionally built forks, and delicate paintwork with flames mark it as a replica rather than a relic. Both share a common style, but their only real similarities are cosmetic.

The violet colored bike at the bottom won the "Best of Show" prize at Villefranche sur Saone in France, besides collecting some other prizes for style. This aesthetic is very typical of the classic chopper style which has recently taken Sweden (yes, Sweden) by storm. The bike's young French builder chose a rigid swingarm frame by Calles, lengthened it 2.25 inches, inclined the column to 40°, installed a Tolle Smooth fork more than ten inches oversized, and mounted 80-spoke wheels. After overhauling the Shovelhead motor he adapted a Morris automotive magneto and a Primo Phase 3 transmission to the chassis. Aerostyl was responsible for repainting the metalwork into violet, candy, and flames. The only thing left to do after that was decide on a name, and the owner chose "Roswell's Bike." The rear wheel is a 15-incher with a 6.5-inch rim and a 195mm tire, while the front is 18 inches tall. The handlebars are a modified Arlen Ness part, as are the headlight and taillight. The controls come from Jay Brake. Now what our talented young Frenchman must do is take this bike to America for the opinions and insights of this country's master builders.

486 top Despite it all, this rather strange Sportster is really rather attractive. It just goes to show once again how it's possible to do almost anything to a Harley, as long as you think it through carefully. The bike's frame was modified to take an Evolution engine and to give the impression of length, lowness, and a certain organic menace. The eye-shaped lights contribute to this feeling, giving the bike's face the look of a small and somewhat nasty tempered Martian.

486-487 bottom This is a splendid Canadian custom bike. The large spoiler on its chin makes one think that the frame is a self-supporting body when in fact it's traditionally tubular. Yet it is the bodywork that constitutes the main technical work executed on this motorcycle. The rear fender alone proved a massive job, as it was made from three parts which had to be individually welded to the frame. A Hexco swingarm holds the rear wheel and three fins were removed from each cylinder to lighten the engine's profile. The staggering paint job is a magnificent work of art worthy of many hours of close examination.

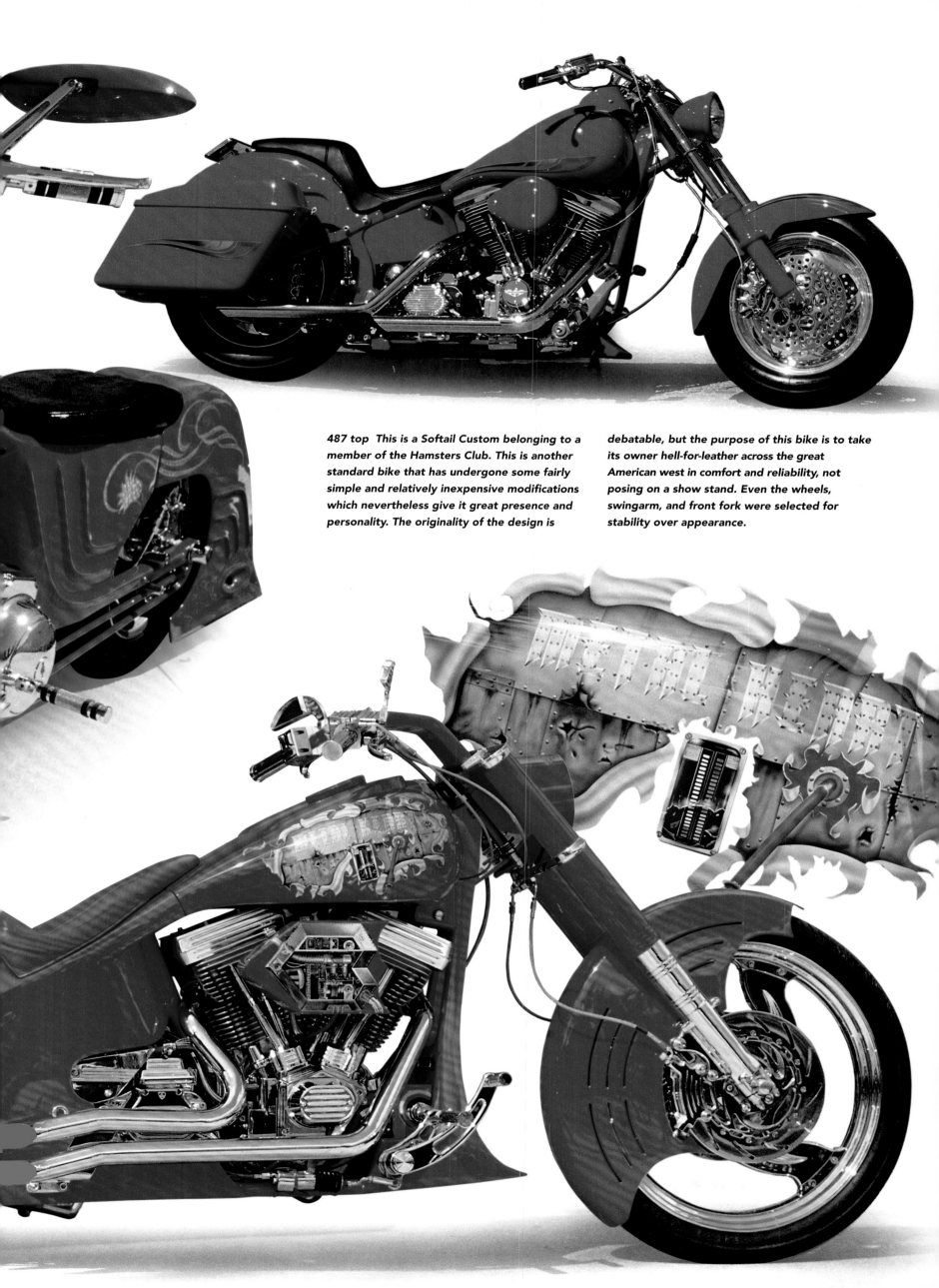

487 top This is a Softail Custom belonging to a member of the Hamsters Club. This is another standard bike that has undergone some fairly simple and relatively inexpensive modifications which nevertheless give it great presence and personality. The originality of the design is debatable, but the purpose of this bike is to take its owner hell-for-leather across the great American west in comfort and reliability, not posing on a show stand. Even the wheels, swingarm, and front fork were selected for stability over appearance.

494 and 495 Two tanks with the same theme but very different messages: While one tiger expresses the power of the wild animal and inspires respect, fear, and prudence, the other is intended to capture its beauty. This calmer treatment still instills respect for the beast but, despite its roar, it is an animal to be admired rather than feared. Note how monochrome and dark colors have been used in both cases to further express the differing concepts of power and beauty.

repeating patterns; easy work for some, more difficult for others, due to the critical balance of shapes and colors which must be achieved.

Sex is another common theme, naturally enough, with the female form sometimes represented as an angel and sometimes as a demon. Interestingly enough, childhood cartoon characters have become almost equally common, though their easily identifiable (and painted) heroes are often further "cartoonized" than usual.

Yet the themes of customization, rich and abundant though they are, can often become a heavy burden for the owner of a Harley. No matter how beautiful his fuel tank looks, its decoration is bound to carry

492 and 493 A superhero in the style of Batman or Superman seems to be protecting the young woman on this tank, and you might almost believe that the figure has succeeded in breaking through the steel to escape from an inferno. To the right another forceful but protective figure, this time a warrior who seems to be tearing off the bike's fender with a single blow. The images found on tanks reflect widely varied scenes and are designed and interpreted at the whim of the owner and artist. All you have to do is find a genius who is capable of discovering your passions, questioning you on the theme you want portrayed, guiding you in your final choice of imagery, and executing it flawlessly...! Anything is possible when one portrays the subconscious; in fact, tank imagery often says more about the owner than he realizes.

488 and 489 At the top is a classic custom bike produced from a Harley Softail. The paintwork has been done to the tastes of the owner, while the wraparound rear fender is similar to the original but differently cut at the bottom and spared of any chrome embellishments. The result is a sober and functional cruiser fit with hard saddle bags, a capacious and elegant tank, and a comfortable double seat. The passenger will have a great view over the head of the rider but will suffer from the lack of wind protection (not included for aesthetic reasons) on long journeys. As for the splendid European-style bike at the bottom with bodywork in the style of Bugatti, it's almost unnecessary to introduce it. The bike has an ostrich-skin seat and is based on a Softail Heritage with an original motor. It is, of course, the Royale 1 by Bob Dron. This is a bike with enormous class; built with millimetric precision and adorned with only the most tasteful accessories, it is considered one of the great custom bikes of our age. It was exactly what the public wanted to see: not just a great paint job, which anyone can have simply by finding a brilliant artist and opening up his wallet, but a true work of creativity. Following the sensation of bikes like Royale 1, SmoothNess, and Miami Nice, fans have come to expect a continuing fount of genius. The modern connoisseur is interested solely in the best, and radical new forms, daring yet successful, are the only thing that will please him. Fortunately, today's top designers have fertile imaginations.

Harley Davidson

490-491 *The light and dark shades of violet for this tormented sky, through which the face of a mythological god appears, are an example of the impeccable technique of the artist-decorator. Perfect knowledge of his tools and superb skill in their use give a result that will always attract admirers.*

The Harley's peanut-shaped gas tank, blown well back with its soft lines and shape that never go out of fashion, is fertile terrain for the designers and artists who wish to improve these machines. They do this most often on the visually critical component, which despite its small size is more than big enough to express their desires, fantasies, regrets, reactions, opinions, emotions, and even dreams. The tank is just another way to launch a message to those capable of decrypting it.

This central part of the bike, the fuel tank cannot be different from the spirit of the rest of the custom. A great deal of time is often spent outlining a scene or an image only to find in the end that it simply doesn't express the same concept as the rest of the motorcycle's imagery. Only when the tank art is correct can the custom be completely successful.

Although I have personally photographed the Harley-Davidson scene and world for several years, I've never been left untouched by the new gas tanks I capture on film at every large event. They are the heart and soul of the custom, and also the most accurate guide to the trend of a certain period (or even a single year).

Take for instance the "Indian" theme, the American-eagle theme (often covered in a Star-Spangled Banner), or the ubiquitous imagery of skeletons, skulls, and monsters (which symbolize defiance of everything the soul cannot accept). Other themes feature simple geometric forms or

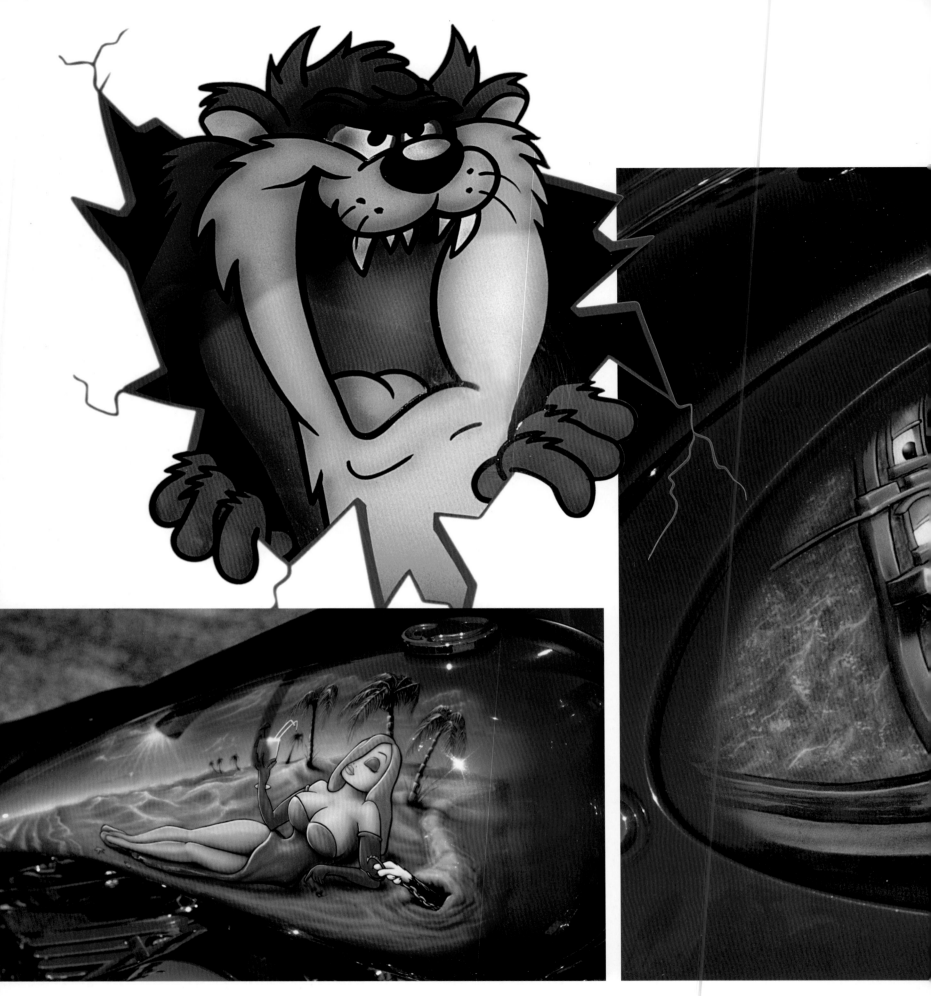

meanings and information of which even he may not be aware.

This is the main reason why one increasingly comes across much simpler gas tanks these days. (The other is simply cost!) It is not at all uncommon now to see the artist's genius reflected merely by a slightly transformed Harley-Davidson logo instead of a veritable tapestry.

The design and embellishment of a Harley-Davidson should never be restricted to drastic changes induced by a large number of mismatched accessories atop the original base. Instead, the effect is best when produced by a few balanced, well-chosen aesthetic changes which may or may not tell a particular story. Of course, one cannot become an Arlen Ness or a Cyril Huze in a few minutes.

Only by living through all the experiences that have allowed these master builders to tackle nearly every technical problem in their day and to stretch all of their aesthetic senses to the limit have they reached their lofty heights. In the case of Ness and Huze, the actual routes were quite different but the destination was the same. Huze arrived on the market when the sky was already the limit, both in terms of financial resources and also in expectations. The investment required for Cyril to become recognized as one of the best can was huge, both financially and emotionally. Only by funding and creating his first works completely by himself was Cyril able to break into the industry. Ness, on the other hand, grew with (and helped form) the very market he now dominates.

496 and 497 Here the artist has produced a series of Warner Brothers cartoon characters for decoration, a style which has become strangely common on the bodywork of custom motorcycles. The Softail Heritage shown has also been fit with a pair of oversized Corbin saddlebags; these offered the owner a further opportunity to indulge his imagination and give the artist plenty of extra space to realize it. Notice that the chosen theme is an evolution of these characters, not a direct copy. As a rule, themes should not be influenced by current fashions in customization or elsewhere; they are only supposed to be based on the passions of the owner.

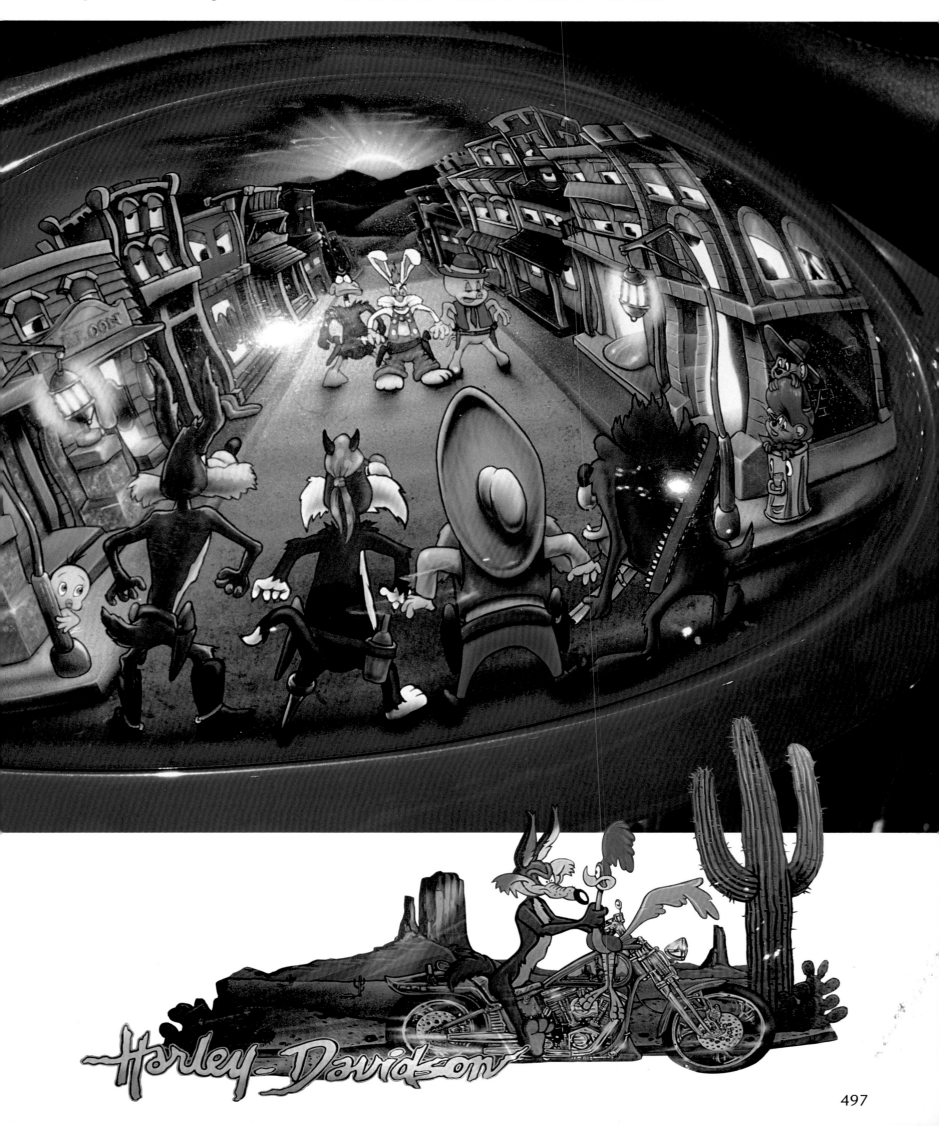

498 and 499 Warriors of all types are a popular theme among bikers. Images of powerful steel-muscled warriors, slaves who have been conquered, and battle-weary skeletons are all likely to be seen as the artist attempts to convey victory, resistance, and domination in his work. (Professionals who work daily for well-known customizers such as Arlen Ness, however, are more dedicated to modernity and commerciality; they will rarely take the risk of indulging in such un-subtle themes.) The tool of choice for the tank artist is the airbrush, with which realistic effects are simpler to create than with a standard brush. On the other hand the airbrush is less precise, so images rendered with this tool are not as clearly defined as those painted by hand. The most talented artists are equally adept at both and will use whichever is most appropriate.

500 and 501 A theme which is based on actual images or objects (in this case an action-movie star) forces the artist to tread lightly with his colors and effects. Whenever humans or machines are to be represented realistically, there is great danger of descending into cartooning rather than painting. The artist must also bear in mind the limitations placed upon him by the curvature of the bodywork, the gloss of its finish, the fact that certain areas will be covered with other parts when the body is reassembled, and the relatively small area on which he is forced to work. Nevertheless, all of the same rules of perspective, light, and shadow which were known to the Great Masters apply to the tank artist. In fact, the limits of his canvas make the rules even more important.

Brothers III

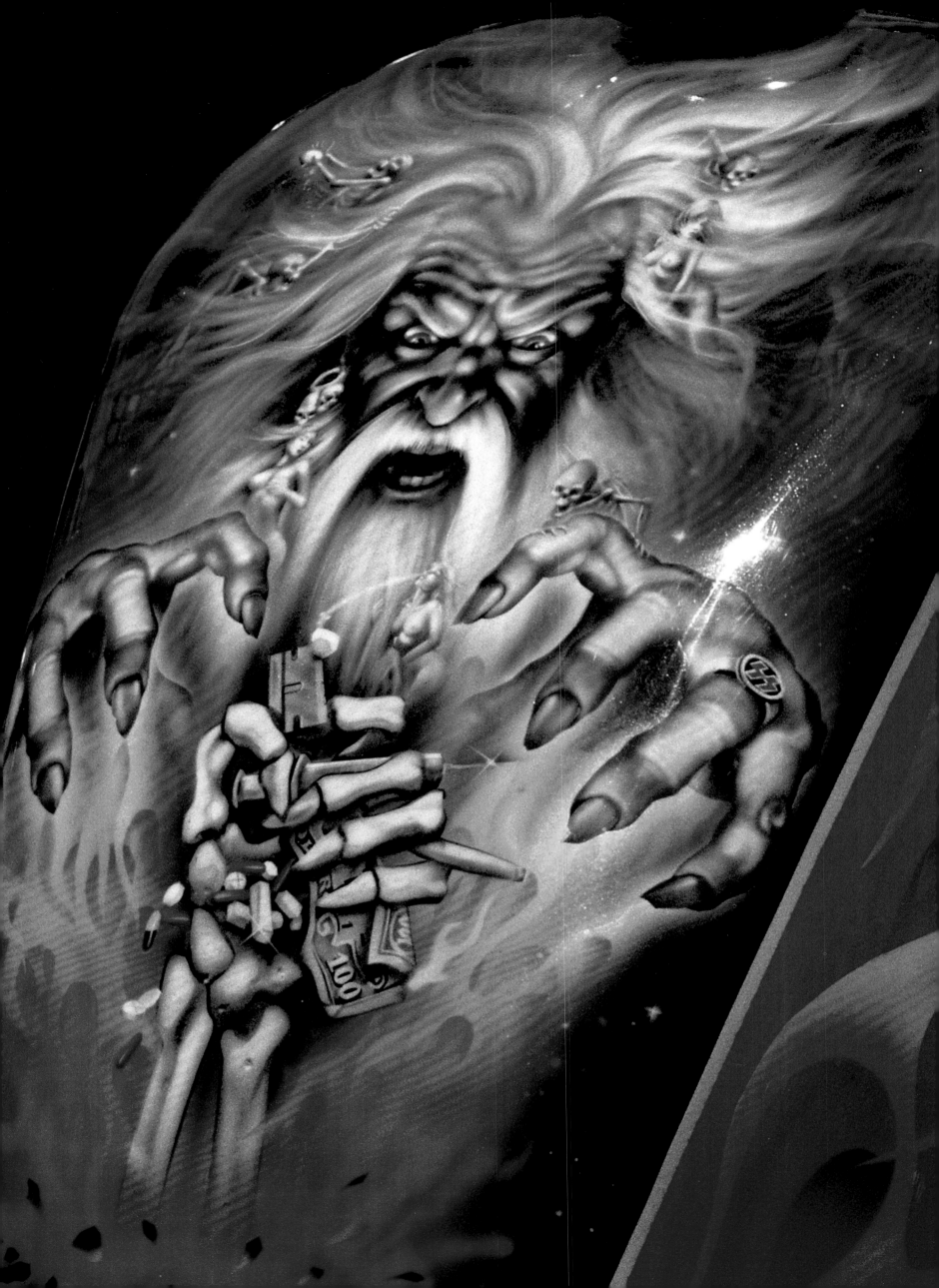

502 and 503 Lascivious, provocative women are one of the most popular themes in the Harley-Davidson world, whether they're shown at ease beside the sea in a hot and luminous paradise or are the most famous stars of film and story. These few examples show that bikers pay their own kind of homage to women; they decorate their tanks with the same abandon that WWII crews decorated their B17s.

A FEW THOUGHTS

Whether professionals or amateurs, all good customizers share a few main qualities. The first two are observation and imagination, two traits which are closely linked. It must always be remembered that a custom is a work of art, and that the creators of custom motorcycles are always attempting to use imagination to surprise, thrill, and startle their audience.

Today's public is also used to quality, however, whether in terms of paintwork, accessories, or even exclusivity. Thus it is important that the customizer temper his imagination with observation of the field's current standards and objectives. It is of little importance whether the motorcycle is supposed to be used daily or merely to display at shows. It must in all cases generate admiration, surprise, and respect.

This is why the custom bike must in its own way symbolize an inaccessible object. It does this through the quality of its construction and through the fact that it's a single, unique, unreproducable model.

There are only a small number of creators who continue to surprise with each new machine and who needn't ever go back to a basic, standard design. The public is particularly interested in this aspect of surprise, and it is this which keeps them coming back every year to discover the latest custom models.

The public continually puts the question of "how far can you go" to the designers, and the designers must walk a fine line between disappointing this curiosity and pushing too far ahead to be understood.

Nevertheless, international coverage of the Harley-Davidson phenomenon, as well as numerous technological advances and a robust Western economy, have allowed a large number of craftsmen to earn an honest living by satisfying Harley-related needs, such as the desire for accessories and gadgets, the organization of rallies, the preparation of specialized trade magazines, etc. This ever-growing phenomenon promotes economic development and, at the same time, rewards those who excel in in each sector through the process of natural selection.

504 and 505 Ever since Harley-Davidson came into existence it has looked to the American bald eagle as an image of strength and freedom. The Harley-Davidson Motor Company uses a stylized version of this symbol with their logo, the Bar and Shield, in which the eagle's wings are spread and its claws grasp the upper part of the frieze. Not only does this add powerful imagery to the logo, it helps make Harley a more "national" company than ever. It was therefore a natural step for bikers to adopt this symbol for use on their bikes. Any technique seems suitable for rendering an eagle: brush, pinstriping, airbrush, and even engraving.

Contrary to popular belief, it is not those who occasionally produce customs for clients that manage to earn a living from their passion. In the end, only two types of artist are likely to succeed commercially. The first is one who, like Arlen Ness, can field an entire catalogue of parts, mostly items of his own design and manufacture, to sell to a very large audience. The other, such as Ron Simms, has perfected the techniques of designing and manufacturing to such a high level that a virtual production line of high-quality, totally individual customs can issue

from his shops in a steady stream. The world of customs is exceedingly selective and competitive.

No matter! Above all, any custom worthy of its name rewards its creator, amateur or pro, with the fulfillment of a dreams. The key is to *keep dreaming*.

With that, we present our section on motorcycle gas-tank art. These are the ultimate steel canvases on which technical realities ride pillion with the customizers' wildest dreams...*bon voyage!*

506 and 507 Native Americans and eagles, two very popular themes in Harley-Davidson decoration, are often used together, as the eagle is not only associated with the United States but also with the earlier inhabitants of the continent. Interestingly, the gestures, faces, poses, and actions of the Native Americans depicted seem to never show a desperate

Harley-Davidson

Indian, on the contrary, they are always portrayed as dignified, wise, strong, and unconquered. The images invariably pay tribute to the Native Americans' race, history, and mythology (including wolves, eagles, and bison) while ignoring their fate at the hands of pioneers and soldiers. Just as the Harley-Davidson is often a nostalgic subject itself, so is the Native American experience when portrayed on the Harley's flanks.

508 and 509 This series does not vary so much in theme as in color. The situations and messages are an indication of the richness of spirit and creativity in the artists and bike designers, the first using airbrushes to express themselves and the second using body sculpture. Skulls are always violent, aggressive, and frightening, just like the dark settings in which they are often placed. The crimson flames of hell are often seen lapping around the tank, and a newer common theme is electric cables so overloaded with current that their colors are reminiscent of a welding flame. Figures which are half-human, half-beast abound, and bones merge with pipes of all sizes in the chromework.

510 Death, usually symbolized by skulls in a variety of expressions, is still one of the most common themes in Harley decoration. The skull not only shows the defiance (or embrace) of death by the owner but also extends the tacit threat of death to his enemies. Whether it's a members of true biker gang or a dentist with a Hog in his reserved parking space, this symbol will likely be found on his T-shirts, belt buckles, key rings, and so on. As you can see from the examples on these tanks, skulls' expressions run the gamut from agony to glee.

510–511 and 511 bottom The tank at the top shows the head of a woman watched by Death. An airbrush was used to soften the edges and multiple layers of paint and clearcoat give the work a depth that's hard to appreciate in a photograph. Colors are also important in creating the perspective of depth: Red, purple, and dark blue in particular help to create this effect, thus lending the artwork that little something extra. The artwork shown below symbolizes the Ghost of Death and is even harder to look at than the previous example. Tank painting often simpler than this, and it rarely offers a true perspective of depth. In this case it is the layout and composition of the image which give strength to the picture. The artwork blends perfectly with the shape of the tank on this Panhead-powered '53 Harley.

512 and 513 Travel, highways, night trains, and twilight landscapes are other favorite biking themes. Years ago it was a rare thrill to come across a bike with skilful decorations, as only the legendary US V-Twins were able to carry it off. French or German bikes could never be decorated the same way, though maybe that was just as much a factor of their riders' mentality as of the limits of the bikes' styling. In any case, decorated Harleys are increasingly common today even in Europe and Asia, and the themes of their artwork often extend to cover the whole bike. This represents a large expense for custom-bike owners, especially as the standards seem to rise every year.

Try and imagine the costs racked up by a new enthusiast who wants to enter the world of custom biking, gain credibility, and possibly win prizes. Still, expense is one of the rules of the game – the cost of living on passion.

514 and 515 The first Terminator film assured the careers of director James Cameron and actor Arnold Schwarzenegger – and also, amazingly enough, launched more than a few custom motorcycles! The creator of this bike, which is again a Softail Custom, even went so far as to create a very special shifter: the hand, fist, and forearm of the fleshless Terminator rendered in life-size. The artist also painted the title character's face (wearing his obligatory biker sunglasses, of course) in several positions and locations. A "romantic" robotic interest, heavily armed and wearing a conveniently ripped swimsuit (and skin), appears across the whole of the rear fender. This bike only goes to reinforce the association between Harleys and film.

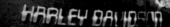

FERMINATOR

516 and 517 The horror film Alien was a great success in the cinemas, and several tank artists have not hesitated to use these monsters as design novelties. The quality of the representation shown on the tank on the left hand page is unquestioned. The sense of proportion, the accuracy of the creature's physiognomy, and the depth of the scene are all magnificently rendered. Note that the colors on this tank are all appropriately dark (as was the tone of the film) and that the red, purple, and brown components are all mixed. The Terminator tank, meanwhile, is a

TERMINATOR

completely different style; the work on both is equally precise and admirable, but the effects are wholly different. The other figures on the right hand page are different yet again. The one at the top was created using the same techniques as seen on the other tanks on this page (most notably a standard brush). The central skeleton was achieved using an airbrush, however, and you will notice that it's less defined (if perhaps more attractive) than the others.

518 and 519 The Stars and Stripes and the Rebel Battle Flag are also widely used on Harley-Davidson tanks, perhaps because the owners of these bikes so fervently loyal to their chosen institutions, be they club, country, marque, or what have you. Whether used for reasons of pride or merely because it is easily rendered and immediately recognizable, the wonderfully adaptable design of the Stars and Stripes is a classic for tanks. Its red, white, and blue color scheme is very adaptable, and the emotional resonance of Peter Fonda's Captain America chopper must never be overlooked. The ubiquitous bald eagle seems even prouder when placed over the American flag, and it's surprising to see how many different versions of this tableau tank artists have come up with in the effort to add life to their work.

520 and 521 Scallops, flames, and cracking stone are other often-seen elements in Harley decoration, although nowadays these classic designs are in danger of becoming cliche. The master builders will rarely employ them, except in extreme circumstances and with creative new twists of color and contrast. Indeed, the modern master builder has to almost become a chemist in his search for a new shade that turns heads, that has never been seen before, and that can truly give a little something extra to a bike that is already considered outstanding. Yellow flames on a black background won't cut it.

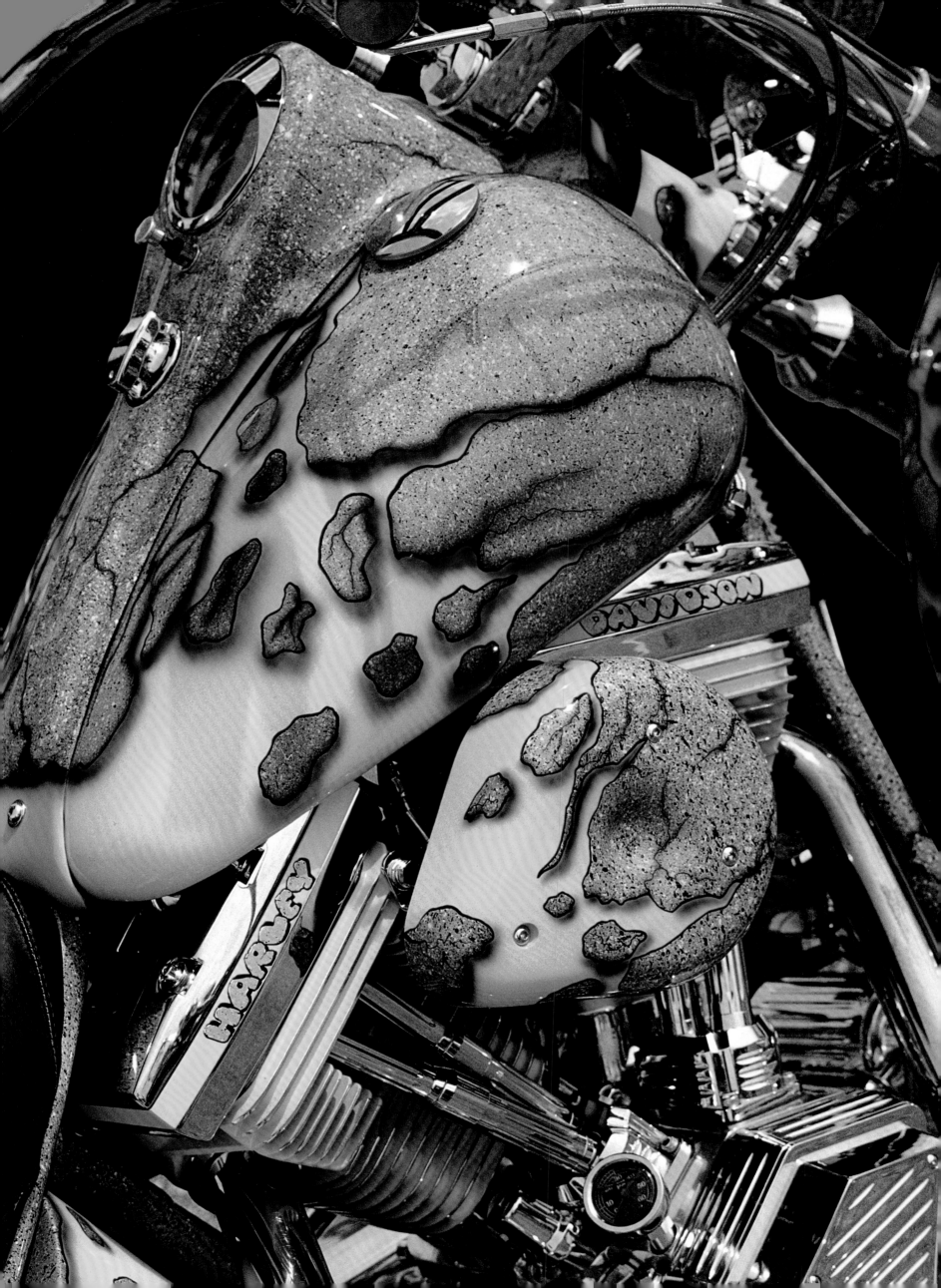

Harley Davidson

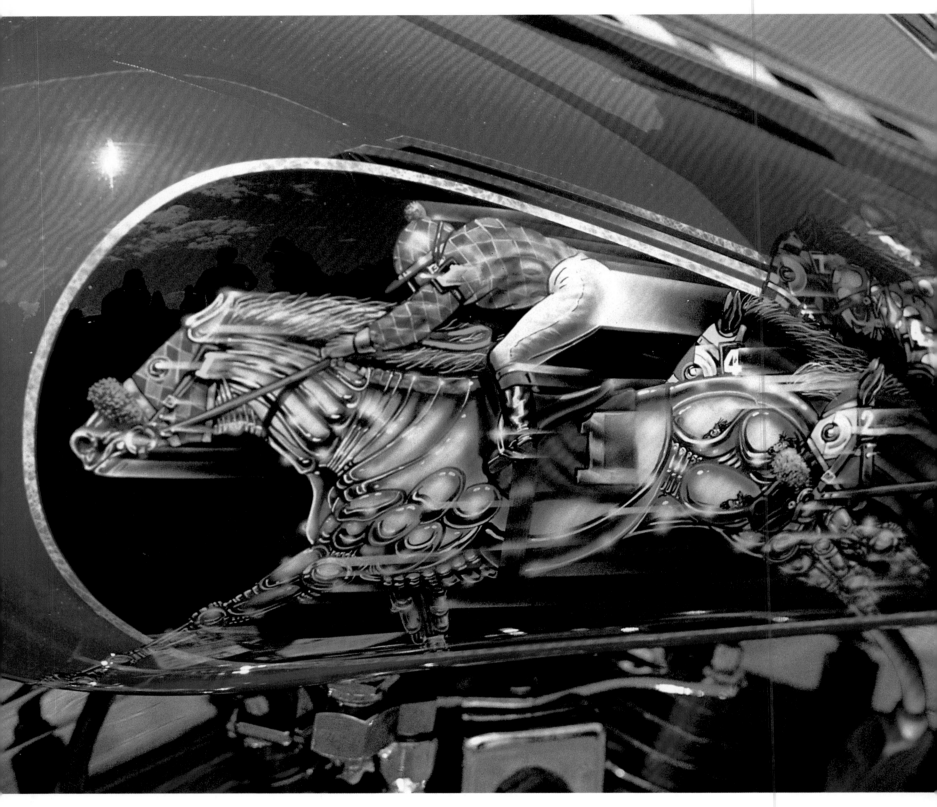

522 and 523 The favorite theme of money, including credit cards, gambling, and even customization costs, could not be neglected on these pages. Some of the simpler expressions include images of a horse race, a shining tank from which money pours out, an Amex Gold Card, or variations on the simple dollar bill (in this case the head of George Washington has been swapped for the head of Death). The fine details in the horse-racing image, particularly in the jockeys and their imaginary weapons, could only be obtained using a standard brush and plenty of patience. Ditto the surprising realism of the American Express Gold Card, which almost looks like a photograph which has been laminated onto the tank rather than a super-realist artwork. In fact, the artist added genuine gold leaf to the painting to increase its realism and depth.

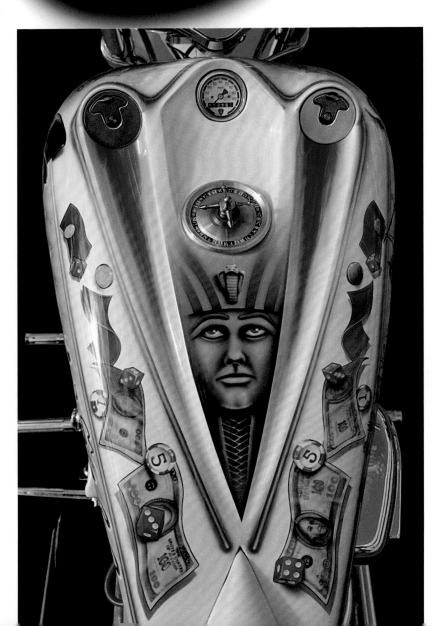

524 top At the end of the century it seems as if gambling is an increasingly popular theme among customizers. This Softail is indicative of that trend, with every available space on the bodywork covered by gambling imagery (so much so that it takes a little time to see beyond the decoration to the elegance of the bike underneath). This custom was assembled by the MH Billet Custom Cycles Design Company, which had no hesitation in using actual gold.

524-525 top and center The frame of this bike was made by Daytec and the engine is an S&S 97-cubic-inch model. The carburetor and oil filter are also from the S&S range. The front fork is an Arlen Ness piece, the 18x3.5-inch front wheel come from RC Components, and so does the 18x5.5-inch rear. This Harley-Davidson is not just notable for its fuel tank but also for its well decorated fenders and oil sump. Casinos couldn't exist without their croupiers, so a friendly face has been added that looks like it just might bring luck. She only appears on the left side; on the right side, a different woman is shown reading a magazine in boredom.

524 bottom and 525 bottom The upper section of the tank is occupied by a roulette wheel that can actually be used while riding. Another amazing detail is the two stacks of chips in purpose-built grooves (which also serve as the indicators). It might be a little overdone, but stylistically this job is one of the best around. Like all excessively customized machines it would be difficult to ride; one suspects that its real purpose is to be displayed around the best casinos in Nevada.

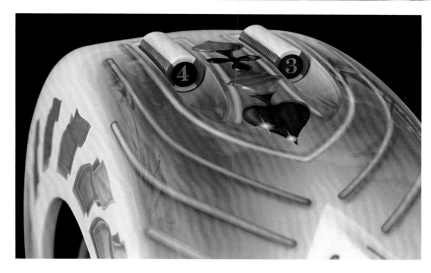

526 and 527 Is riding a custom with hyper-realistic images just another way to exorcise death? Could be. Themes of this type always seem to include a skull surrounded with decanters, test tubes, beakers, explosives, drugs, or other objects which are meant to represent evil. Of course we must not forget the Devil, either. He generally appears not as himself but in the form of a dragon, a ghoul, or a human-faced sharp. Imagine how much work is involved in painting an entire frame with flames before even starting on the tank and fenders! This work has brought the bike's owner several prizes for the quality of its paint job, even though some might consider that the decoration has gone a little too far over the top.

Acknowledgments

The authors would particularly like to thank

Cyril and Brigitte Huze
Arlen and Beverly Ness
Cory Ness
Keith Randall Ball
Bridget Ferrara
Willie G. and Nancy Davidson
Bill Davidson
Steven J. Pielh
Martin Jack Rosenblum
Bob and Tracey Dron
Dave Perewitz
Donnie Smith

Jay Brake
Bob Lowe
Tom Worrel
Ed Kirms
Ron Simms
Wyatt Fuller
Jim Betlach
Charlie Saloway
Rick Dos
Karl Smith
Claude Babot
Christian Dupont

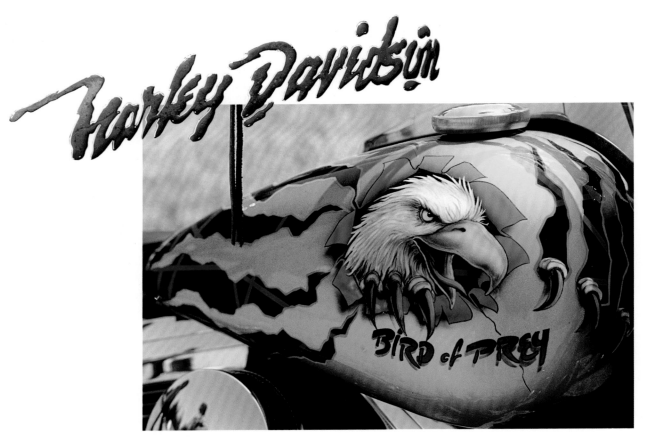

528 The original form of a typical Harley-Davidson tank has undergone alterations with the transformations of the V-Twins over the years and, despite retaining its teardrop shape, it has been subjected to lengthening, cutting, reshaping (to suit the frame or the seat), excessive widening (to give more weight to the original lines), stretching (to make it more elegant), or accentuation of its curvature (which some consider erotic). None of these transformations should do anything to harm a Harley's vocation or its gentle, timeless lines. These are what make a Harley-Davidson, after nearly a century of life, still the loveliest bike on the road.

All the pictures supplied by the authors except the following:
343 right Corbis Bettmann,
346-347 Markus Cuff.

Translation
For Harley Davidson - Evolution of the myth
English translation: C.T.M., Milan
English translation editor: Jay Lamm
For Harley Davidson - A way of life - A hundred year old myth
English translation: Hugh Swainston, Studio Traduzioni Vecchia, Milan